THE

CREDIT
REPAIR
KIT

SECOND EDITION

JOHN VENTURA

Dearborn
Financial Publishing, Inc.

This publication is designed to provide accurate and authoritative information in regard to the subject matter covered. It is sold with the understanding that the publisher is not engaged in rendering legal, accounting or other professional service. If legal advice or other expert assistance is required, the services of a competent professional person should be sought.

Acquisitions Editor: Christine E. Litavsky
Managing Editor: Jack Kiburz
Project Editor: Karen A. Christensen
Cover and Interior Design: S. Laird Jenkins Corporation

© 1993 and 1996 by John Ventura

Published by Dearborn Financial Publishing, Inc.®

All rights reserved. The text of this publication, or any part thereof, may not be reproduced in any manner whatsoever without written permission from the publisher.

Printed in the United States of America

97 98 10 9 8 7 6 5 4 3

Library of Congress Cataloging-in-Publication Data

Ventura, John.
    The credit repair kit / by John Ventura. — 2nd ed.
      p.   cm.
    Includes index.
    ISBN 0-7931-1779-8
    1. Credit ratings—United States. 2. Credit bureaus—United States. 3. Consumer credit—United States. 4. Consumer protection—Law and legislation—United States.
I. Title.
HG3751.7.V46 1996
332.7′43—dc20   95-51275
                                                          CIP

Dearborn Financial Publishing books are available at special quantity discounts to use as premiums and sales promotions, or for use in corporate training programs. For more information, please call the Special Sales Manager at 800-621-9621, ext. 4384, or write to Dearborn Financial Publishing, Inc., 155 N. Wacker Drive, Chicago, IL 60606-1719.

Dedication

To Ernesto and Rosario Gomez
For all your support and good times.

Books by John Ventura

The Bankruptcy Kit

The Credit Repair Kit

Fresh Start!

The Small Business Survival Kit

Contents

Preface

I wrote the first edition of *The Credit Repair Kit* in the early 1990s when the credit reporting industry was under fire from state attorneys general, the Federal Trade Commission (FTC) and consumer groups. Among the complaints: Problems in consumer credit records were causing consumers to be turned down for credit, jobs and insurance; credit bureaus were not responsive to consumers' efforts to correct the problems; and credit reporting agencies were making money selling personal information about the consumers whose records were in their databases.

Since that time, the credit reporting industry has gone through tremendous changes for the better that have necessitated a new version of this book. Some of the changes were the result of actions by state attorneys general and the FTC. Other industry reforms were initiated by the credit reporting industry itself. For example, TRW, Trans Union and Equifax, the three credit reporting agencies that dominate the industry, have made their credit reports more readable and have begun sharing information that needs to be corrected in a consumer's credit record.

Despite these and other reforms, understanding your credit report, dealing with any problems in it and rebuilding your credit after financial difficulties can still be confusing and difficult at times. Therefore, my goal remains the same—to provide you with the knowledge and tools you need to deal with credit bureaus and rebuild your credit history, whether it was damaged because your credit was overextended or because of circumstances beyond your control. To help you, the second edition of *The Credit Repair Kit* includes

- time-saving sample letters that get results and create a paper trail that you may need later;

- updated instructions on obtaining your report from the "big three" credit bureaus—TRW, Equifax and Trans Union;

- up-to-date sample reports from the big three with easy-to-understand explanations of how to read them;

- addresses of government agencies and consumer groups that can help you; and

- a full explanation of your rights under the Fair Credit Reporting Act (FCRA).

This new edition of *The Credit Repair Kit* also includes a chapter on the special credit-related issues that women face as well as a chapter about divorce and credit.

The Credit Repair Kit is not just for the financially distressed. I firmly believe that everyone should monitor their reports on a regular basis. After all, you don't want to find out in the middle of your mortgage application that somebody else's negative history has turned up on your report. Furthermore, technology and a lack of adequate regulation allow unauthorized persons accessibility to consumers' personal credit data.

It makes good sense to actively ensure the accuracy of your credit history and to develop and protect your own credit identity. Women should build a credit history separate from their husbands' to protect themselves and their families in case of divorce, widowhood or financial setbacks. Couples contemplating divorce should modify their credit arrangements before they initiate divorce proceedings to minimize their postdivorce financial ties.

I have seen many sad cases of people whose lives have been damaged by negative credit histories. Sometimes those histories were the result of credit bureau mistakes; sometimes the result of creditors' supplying credit bureaus with erroneous information; and sometimes the result of credit misuse. Regardless of the reasons, bad credit can make your life tougher than it needs to be by removing many opportunities for success.

You and you alone must take responsibility for the accuracy of your credit record and for maintaining or rebuilding a good credit history for yourself. Your wise use of credit combined with the information in this book can help you secure a positive financial future for yourself and your family. Good luck!

Acknowledgment

Special thanks to all the people at Dearborn whose dedication helps make working with them such a pleasure.

CHAPTER ONE

The Power of Credit Bureaus

Margaret and Joe O. were unaware that a "sleeping giant" was following them through their credit life. Not until they applied for a loan to buy their first home did they realize how important that giant was—and how much trouble it would cause them. The sleeping giant was the credit bureau.

When Margaret and Joe were refused a loan for their dream house, they came to see me about what they could do. The mortgage lender they had applied to for a loan had told them that information in their credit file was responsible for the denial of their credit application. They brought with them a copy of the credit report that reflected the negative information.

"We have worked hard to keep our credit clean," Joe said. "We just don't understand what's wrong."

After reviewing their report with them, we discovered credit information on a bad debt that Margaret and Joe didn't know anything about.

I explained Margaret and Joe's rights under the Fair Credit Reporting Act, and we sent a letter to the credit bureau disputing the bad debt. After a wait that almost lost the couple their dream home, the credit bureau determined that the incorrect information actually belonged to someone else with a name similar to Joe's. The mistake in Margaret and Joe's credit record was subsequently corrected; however, they experienced a lot of anguish and worry waiting to find out if their credit record would be corrected and if they would get the home loan.

This is just one example of the role that credit reporting agencies can play in your life. It's also a good example of why it's important to regularly monitor your own credit record for problems and inaccuracies. If you don't, you may not learn that there is a problem in your credit record until, like Joe and Margaret, you've filled out an important loan application.

The *Fair Credit Reporting Act* (FCRA) was passed by Congress in 1970 to regulate the credit reporting industry and to establish the rights of consumers in dealing with credit reporting agencies. In spite of this legislation, dealing with credit bureaus can sometimes be time-consuming and frustrating for consumers. The size and influence of the credit reporting industry can best be understood by taking a closer look at what credit bureaus are and how they play such an important role in our lives.

What Are Credit Bureaus?

Credit reporting agencies or credit bureaus are part of a $1 billion industry. According to Associated Credit Bureaus, Inc., a trade association of credit bureaus and mortgage reporting companies in the United States, this industry consists of approximately 900 credit bureaus, most of which are association members. Most credit bureaus are either owned by or affiliated with one of the three national companies that dominate the industry—*TRW*, *Equifax* and *Trans Union*—and are linked to their computer systems. These companies are often referred to as *the big three*. There are also smaller local or regional credit bureaus that have no relationship with the big three as well as large, national information brokers that purchase consumer credit information from the big three and resell that information to other businesses. These national information brokers often maintain mutiple databases, consumer credit information being just one of those databases.

The vast computerized libraries maintained by credit bureaus act as clearinghouses for credit-related information about most American adults. Credit bureaus sell this information to their subscribers—retailers, credit card companies, insurance companies, banks and savings and loans, credit unions, finance companies and the like. It is estimated that the big three update almost 2 billion pieces of credit file information each month, received from thousands of businesses across the country, and generate more than 550 million consumer credit reports annually.

Information in Your Credit Record

A credit bureau maintains the information it collects on you in a credit record or file, which is actually a history of your use and management of credit.

Basic information in your credit record tells who has extended credit to you, whether you pay your bills on time and how much you owe each of your creditors. A more complete discussion of credit record information can be found in Chapter 2.

Where Do Credit Bureaus Get Their Information?

Credit reporting agencies obtain information about you from three basic sources: *subscribers, public records* and *you.* Credit bureaus update their information regularly to provide a month-to-month profile of your use of credit.

In most instances credit bureau subscribers are companies that extend credit to consumers. They provide credit bureaus with information on the bill-paying habits of their account holders. Many credit bureaus require that their subscribers provide consumer account information each month. Increasingly, creditors are using computers to relay consumer account information to credit reporting agencies, but some creditors continue to use manual methods.

Public records, the second source of credit bureau information, include bankruptcy filings, tax liens and judgments. This information also appears in your credit record.

You are the third source of the data gathered and maintained by credit bureaus. When you fill out a credit application, you list identifying information, such as your name, current and former addresses, age and Social Security number. This information becomes a part of your credit file.

Who Sees Your Credit Record?

A credit record is an extremely important document because it contains information that can affect many aspects of your life. Among other things, your credit record can influence your ability to obtain new or additional credit and the terms of that credit, as well as your opportunity to have the type of job you would like, especially if you will have responsibility for money or expensive equipment.

Employers are increasing their use of credit reports since lie detector tests and other screening devices have been banned.

Credit record information may also affect your ability to get adequate insurance or to rent or buy a home or apartment. In addition, credit report information may prevent you from being granted a government security clearance or special license.

The FCRA specifies who may review your credit record and for what purposes. According to that law, access to your file is limited to the following:

- *Potential creditors.* Creditors may access consumer credit records to decide whether to extend credit, to review an account or to collect a debt.

- *Potential insurers.* Insurers may access consumer credit records for information that will assist them in the underwriting of a personal, automobile, family, household or medical insurance policy.

- *Employers.* Consumer credit record information is made available to employers or potential employers to help them make decisions regarding hiring, firing, reassignment or promotion.

- *Others.* Others may review your credit record if you give them written permission to do so.

Additionally, your credit record may be reviewed by issuers of a court order or an IRS subpoena and anyone with a "legitimate business need."

Insurers

Under the FCRA, insurers may review your credit record before granting you insurance. Some companies use the information in credit records to screen out high-risk applicants. Others use consumer credit record information to determine whether to give someone who is already insured additional coverage, to raise that person's insurance rate, or to terminate coverage altogether.

Employers

The FCRA says that if a company or organization orders a credit report on an applicant for a new job or a promotion, the employer must notify the applicant in writing within three days after ordering the report. This has to be done whether or not the applicant is hired or promoted. However, an employer does not have to provide this kind of notification if someone is just being screened for a possible job but has not officially applied for it.

To help protect the rights of job applicants, members of Associated Credit Bureaus, Inc. have voluntarily decided to sell credit reports to employers for hiring purposes only if the employer certifies in writing that the current or potential employee is aware that the credit report will be reviewed.

Credit bureaus will not provide an employer certain kinds of information from a consumer's credit record. This information includes: the consumer's age, marital status and account numbers.

Government Agencies

Any government agency may review your credit record for purposes of granting credit, hiring or insuring. Government agencies also may review your credit file if you are being considered for a special license or a security clearance. For cases in which the law requires that your financial status or financial responsibility be reviewed, a government agency may use the information in your file to help determine your eligibility for a government benefit, including eligibility for welfare benefits.

Other than the specific purposes listed above, a government agency may access only *identifying information* from a credit report, such as name, address and employer.

Legitimate Business Need

The FCRA provides that anyone with a "legitimate business need" may gain access to your file; however, the law fails to define this term, creating a major loophole in the FCRA.

In the absence of a clear definition of *legitimate business need,* credit reporting agencies have interpreted the term broadly, often turning consumer credit information into a profitable commodity. Many have used the information in their files to develop new products and services not directly related to the extension of credit. Some of these products and services are reviewed later in this chapter.

During the early 1990s, the buying and selling of your credit data came under attack by consumer advocates, who cited this practice as a violation of consumer privacy. They pointed out that you provided the information in your credit files on the assumption that it would be used for a single purpose—to evaluate your creditworthiness. These advocates also pointed out that, although credit bureaus are making money buying and selling consumer credit record information, they are not required to remunerate consumers for the use of that information.

In response to the criticism, state attorneys general and the Federal Trade Commission (FTC) began taking a closer look at the buying and selling of consumer credit record information. As a result, the FTC has placed specific restrictions on repackaging and selling consumer credit data. In addition, TRW and Equifax no longer sell direct marketing lists based on consumer account data, although they still market lists based on demographic data gleaned from consumer credit files. Whether Trans Union will continue selling lists based on consumer account data was on appeal in the courts at the time this book was written.

The subject of credit bureaus and the buying and selling of consumer credit record information is discussed in detail in Chapter 10.

Credit Bureau Security

To become a credit bureau subscriber, a company must meet certain qualifications—and prove that it is in business. To verify this, someone from the credit bureau must actually visit the business. These security measures help protect credit bureau information from being scrutinized by companies that are not going to use it for authorized purposes.

Once accepted as a subscriber, a company is given a special code and a security number. These numbers are part of the security system that credit reporting agencies are required to have in place for preventing unauthorized access to consumer credit files. Upon presentation of the correct code and security number, the credit bureau will produce a computer-generated copy of the information it has in its files about you—your credit report.

Credit bureau security systems have been known to fail. Therefore, when reading your credit report, *take note of who has reviewed your file.* Whenever someone asks to review your credit file, that request will be indicated on your report as an *inquiry.* If you do not recognize the name of the company or organization that has made an inquiry into your credit file, contact the credit reporting agency. For more information about the inquiries section of a credit report, see Chapter 2.

The Evolution of the Consumer Credit Industry

Credit records and credit reporting agencies were not always as important as they are today. Until the 1950s most businesses loaned money to people they knew something about—people in their neighborhood or community, for example. As a result, creditors usually knew something about a consumer's personal background, family and bill-paying habits before making a loan. Companies therefore did not make extensive use of credit bureaus. As the number of national and regional consumer-oriented businesses grew during the 1950s and 1960s, however, consumer/creditor transactions became increasingly impersonal. Businesses began making greater use of credit reporting agencies for information needed to judge a consumer's credit-worthiness.

Over the years the credit reporting industry expanded and grew increasingly sophisticated. Automation began to play a major role in the industry's evolution, allowing companies to move from paper-based to computerized records and thus making it easier for credit agencies to collect and access consumer data.

The Federal Fair Credit Reporting Act (FCRA)

The FCRA was a response to changes in the credit reporting industry. The major purposes of this national legislation were to ensure that credit-related information would be collected and used in a way that would protect consumers' right to privacy while guaranteeing consumers access to their own credit records.

The act, which is enforced by the FTC, states that its purpose is "to require that consumer reporting agencies adopt reasonable procedures for meeting the needs of commerce for consumer credit, personnel, insurance and other information in a manner which is fair and equitable to the consumer, with regard to confidentiality, accuracy, relevancy, and proper utilization of such information."

Figure 1.1 summarizes consumer rights under the FCRA. The complete text of the FCRA is contained in Appendix A, and detailed discussions of consumer rights covered by the FCRA may be found throughout this book.

 **HOT TIP**

The policy of Associated Credit Bureaus, Inc. is that a completed Chapter 13 bankruptcy should be reported for seven, not ten, years.

FIGURE 1.1   Summary of Consumers' Rights under the Fair Credit Reporting Act

The FCRA grants you a number of important rights, including the following:

- The right to know what your credit records contain

- The right to be told by a credit bureau the nature, substance and sources (except investigative sources) of the information collected about you

- The right to know the name and address of the credit bureau responsible for preparing a credit report used to deny you credit, insurance or employment, or to increase the cost of your insurance or credit

- The right to a free copy of your credit report if you are denied credit and the denial is due at least in part to credit record information (By law, requests for a free copy must be made within 30 days of your receipt of a notification of denial, although in 1994 the industry adopted a new consumer-friendly policy of 60 days.)

- The right to review your credit report in person at the credit bureau, by phone or by mail

- The right to take someone with you to review your file if you visit a credit bureau in person

- The right to have investigated within a reasonable period of time any information in your credit record that you dispute (If the credit bureau deems your request "frivolous or irrelevant," the law says that the credit bureau need not investigate.)

- The right to have inaccurate information deleted from your credit record if a credit bureau investigation finds the information to be erroneous

- The right to have information deleted if the credit bureau cannot verify it through its investigation

- The right to have the credit bureau notify—at no cost to you—those you name who previously reviewed the incorrect or incomplete information in your credit file that the information has been removed or changed

- The right to know who has received a copy of your credit report over the past six months for credit granting purposes

- The right to know the names of everyone who has seen your credit record over the last two years for employment purposes

- The right to include a brief written statement that will become a permanent part of your credit record explaining your side of any dispute that cannot be resolved with a credit bureau (You may ask that the credit reporting agency share your written statement with certain businesses. The agency must do so without charge if you make your request within 30 days of being denied credit.)

(continued)

FIGURE 1.1   Summary of Consumers' Rights under the FCRA *(continued)*

- The right to have negative credit-related information deleted from your credit record after seven years

- The right to have a bankruptcy deleted after ten years

- The right to sue a credit bureau for damages if it willfully and negligently violates the law (If you are successful in your lawsuit, you may collect attorney fees and court costs as well.)

- The right to be notified by a company that it has requested an investigative report on you

- The right to request from a company pursuing an investigative report more information about the nature and the scope of the investigation

- The right to know the nature and the substance of the investigative report but not the sources

The FCRA does *not* require that

- a credit bureau provide you with a copy of your credit file (Some bureaus will do so, however, if you request it.);

- a business or individual do business with you;

- any federal agency intervene on your behalf; or

- a credit bureau add information on accounts not already in your file (Some credit bureaus will do this for a fee.).

Also, the FCRA does not apply to applications for commercial credit or business insurance. According to the FCRA, most information in a consumer's credit file cannot be reported after seven years. However, the following are exceptions:

- Bankruptcies can be reported for ten years.

- There are no time limitations on reporting information when you apply for a job with a salary of more than $20,000 if the employer requests a credit report as part of the application process.

- There are no time limitations on reporting information when you apply for more than $50,000 worth of credit or life insurance.

- Information concerning a lawsuit or judgment against you can be reported for seven years.

Penalties for Violating the FCRA

If your rights are violated under the provisions of the FCRA, you may sue for damages in a civil court. However, you must be able to prove that the company named in the suit willfully and knowingly violated the law. If you win, you may collect attorney fees and court costs.

The FCRA also makes it a criminal offense for an individual or a company to gain access to information in your credit file under false pretenses and for an employee or an officer of a credit bureau to provide such information to an unauthorized individual.

Fines of up to $5,000, a prison sentence, or both may be imposed on anyone convicted of using false pretenses to obtain credit information about you from a credit bureau. The same penalties and fines apply to officers and employees of credit bureaus who make unauthorized disclosures of credit record information.

Investigative Reports

A few credit reporting agencies provide investigative reports for companies, primarily insurance companies and potential employers. Although they are not new, these reports are not familiar to most consumers. Members of Associated Credit Bureaus, Inc. rarely prepare this type of report.

Investigative reports contain subjective information about an individual such as details about that person's lifestyle, personal habits and character, gathered through personal interviews with individuals who know you.

The FCRA requires that the user of an investigative report must notify you in writing at the time the report is requested; however, the law does not require that you be told who was contacted to prepare the report.

If your application for insurance is denied as a result of information about you in an investigative report, the law says that the company requesting the report must give you the name and address of the company that prepared the report so you can review exactly what was reported. If you discover something that is not true in your report, the process for correcting it is the same as the process for correcting adverse information in your credit report.

Recent Developments in the Credit Reporting Industry

During the 1980s, the consumer credit reporting industry changed dramatically. Technological advances only dreamed about at the time the FCRA was written transformed the face of the industry and the ways in which consumer data could be used. For example, businesses can now gain immediate, online access to a credit bureau's databases.

Computer technology has also facilitated the development of many of the new specialized products and services that the larger credit bureaus market to their subscribers and others. These new products and services help creditors evaluate, analyze and monitor consumer accounts, highlighting those that are at a high risk for delinquency, default and the like. Also included among the new products and services are those that help create more effective direct mailing lists or better marketing databases.

As discussed earlier, some new credit-specific products and services are the direct result of a loophole in the FCRA. They are also the result of technological advances that policymakers never envisioned when the law was drafted.

Most consumers are not aware of the additional products and services marketed by credit bureaus because these products and services are not consumer-oriented. A review of some of these products and services follows.

Credit Bureau Products and Services for Subscribers

Not all credit bureaus offer each of the products and services described in this section. However, this list illustrates the many ways that credit reporting agencies can generate additional income by using consumer credit information.

- *Fraud detection databases.* To help creditors detect fraudulent credit applications, credit reporting agencies have developed computerized systems that allow identifying information from a credit application to be compared to the agency's fraud file. When a match is found, the creditor is notified of the possibility for fraud.

- *Automated cross-directories.* Credit reporting agencies can help creditors locate missing or delinquent consumers by offering them direct on-line access to the names and addresses of hundreds of thousands of consumers all over the country.

- *Collections.* Many credit reporting agencies offer collection services to their subscribers.

- *Risk Scores.* Credit reporting agencies can provide creditors with risk scores on consumers based on a statistical evaluation of information in their credit files. These scores rate how well a consumer is likely to manage additional or new credit. Some creditors rely more on these ratings than they do on the actual content of a consumer's file when evaluating that consumer's credit-worthiness.

- *Account monitoring.* To help creditors minimize the number of accounts that are in default or delinquent, the credit bureaus let creditors know when one of their consumer accounts has moved, become delinquent and so forth by monitoring consumers' payment histories and patterns of using credit.

- *Weekly compilations of information from courthouse records, including federal tax liens, civil judgments, bankruptcies, divorces and mortgages.* This information is not necessarily used by creditors to help them make decisions about the extension of credit but rather helps them pinpoint those accounts that may end up delinquent and/or in collections.

- *Delinquency/bankruptcy predictors.* Credit reporting agencies are able to combine the information in their files with risk evaluation measures to identify consumers likely to become delinquent or to file for bankruptcy.

- *Prescreening.* Cross-checking the credit information in consumer files with company-provided credit granting criteria or against a list of consumer names, credit bureaus can help a company identify individuals to whom credit should be offered. This practice is called prescreening. Credit granting criteria might include age, sex, ethnicity, income and similar facts. The industry has received a lot of criticism about prescreening and the big profits the practice generates for credit reporting agencies. Although the FCRA is vague on the issue, the FTC has ruled that prescreening is permissible so long as each person on the list—after prescreening—receives a "firm offer of credit." See Chapter 9 for a more detailed discussion of prescreening.

- *Database enhancement.* Some credit bureaus extract very specific, limited information from their consumer files to help companies improve their marketing databases. By carefully defining exactly what information it provides, a credit reporting agency can circumvent the restriction placed on prescreening by the FTC.

- *Targeted marketing lists.* Because of pressure from the FTC, TRW and Equifax no longer sell consumer account-related data to marketers. However, they do sell lists based on consumer identification data, such as your address, age and the like, that businesses can use to target segments of their markets. A case involving Trans Union's sale of consumer account-related data to marketers was under appeal at the time this book was written. Depending on its outcome, Trans Union may ultimately be held to the same standards as TRW and Equifax.

Criticism of Credit Reporting Agencies

During the late 1980s and early 1990s, the credit reporting industry came under considerable criticism from consumer watchdog groups, policymakers, state attorneys general and the media. Reasons for this criticism included

- well-publicized high rates of error and inaccuracy in consumers' credit records (To be fair, some of these problems were the result of credit grantors providing inaccurate information to credit bureaus.);

- consumer difficulty correcting problems in their records;

- invasion of consumers' privacy through the collection, storage and resale of massive amounts of sensitive and highly personal consumer information without the consumers' knowledge.

Consumers became increasingly aware that the credit reporting industry may have been abusing their privacy through its use of consumer credit information and that they needed help dealing with credit reporting agencies. The result was that attorneys general in several states as well as the FTC became more aggressive and in several instances took legal action against one or more of the big three. Several important reforms that resulted have changed the way credit reporting agencies relate to consumers and the way the industry does business.

Legal Actions

During the summer of 1991, the FTC and attorneys general from Alabama, Arkansas, California, Connecticut, Delaware, Florida, Idaho, Illinois, Louisiana, Michigan, Missouri, Nevada, New Hampshire, New Mexico, New York, Ohio, Pennsylvania, Rhode Island and Texas sued TRW.

As a result of the lawsuit, TRW agreed to make changes in its computer system to improve the accuracy of its credit files; to respond within 30 days to consumer complaints about errors and inaccuracies in their credit records or to delete the disputed information; to accept consumers' documentation in disputes over credit record errors; and to mail consumers a copy of their credit records within four business days after receiving a request. TRW also agreed to charge consumers living in the 19 states that brought the lawsuit no more than $7.50 for a copy of their credit reports, adjusted annually for inflation.

In addition, TRW promised to offer toll-free service to consumers denied credit; notify consumers of their right to dispute information in their credit records; and inform those who inquired of the names of the companies that have bought TRW's credit reports. TRW also agreed to tell consumers what their credit risk scores are—a score TRW previously made available only to creditors. TRW also announced that it would provide consumers with one free credit report each year, whether a consumer had been denied credit or not, and it revamped the format of its credit report to make it easier to understand.

Also under pressure from attorneys general in nearly 20 states, Equifax promised to improve consumer access to credit records and the timeliness of its dispute investigation and resolution process. The company also agreed to make credit reports available to consumers within four business days of receiving a request and revised the format of its credit report to make it easier to understand. In addition, Equifax established a toll-free consumer assistance line; announced that it would send a free report to anyone who had ever been denied credit, no matter how long ago; and reduced the cost of its reports from $15 to $8 in most states. As mentioned earlier in this chapter, Equifax also stopped selling consumer credit data to businesses for direct marketing purposes.

Although fewer and less drastic, Trans Union also has made some changes. In a nationwide settlement announced in the fall of 1992, Trans Union agreed to reinvestigate all consumer complaints about inaccurate credit record information within 30 days and to make necessary corrections. It also agreed to provide consumers with copies of their credit reports within four business days of a request. Trans Union has also made some small changes in the format of its credit report to make it more consumer-friendly; and it has installed new software to cut down on credit bureau errors.

Actions of the Federal Trade Commission

The FTC also became stricter with the credit reporting industry during the early 1990s. For example, in a 1995 reinterpretation of the FCRA, the FTC ruled that when a credit reporting agency develops credit risk scores or other types of point systems to help creditors evaluate the credit-worthiness of a consumer, it must disclose those scores to consumers who request a copy of their credit files as well as provide an explanation of the scores. Although many creditors use their own scoring systems to evaluate credit applicants, others use the score provided by the reporting agency. According to the FTC, the score may be the *only* information a creditor receives from a credit bureau after requesting a consumer's credit history.

The FTC also began to crack down on the sale of consumer credit data to businesses that use such information to develop new business. The FTC's actions in this area are covered in greater detail in Chapter 10.

Congressional Hearings

Every year from 1991 through 1994, the U.S. Congress held public hearings to examine industry practices and to review possible revisions to the FCRA.

The revisions considered by various Senate and House subcommittees would have made the credit reporting industry fairer and friendlier to consumers by

- reducing the cost of credit reports to consumers;

- requiring credit bureaus to provide toll-free numbers for consumers to call with complaints;

- increasing the accuracy of credit reports;

- making it easier for consumers to correct their credit records;

- placing greater responsibility on creditors to report accurate, up-to-date information to credit bureaus;

- requiring greater disclosure of consumers' rights in regard to their credit records and credit reporting in general;

- providing consumers with greater protection against privacy invasion; and

- regulating credit repair firms.

Despite the compelling testimony offered during the subcommittee hearings, the FCRA has not been revised because of intense pressure from special interest groups and lack of commitment by Congress. However, as already discussed, despite the lack of congressional action, changes have nevertheless been taking place in the credit reporting industry.

The Future

Although recent reforms are steps in the right direction, most industry watchdogs and critics agree that they are not enough. In part this is because the reforms made by one credit reporting agency do not apply to all other agencies, including the smaller regional and local independent credit bureaus. Also, some problems need to be addressed at the national level by reforming the FCRA.

According to the FTC, two reforms in particular are needed: (1) Creditors need to be held to the same standards of accuracy in maintaining and reporting consumer account information as are credit reporting agencies and (2) the FTC's powers to enforce the provisions of the FCRA need to be strengthened by allowing it to impose monetary penalties against those who violate the law.

Congressional observers predict that these FCRA reforms are unlikely to take place any time soon. On the other hand, however, we may see the states continuing to enact their own fair credit reporting laws—24 already have such laws on the books.

CHAPTER
TWO

Credit Report Basics

Constance M. was referred to me by a friend. An intelligent, successful woman who had reached a senior management position in an insurance company, Constance had no financial problems. She was following up on some good advice she had received about the importance of reviewing her credit file at least twice a year. Sitting across from me, Constance removed a file from her briefcase neatly marked "Credit Report."

This was the first time Constance had ever seen her credit report, and she wanted to make sure that she understood all of it. We went through each item in her report.

As we did so, Constance was relieved to discover that her report was problem-free. I told her that she was lucky—I had worked with many consumers who had found problems in their credit records. I also explained to Constance that each of the major credit reporting agencies may keep a file on her and that the credit-related information in each file may be different. Disconcerted to learn this, Constance left my office prepared to obtain a copy of her credit report from each of the other major credit reporting agencies.

This chapter provides the information and the tools that you need to determine the status of your credit files. If you have a good credit history, checking your credit record once a year is a wise preventive measure. If you have had credit problems in the past, however, the first step in the credit rebuilding process involves reviewing your credit history regularly. Also, before applying for an important loan, it is always a good idea to review your credit file to make sure that there are no problems that could cause a delay in the loan approval process or could cause your application to be denied. It is also advisable to review your file if you are applying for insurance or a new job.

Some of the more subtle—but very important—ways that credit record information can affect your life will be explained in this chapter. Such information underscores the importance of regularly monitoring what credit reporting agencies are saying about you.

Which Credit Bureaus Maintain a Record on You?

To gain a comprehensive picture of yourself as a credit managing consumer, it is a good idea to request a copy of your credit report from each of the big three credit reporting agencies. You also may need to get copies of your credit record from regional and local credit reporting agencies in your area not affiliated with one of the nationals, although the number of independent credit bureaus is declining.

Credit bureaus, as mentioned in Chapter 1, obtain much of their information from the businesses and organizations that subscribe to their services. Because different companies subscribe to the services of different credit reporting agencies, each credit bureau may have slightly different information on a consumer. For example, Company A may report to TRW and Equifax, whereas Company B reports to Trans Union and Company C reports only to TRW. However, most large credit grantors now report data to each of the big three. In addition, although each of the big three credit reporting agencies are separate businesses that compete with one another for the same subscriber base, they have begun sharing some of their consumer credit information. Therefore, all of the major credit bureaus increasingly will have the same information about you in their computer files. This also means that an error in the files of one of the big three is likely to appear in the files of the others.

To locate the credit reporting agencies in your area, look in your local yellow pages under "credit reporting agencies" or "credit bureaus." If you live in a small town or rural community, go to the library and use the yellow pages for the city nearest you. If you see a listing for any of the major credit reporting agencies, jot down an address and telephone number for each. Do the same for any local or regional credit bureaus you may find listed. Then call each of the credit bureaus you've identified to find out if any of them maintain a file on you.

If you don't see a local listing for any of the big three in the yellow pages, you can order a copy of your report from their national offices. Instructions on how and where to order are in the next section.

Requesting a Copy of Your Credit Report

Once you've developed a list of the credit bureaus to contact, you will need to prepare a credit report request letter. In your letter, print your full name, including your middle name, and be sure to include "Jr.," "Sr.," "III," and so forth when applicable. Also include your date of birth, Social Security number, current address and former address if you've not been at your current address for at least five years. (TRW wants consumers requesting a copy of their credit report to list their full addresses for the past five years.) Include your spouse's name if you're married and your daytime and evening phone numbers with area codes. Also, send along a copy of a billing statement from a major national bankcard, a utility bill, your driver's license—any document that reflects your current name and address. This is for security purposes to help the credit reporting agency verify that you are in fact the person requesting the copy of your credit report. Finally, be sure to sign your letter so the credit bureau has your signature on file; it too is needed for security purposes.

Once a credit bureau receives your request for a copy of your report, it should respond to your request within three business days. For a sample credit report request letter, see Figure 2.1.

Where To Direct a Credit Record Request Made to One of the Big Three

Instructions for ordering a copy of your credit report from one of the big three will vary depending on why you are ordering it—you have been denied credit, employment or insurance because of information in your credit file, or you want to review your report to make sure it contains no errors or omissions. TRW offers all consumers one free copy of their credit report every year, including special instructions for getting it that are provided later in this chapter.

HOT TIP

The credit report-ordering information reported in this chapter can change. Therefore, to avoid delays in processing your credit report requests from the big three, it's always a good idea to call their national consumer assistance offices for up-to-date instructions.

If You Want To Check Your Credit Report for Errors or Omissions

If you're requesting a copy of your credit report because you want to make sure that it contains no errors or serious omissions, write to the national consumer assistance offices for each of the big three. To help ensure that your request is processed without delay, be sure to include in your letter all of the information

FIGURE 2.1   Sample Credit Report Request Letter

Date

Address of Credit Bureau

Dear Sir or Madam:

I am writing to request a copy of my credit report.

My complete name is: _____

My Social Security number is: _____

My date of birth is: _____

My spouse's complete name *(if applicable)* is: _____

My spouse's Social Security number is: _____

My current address *(do not use a PO Box number)*: _____
_____

My previous address/es over the past five years are:
_____
_____
_____
_____
_____

My daytime phone number is: (_____) _____

My evening phone number is: (_____) _____

To pay for the cost of the report, I have enclosed a check *(or money order)* in the amount of $_____.

Please send the report to me at the following address: _____
_____

Thank you for your cooperation. If you have any questions, you may contact me at: *(area code/telephone number)*.

Sincerely,

Signature

detailed in the previous section of this chapter entitled "Requesting a Copy of Your Credit Report." Mail your request letters to:

TRW National Consumer Assistance
PO Box 2104
Allen, TX 75013
800-682-7654
You can pay for a TRW credit report with a check or money order.

Trans Union
Consumer Disclosure Center
PO Box 390
Springfield, PA 19064-0390
610-690-4909
You can pay for your Trans Union credit report with a check or money order.

Equifax
Office of Consumer Affairs
PO Box 105873
Atlanta, GA 30348
800-685-1111
You can pay for your Equifax report with a check or money order; you can pay with a credit card by using the company's automated dialing system. Access it by calling 404-612-3200. You can also order via fax at 404-612-3150 and pay with a credit card.

The Cost of Your Report

At the time this book was researched, the cost of a credit report in most states was $8, plus applicable state sales tax. However, the cost of a report may increase slightly every year based on inflation. Some states, however, have set caps on the cost of a credit report. These states include but are not limited to:

States	Fee
Connecticut	$5.00
Maine	2.00
Maryland	5.00
Vermont	7.50
Washington	8.00

These same states also require credit bureaus to provide consumers one free copy of their credit report each year upon request. This means that you can review your credit report for free each year if you reside in one of these states and that if you want to review it a second time in a year and have not been denied credit, you'll pay less than consumers in the rest of the country.

HOT TIP

Before ordering a copy of your credit report, call the consumer information or credit practices office at your state attorney general's office to confirm the cost of a credit report in your state and your state's law regarding free reports. Consumer assistance lines of the big three do not always provide complete and up-to-date information on the cost of a credit report nor on the availability of a free report for residents of your state.

How To Request TRW's Free Credit Report

TRW offers one free report a year to all consumers regardless of their state of residence or whether they have been denied credit. To obtain a free copy of your TRW credit report, call 800-682-7654 for ordering instructions.

If You've Been Denied Credit, Employment or Insurance

If you're contacting a credit reporting agency because you've been denied credit, employment or insurance as the result of information in a credit or investigative report, the FCRA says that you are entitled to a free copy of the report if you make the request within 30 days of the denial. However, most credit bureaus, including the big three, have extended that period to 60 days. The company that denied you credit should give you the name and address of the credit bureau that provided the negative information.

 HOT TIP

The big three have adopted a policy that allows a consumer denied credit because of information in the credit file of any one of them to obtain a free credit report from *each* of the big three, not just from the one that provided the negative information.

Mail your credit report request together with a copy of your denial letter to the address provided in the letter. If you are not given an address or if you lose it, you can also mail your requests to the addresses provided at the end of this section. Be sure your request letter includes all necessary information.

TRW
National Consumer Assistance Center
PO Box 949
Allen, Texas 75002-0949
800-682-7654

Trans Union
National Consumer Disclosure Center
PO Box 390
Springfield, PA 19064-0390
610-690-4909
Trans Union also offers consumers an interactive phone number you can call
to order a copy of your credit report by phone if you've been denied credit.
That number is 316-636-6100.

Equifax
PO Box 105873
Atlanta, GA 30348
800-685-1111

What's in a Credit Report?

All credit reports include the same basic types of information: an identification number, identifying data, credit history, inquiries and public record information. Each credit reporting agency, however, uses a different format for presenting this information.

In recent years, each of the big three has made an effort to simplify its credit reports so they are easier to understand. These new reports are a response to pressure from the Federal Trade Commission, consumer advocacy groups and state attorneys general. Taking the lead, for example, TRW's credit report dispenses with all codes and symbols, instead using a narrative format to present consumer account information. Its credit report is the most readable of any of the big three's. Trans Union has simplified its report format somewhat, adding some explanatory text and removing codes. Equifax has made some improvements in its report but continues to rely primarily on codes and symbols. To help you understand your credit report, explanations of the formats used by each of the big three are provided in Chapter 3.

If you are unable to understand any of the information in your credit report, the FCRA requires the credit bureau that generated the report to have personnel available who can help you. Your credit report should include either a toll-free number to call with your questions or the address and phone number of an affiliated bureau you can call for help.

Identifying Data

The identifying information in your credit report usually includes the following:

- Name and address

- Birthdate

- Spouse's name

- Current place of employment and address

- Social Security number

This information generally comes from credit and loan applications that you have filled out.

Credit History

The heart of any credit report is the payment history on accounts that were reported to the credit reporting agency. Despite the slightly different credit report format used by each credit bureau, most reports reflect the following types of account information:

- Name of the creditor and account/loan number

- Nature of the account/loan (i.e., whether it is joint or individual)

- Type of account/loan—revolving, installment, student loan, mortgage

- Date account was opened or loan was established

- Credit limit on account/loan amount

- Current balance on account/loan (*Note*: The dollar amount shown in this section of a consumer's report reflects the account balance at the time the information was obtained. It will not reflect what has been paid on the account or charged on the account since that time.)

- Account payment history, including number of late payments and whether an account has been referred to collections or has been closed by the consumer or the creditor (*Note*: Just as with the item above, this part of a consumer's credit report reflects what was history at the time the account information was reported and will not reflect subsequent account activities.)

- Date information on the account/loan was last reported

- Number of months for which information has been reported

- Amount of credit that has been extended to a consumer

- Whether the consumer is disputing information related to an account

Inquiries

The inquiries section of a credit report indicates those creditors and others who have checked your credit file. Some of the inquiries listed will be preceded by such abbreviations as *PRM, AM* and *AR*. PRM indicates that the inquiry was made for *promotional* purposes—your credit file was reviewed or screened for a preapproved credit offer. AM stands for *account monitoring* and AR for *account review*, both of which mean that one of your creditors reviewed the information in your file, perhaps to determine whether your line of credit should be increased or your credit card canceled. The only inquiries that are reported to businesses when they review the information in your credit file are those that result from your application for new or additional credit.

The FCRA does not specify the amount of time that an inquiry can and/or should remain on a credit report, but it does indicate the minimum amount of time that an inquiry should stay there. That minimum is two years for employment purposes and six months for all other purposes.

Although the inquiries section of a credit report may seem relatively unimportant, it can have a significant bearing on your ability to get credit because lenders consider the number of credit-related inquiries in your file to be an indicator of how much credit you are trying to obtain. If they see a lot of inquiries, they may assume that you are applying for too much credit and are likely to conclude that you will not be a responsible user of credit. In such cases, lenders are apt to deny your credit request.

 HOT TIP

Every time you apply for a credit card, a mortgage loan, a loan from a car financing company or some other type of credit, your credit record is likely to reflect an additional inquiry. To minimize the number of inquiries in your file, apply only for the credit you most need or want.

The FCRA does not provide consumers any rights with regard to inquiries. Regardless, it is always a good idea to challenge any inquiries that you do not recognize as the credit reporting agency may be willing to investigate them for you.

Public Record Information

The information in this section of a credit report refers to credit-related events that are a matter of public record. They include bankruptcies, foreclosures, judgments and tax liens. The public information section also may make note of convictions. In an effort to reduce the number of parents who are falling behind or totally ignoring their child support payments, state or local agencies that enforce child support agreements are beginning to report child support delinquencies to credit bureaus.

What Your Credit Report Says about You

After you receive a copy of your credit report, you'll probably be surprised to discover what is and isn't in the report and that it is really quite incomplete.

The fact that a credit record is not a truly comprehensive portrait of you as a consumer is the result of a number of factors. First, as mentioned earlier in this chapter, different credit reporting agencies may get their information from different subscribers. Therefore, no credit bureau maintains a comprehensive credit file on a consumer.

Second, not all creditors maintain ongoing subscriber relationships with credit reporting agencies and therefore do not regularly report consumer account information to credit bureaus. In fact, some may only do so when an account is in collection or in default. Examples of the types of companies that tend not to report regularly to credit bureaus include: auto dealers; mortgage companies; small department stores and local retailers; utility companies; and medical providers. Figure 2.2 summarizes reporting patterns of key subscribers.

You may find that significant account information is missing from your credit record, whereas information that you would rate as relatively unimportant is included. For example, unless you have ever been 90 days late or more on your mortgage payment, it is unlikely that your credit history will reflect your payment history on that loan. Yet for most consumers a mortgage is the single largest financial commitment they make! On the other hand, the fact that you may have been a couple of days late with a small monthly bankcard payment *will* most likely appear in your report.

FIGURE 2.2   Regularly Reported Consumer Account Data

Consumer account data are reported regularly for the following accounts:

- Bankcards
- Large retailers such as Sears and J. C. Penney
- American Express and other travel and entertainment cards
- Airline charge cards
- Federally guaranteed student loans

In most cases, consumer data on the following accounts are not reported to credit bureaus unless the account is past due, in collection, or results in a lawsuit or a judgment against the consumer:

- Utility bills
- Oil and gas cards (Some oil and gas companies report regularly.)
- Medical bills
- Attorneys' bills
- Rent
- Mortgages that are at least 90 days past due
- Auto dealer loans
- Credit union loans (Some credit unions report regularly.)
- Accounts with smaller department stores and local retailers

CHAPTER
THREE

How To Read
Credit Reports from
the Big Three

Mike R. came to see me about rebuilding his credit. Following my advice, he got a copy of his credit report from each of the big three credit bureaus. He was going to review them for misinformation, incorrect entries or information he disputed.

Several weeks after our first meeting, Mike showed up in my office. He had gotten his credit reports but had questions about some of the information.

Mike and I sat down and looked over each of his credit reports. He was amazed to learn how much information each report contained. As I explained what some of the abbreviations and symbols in the reports meant and discussed which accounts presented the biggest problems for him, we also noted two items that we thought were incorrect and might cause Mike problems in the future if he didn't get them removed from his record.

During the early 1990s, the big three were under increasing pressure from consumer advocates, consumers, state attorneys general, elected officials, the FTC and the media to become more consumer-friendly. Each of the big three responded by making changes in the way they do business. To a greater or lesser degree, for example, each company changed the formats of their credit reports to make them more readable and more understandable so that it is easier for consumers to identify problems in their credit records.

In this chapter I will review the credit report formats of each of the big three credit reporting agencies and explain how to read them. I will also review the format of the credit report produced by CREDCO, Inc., which consolidates credit information from each of the big three into a single report. If after reading this chapter you are confused about how to interpret anything in your credit report, call the appropriate credit bureau for help using the number listed on your credit report, or call the consumer assistance numbers provided in the previous chapter. As has already been mentioned, the FCRA requires that credit bureaus have personnel available to help consumers make sense of their reports.

Systems for Reporting Consumer Information

As reported in Chapter 2, although the types of information found in the credit reports of the big three are basically the same, the presentation of that information varies from company to company.

Traditionally, there have been two basic systems for reporting a consumer's account payment history: *Method of Payment* (MOP) and *Historical Method of Payment* (HOP).

MOP classifies all accounts as *Revolving* (R), *Installment* (I) or *Open-End* (O) loans and then notes the timeliness of payments on each account, using a number code.

HOP focuses on the frequency with which a consumer has been late with an account payment, how late the payments have been and the like.

Credit reporting agencies typically combine elements of both MOP and HOP. TRW, however, has broken with tradition with its introduction of a narrative format for credit reporting.

The Equifax Credit Report

Figure 3.1 is a sample of an Equifax credit report with its detailed explanation of each section and how to read its codes and abbreviations. The Equifax report also comes with a *Research Request Form* to use if you find a problem with anything in your report.

The Equifax address to which you should direct correspondence about credit record corrections, omissions or other queries is listed in the upper right-hand corner of the report. Below that address is basic consumer identification information, including current address, Social Security number, date of birth and name of spouse (if applicable).

Credit History

Proceeding down the page, you will find a section labeled *Credit History,* the heart of your credit report. Under this major heading is a series of subheadings. Moving from left to right, the first subheading is *Company Name.* Companies

FIGURE 3.1 Sample Equifax Credit Report

Note: This is a copy of an actual credit file. Identifying information (i.e., name, address, Social Security number, date of birth, account numbers, etc.) has been removed to protect consumer's identity.

Source: Reprinted by permission of Equifax, Inc.

listed under this subheading are the creditors who report to Equifax. Account numbers for each of the creditors are listed to the right.

To the right is a series of narrow columns, each with a heading, that contain specific information for each of the accounts listed on the credit report. A brief explanation of these columns follows.

Whose Account

Equifax uses nine different letter codes to indicate who is responsible for an account and the type of participation you have with each account. For example, on the sample credit report, three letter codes appear: *I* (individual), *J* (joint) and *U* (undesignated).

Your credit report might also include codes for authorized user, cosigner or some other category. Explanations for each of the letter codes are provided in the material Equifax encloses with its consumer credit reports.

Date Opened

Date Opened indicates the month and year you opened the account with the credit grantor.

Months Reviewed and Date of Last Activity

Months Reviewed refers to the number of months of account payment history reported to Equifax by a creditor. On the sample report, those numbers range from 10 months to 99 months.

Date of Last Activity is the last date for which there was any activity on an account. That activity could include the last time you made an account payment or the last time you charged something to the account.

High Credit and Terms

High Credit indicates either the maximum amount you have ever charged to an account or your credit limit on an account.

Terms indicates the number of installment payments for a revolving account—signified by a number, or the monthly payment for an installment account—signified by an *M*.

Items as of Date Reported

This subheading contains three columns of information. *Balance* refers to the amount you owe on an account at the time that it is reported to Equifax by your creditor. The *Past Due* column reflects any amount past due at the time the account information was reported.

Two kinds of information are represented by the letter/number codes found in the *Status* column of the Equifax report. The letter part of each code indicates the type of account being reported. *O* refers to an *Open* account, one in which the entire balance is due each month. *R* refers to a *Revolving* account, and *I* signifies an *Installment* account.

The number part of the code provides information regarding the timeliness of your account payments to your creditors. For example, *1* indicates that you have made your account payments as agreed and that your account is in good standing; *2* means that the account is 30 days or more past due; *7* signifies that regular payments are being made under a wage earner plan (Chapter 13 bankruptcy) or similar arrangement.

Date Reported

The *Date* the account was last reported to the credit bureau is indicated in the far right column of the credit history section.

Other Account Information

For some accounts listed in the *Credit History* section, your Equifax credit report may reflect *prior paying history* data. For example, on the sample credit report, this information is provided for the Wells Fargo and Frost Bros. accounts.

Prior paying history information tells how frequently you were 30, 60 or 90 days past due making payments on an account during the number of months of account information provided by a creditor. For example, in the case of the Wells Fargo account on the sample report, the consumer was 30 days late four times—30 (04)—and 60 days late one time—60 (01). This section of the report also provides the date when the two most recent payment delinquencies occurred as well as the date of the most serious delinquency. The two most recent times that payment on the Wells Fargo account were late were June 1991 and May 1991, and the account was most seriously delinquent on February 1991.

Other data that would appear in this section of your Equifax report includes information about you or a creditor closing one of your accounts, or details of an account being transferred or sold.

Collection Accounts

This section of the Equifax report notes any accounts that have been referred to collections. This information will appear after your basic credit history and before the section labeled *Courthouse Records.*

The sample credit report shows no collection accounts. When collection accounts are listed, the following information is provided for each account turned over to a collection agency:

- When the collection was reported

- The date the account was assigned to a collection agency

- The dollar amount in collection

- The date of last activity on the account

- The type of account (i.e., individual, joint, etc., and the account number)

Courthouse Records

This section of the Equifax report presents public record information that is pulled from local, state and federal court records and reflects your history of meeting financial obligations.

Looking at the sample report, you see that this section shows a lien was filed by the federal government on 11/89 against a piece of property owned by the consumer to satisfy a $2,056 debt the consumer owed the government. It also shows that the lien was released on 4/90 once the debt was paid in full.

If you have filed for bankruptcy, relevant related information would also be presented in this section of your Equifax credit report. Bankruptcy-related information would include: the date the bankruptcy was filed, the case number, the dollar amount of your assets and liabilities, and whether your bankruptcy had been discharged at the time the report was issued.

If anyone or any company had won a judgment against you, that too would appear in your credit report. Information regarding the judgment would include: the date the judgment was filed, the case number, the names of the defendant and the plaintiff, amount of the judgment, when the judgment was satisfied or paid and how it was satisfied.

Additional Information

This section of your Equifax credit report provides additional creditor-reported identification information. Typically, this will include your former addresses as well as details regarding your current and former employment—job title, company name, location and dates of employment.

Companies That Requested Your Credit History

At the bottom of the Equifax report is a list of those businesses that requested a copy of your credit report over the past 24 months. The full names of the requesters or abbreviations of their names are provided.

A letter code will precede some requesters' names. Possible codes include: *PRM, AM* and *AR*. As explained in Chapter 2, PRM stands for promotional and means that the creditor obtained your name and address from Equifax so that it could offer you credit. *AM* and *AR* appear when one of your creditors makes a periodic review of your Equifax report. *Equifax* appears in those instances when you requested a copy of your own credit report.

The Trans Union Credit Report

Figure 3.2 is a sample Trans Union credit report. Of the big three agencies, Trans Union's credit report used to be the most difficult to understand because it relied heavily on symbols and codes and included extraneous information. The company has now made significant improvements to its credit report format for easier understanding.

The Trans Union report comes with an *Investigation Request Form* that serves the same purpose as the Equifax *Research Request Form*. Consumers are supposed to use this form to contest information in their credit reports as well as to present credit-related information they would like to have added to their reports.

File Number

Trans Union's report contains a file or identification number that should be referenced when you contact the company about information in your credit report. The number is located in the upper right-hand corner of the first page of the report.

Identifying Information

Just below the file number at the start of the Trans Union credit report is your Social Security number. Below that and to the left is your name, current address and any former addresses reported. Employment data may also be reported in this section of the report although it does not appear on the sample report.

FIGURE 3.2 Sample Trans Union Credit Report

```
⊔ TRANS UNION                      YOUR TRANS UNION FILE NUMBER:
   Solutions From The Company That Listens   PAGE  1 OF  5 (INTL USE:
   760 SPROUL RD. P.O. BOX 390     DATE THIS REPORT PRINTED: 08/15/95
   SPRINGFIELD, PA 19064-0390
                                   SOCIAL SECURITY NUMBER:

                                   YOU HAVE BEEN IN OUR FILES SINCE: 09/86



   CONSUMER REPORT FOR:


       ‖⊔‖‖⊔‖‖⊔‖‖‖⊔‖‖⊔‖



   FORMER ADDRESSES REPORTED:



                        YOUR CREDIT INFORMATION
   ───────────────────────────────────────────────────────────────────
   THE FOLLOWING ITEMS OBTAINED FROM PUBLIC RECORDS APPEAR ON YOUR REPORT. YOU M/
   BE REQUIRED TO EXPLAIN PUBLIC RECORD ITEMS TO POTENTIAL CREDITORS.  ANY BANK-
   RUPTCY INFORMATION WILL REMAIN ON YOUR REPORT FOR 10 YEARS FROM THE DATE OF
   FILING.  ALL OTHER PUBLIC RECORD INFORMATION, INCLUDING DISCHARGED CHAPTER 13
   BANKRUPTCY AND ANY ACCOUNTS CONTAINING ADVERSE INFORMATION, REMAIN FOR 7 YEARS

   DOCKET #            COUNTY CLERK        FEDERAL TAX LIEN
   PLAINTIFF:          FEDERAL TAX LIEN                      ENTERED:
   PLAINTIFF ATTORNEY:                                       AMOUNT:      $
                       STATE: TX                             PAID:        0

   ───────────────────────────────────────────────────────────────────
   THE FOLLOWING ACCOUNTS CONTAIN INFORMATION WHICH SOME CREDITORS MAY CONSIDER T
   BE ADVERSE.  THE ADVERSE INFORMATION IN THESE ACCOUNTS HAS BEEN PRINTED IN
   >BRACKETS< FOR YOUR CONVENIENCE, TO HELP YOU UNDERSTAND YOUR REPORT.  THEY ARE
   NOT BRACKETED THIS WAY FOR CREDITORS. (NOTE: THE ACCOUNT # MAY BE SCRAMBLED BY
   THE CREDITOR FOR YOUR PROTECTION).

   FROST BROS   - #                        REVOLVING TERMS ACCOUNT
      REPT'D   09/90   BALANCE:        $0   INDIVIDUAL ACCOUNT
      OPENED   11/83   MOST OWED:    $396   PAY TERMS:  MINIMUM $15
    >IN PRIOR  6 MONTHS  1 TIME  60 DAYS LATE<
      STATUS AS OF 09/90: PAID AS AGREED

   WELL FARG VS - #                        REVOLVING TERMS ACCOUNT
   ACCOUNT CLOSED                           CREDIT CARD
      REPT'D   05/95   BALANCE:        $0   INDIVIDUAL ACCOUNT
      OPENED   04/84   MOST OWED:   $3000   CREDIT LIMIT:     $3000
      CLOSED   07/93
    >IN PRIOR 45 MONTHS  1 TIME  60 DAYS LATE<
      STATUS AS OF 05/95: PAID AS AGREED
```

Note: This is a copy of an actual credit file. Identifying information (i.e., name, address, Social Security number, date of birth, account numbers, etc.) has been removed to protect consumer's identity.

Source: Reprinted by permission of Trans Union.

FIGURE 3.2 Sample Trans Union Credit Report *(continued)*

```
REPORT ON                                                    PAGE  2 OF  5
SOCIAL SECURITY NUMBER:            TRANS UNION FILE NUMBER:


  ANBCC       - #                  REVOLVING TERMS ACCOUNT
                                   CREDIT CARD
    REPT'D  06/95  BALANCE:      $0  INDIVIDUAL ACCOUNT
    OPENED  04/84  MOST OWED:  $1935  PAY TERMS:  MINIMUM $15
                                   CREDIT LIMIT:      $2200

   >IN PRIOR 48 MONTHS  1 TIME  30 DAYS LATE<
    STATUS AS OF 06/95: PAID AS AGREED


THE FOLLOWING ACCOUNTS ARE REPORTED WITH NO ADVERSE INFORMATION

  CHASE       - #                  REVOLVING TERMS ACCOUNT
    REPT'D  08/95  BALANCE:     $10  INDIVIDUAL ACCOUNT
    OPENED  04/84                   PAY TERMS:  MINIMUM $10
                                   CREDIT LIMIT:      $1200

    IN PRIOR 12 MONTHS NEVER LATE
    STATUS AS OF 08/95: PAID AS AGREED

  FROST NTL BK - #                 INSTALLMENT ACCOUNT
    REPT'D  07/95  BALANCE:   $3624  JOINT ACCOUNT
    OPENED  08/94  MOST OWED: $5000  PAY TERMS: 36 MONTHLY $163
    IN PRIOR 11 MONTHS NEVER LATE
    STATUS AS OF 07/95: PAID AS AGREED

  FROST NTL BK - #                 INSTALLMENT ACCOUNT
    REPT'D  07/95  BALANCE:  $13708  JOINT ACCOUNT
    OPENED  04/94  MOST OWED: $14436  PAY TERMS: 180 MONTHLY $137
                                   LOT 3 A AMENDED PLAT L 2   3
    IN PRIOR 15 MONTHS NEVER LATE
    STATUS AS OF 07/95: PAID AS AGREED

  CENTURIONS&T - #                 REVOLVING TERMS ACCOUNT
                                   CREDIT CARD
    REPT'D  07/95  BALANCE:   $1562  INDIVIDUAL ACCOUNT
    OPENED  12/89  MOST OWED: $1562  CREDIT LIMIT:      $5500
    IN PRIOR 48 MONTHS NEVER LATE
    STATUS AS OF 07/95: PAID AS AGREED

  AMERICAN EXP - #                 OPEN TERMS ACCOUNT
                                   CREDIT CARD
    REPT'D  07/95  BALANCE:    $129  INDIVIDUAL ACCOUNT
    OPENED  04/75  MOST OWED:  $129
    IN PRIOR 48 MONTHS NEVER LATE
    STATUS AS OF 07/95: PAID AS AGREED

  :HEVRON      - #                 REVOLVING TERMS ACCOUNT
    REPT'D  07/95  BALANCE:     $47  INDIVIDUAL ACCOUNT
    OPENED  09/66  MOST OWED:  $217
    IN PRIOR 48 MONTHS NEVER LATE
    STATUS AS OF 07/95: PAID AS AGREED
```

Note: This is a copy of an actual credit file. Identifying information (i.e., name, address, Social Security number, date of birth, account numbers, etc.) has been removed to protect consumer's identity.

FIGURE 3.2 *(continued)*

```
REPORT ON                                            PAGE  3 OF  5
SOCIAL SECURITY NUMBER:              TRANS UNION FILE NUMBER:


   FFB MTG CAP   - #                 MORTGAGE ACCOUNT
                                     REAL ESTATE
     REPT'D   07/95   BALANCE:      $26088   JOINT ACCOUNT
     OPENED   03/81   MOST OWED:    $30500   PAY TERMS: 360 MONTHLY $417
     IN PRIOR 28 MONTHS NEVER LATE
     STATUS AS OF 07/95: PAID AS AGREED


   PHILLIPS 66   - #                 REVOLVING TERMS ACCOUNT
                                     CREDIT CARD
     REPT'D   07/95   BALANCE:          $0   INDIVIDUAL ACCOUNT
     OPENED   12/87   MOST OWED:       $166
     IN PRIOR 24 MONTHS NEVER LATE
     STATUS AS OF 07/95: PAID AS AGREED


   NEIMAN MARCU - #                   REVOLVING TERMS ACCOUNT
     REPT'D   08/95   BALANCE:          $0   INDIVIDUAL ACCOUNT
     OPENED   04/88   MOST OWED:       $180
     IN PRIOR 48 MONTHS NEVER LATE
     STATUS AS OF 08/95: PAID AS AGREED


   FROST NTL BK - #                   INSTALLMENT ACCOUNT
     REPT'D   11/94   BALANCE:          $0   JOINT ACCOUNT
     OPENED   07/93   MOST OWED:    $25000   PAY TERMS: 180 MONTHLY $231
     CLOSED   12/93                    B   M LIEN
     IN PRIOR 16 MONTHS NEVER LATE
     STATUS AS OF 11/94: PAID AS AGREED


   BLOMINGDALES - #                   REVOLVING TERMS ACCOUNT
     REPT'D   07/95   BALANCE:          $0   INDIVIDUAL ACCOUNT
     OPENED   01/74   MOST OWED:       $153   PAY TERMS:  MINIMUM $20
                                      CREDIT LIMIT:        $500

     IN PRIOR 44 MONTHS NEVER LATE
     STATUS AS OF 07/95: PAID AS AGREED


   BK OF AMER    - #                  REVOLVING TERMS ACCOUNT
     REPT'D   04/93   BALANCE:          $0   INDIVIDUAL ACCOUNT
     OPENED   11/83                         PAY TERMS: 10 MONTHLY
                                      CREDIT LIMIT:       $6000

     IN PRIOR 41 MONTHS NEVER LATE
     STATUS AS OF 04/93: PAID AS AGREED


   FRANKLIN SAV - #                   MORTGAGE ACCOUNT
                                     REAL ESTATE
     REPT'D   02/93   BALANCE:          $0   JOINT ACCOUNT
     OPENED   03/81   MOST OWED:    $30500   PAY TERMS: 360 MONTHLY $347
     IN PRIOR 39 MONTHS NEVER LATE
     STATUS AS OF 02/93: PAID AS AGREED


   CITIBANK MC   - #                  REVOLVING TERMS ACCOUNT
   ACCOUNT CLOSED BY CONSUMER         CREDIT CARD
     REPT'D   04/92                   INDIVIDUAL ACCOUNT
     OPENED   07/83   MOST OWED:    $2300   PAY TERMS:  MINIMUM $20
                                      CREDIT LIMIT:      $2300

     IN PRIOR 29 MONTHS NEVER LATE
     STATUS AS OF 04/92: PAID AS AGREED
```

Note: This is a copy of an actual credit file. Identifying information (i.e., name, address, Social Security number, date of birth, account numbers, etc.) has been removed to protect consumer's identity.

FIGURE 3.2 Sample Trans Union Credit Report *(continued)*

```
REPORT ON                                             PAGE  4 OF  5
SOCIAL SECURITY NUMBER:           TRANS UNION FILE NUMBER:


  SEARS        - #                REVOLVING TERMS ACCOUNT
     REPT'D   03/92   BALANCE:          $0   INDIVIDUAL ACCOUNT
     OPENED   09/81   MOST OWED:      $1300  PAY TERMS:  MONTHLY $10
                                             CREDIT LIMIT:      $3200
     IN PRIOR 28 MONTHS NEVER LATE
     STATUS AS OF 03/92: PAID AS AGREED

  COOLIDGE BK  - #                LINE OF CREDIT ACCOUNT
     REPT'D   10/91                INDIVIDUAL ACCOUNT
     OPENED   10/76   MOST OWED:        $0   PAY TERMS: 10 UNSPECIFIED $38
     IN PRIOR  2 MONTHS NEVER LATE
     STATUS AS OF 10/91: PAID AS AGREED

  COOLIDGE BK  - #                LINE OF CREDIT ACCOUNT
  CLOSED
     REPT'D   05/91                INDIVIDUAL ACCOUNT
     OPENED   10/76   MOST OWED:        $0   CREDIT LIMIT:        $0
     IN PRIOR 18 MONTHS NEVER LATE
     STATUS AS OF 05/91: PAID AS AGREED

  FST OMNI BK  - #                REVOLVING TERMS ACCOUNT
     REPT'D   05/91   BALANCE:          $0   INDIVIDUAL ACCOUNT
     OPENED   07/80   MOST OWED:      $1211  CREDIT LIMIT:      $1000
     IN PRIOR  3 MONTHS NEVER LATE
     STATUS AS OF 05/91: PAID AS AGREED

  FIB BKCRD    - #                REVOLVING TERMS ACCOUNT
  TRANSFER
     REPT'D   12/90   BALANCE:          $0   INDIVIDUAL ACCOUNT
     OPENED   04/84                CREDIT LIMIT:      $1900
     IN PRIOR  3 MONTHS NEVER LATE
     STATUS AS OF 12/90: PAID AS AGREED

  COMMERICAL   - #                INSTALLMENT ACCOUNT
                                  NOTE LOAN
     REPT'D   08/89   BALANCE:          $0   INDIVIDUAL ACCOUNT
     OPENED   07/86   MOST OWED:      $6951  PAY TERMS: 36 MONTHLY
     STATUS AS OF 08/89: PAID AS AGREED

  LORD&TAYLOR  - #                REVOLVING TERMS ACCOUNT
     REPT'D   08/94   BALANCE:          $0   INDIVIDUAL ACCOUNT
     OPENED   06/72   MOST OWED:       $502  CREDIT LIMIT:       $400
     STATUS AS OF 08/94: PAID AS AGREED


THE FOLLOWING COMPANIES HAVE RECEIVED YOUR CREDIT REPORT.  THEIR INQUIRIES
REMAIN ON YOUR CREDIT REPORT FOR TWO YEARS.  (NOTE: "CONSUM DISCL" REFERS TO
TRANS UNION CONSUMER RELATIONS AND ARE NOT VIEWED BY CREDITORS).

                        INQUIRY TYPE                      INQUIRY TYPE
  CONSUM DISCL 08/15/95 INDIVIDUAL    FROST BK-CON 08/17/94 JOINT
```

Note: This is a copy of an actual credit file. Identifying information (i.e., name, address, Social Security number, date of birth, account numbers, etc.) has been removed to protect consumer's identity.

FIGURE 3.2 *(continued)*

```
                                                              PAGE  5 OF  5
REPORT ON
SOCIAL SECURITY NUMBER:                   TRANS UNION FILE NUMBER:
```

```
THE FOLLOWING COMPANIES DID NOT GET YOUR FULL REPORT, BUT INSTEAD RECEIVED ONLY
YOUR NAME AND ADDRESS INFORMATION FOR THE PURPOSE OF MAKING YOU A CREDIT OFFER,
OR TO REVIEW YOUR ACCOUNT. THEIR INQUIRIES ARE NOT SEEN BY CREDITORS.

  FOLEYS DEPT    07/95     FST DEPOSIT    07/95     SEARS         07/95
  FST DEPOSIT    05/95     ANBCC          04/95     CITIBK GOLD   04/95
  SEARS          04/95
```

```
IF YOU BELIEVE ANY OF THE INFORMATION IN YOUR CREDIT REPORT IS INCORRECT,
PLEASE LET US KNOW.  FOR YOUR CONVENIENCE, AN INVESTIGATION FORM IS INCLUDED.
PLEASE COMPLETE IT AND MAIL TO:
```

Note: This is a copy of an actual credit file. Identifying information (i.e., name, address, Social Security number, date of birth, account numbers, etc.) has been removed to protect consumer's identity.

Credit History

This section of the Trans Union report begins by presenting any credit-related public record information your credit file may contain. This could include tax liens as on the sample credit report, bankruptcies and judgments against you.

Your history with creditors that report accounts to Trans Union can be found immediately following the public record information. Unique to the Trans Union report, accounts with adverse information are grouped together and presented first. Adverse account information is highlighted with arrowed brackets, but is not bracketed this way when provided to a consumer's creditors.

Account information for both accounts with and without adverse information is organized in blocks with each block divided into two separate sections. The left section of each block includes the name of the creditor reporting to Trans Union and the applicable account number. Below that is the last date account information was reported to Trans Union, the current account balance, the date the account was opened and the most ever owed on the account. For example, the sample report shows that the Frost Bros. account was opened in 11/83 and that the last time account information was reported to Trans Union was 9/90. Below this is the adverse information with the arrowed brackets showing that in the six months prior to the date the account was last reported to Trans Union, the consumer was 60 days late one time on an account payment. The last line in this section indicates the account's status as of the date it was reported to Trans Union. The sample report shows that the Frost Bros. account was "paid as agreed" as of 9/90.

The section to the right in each block of account information identifies the kind of account (revolving or installment account, credit card, mortgage account, line of credit account, for example), payment terms and credit limit.

The information on accounts with no adverse information is organized just like the information on accounts with adverse information.

Inquiries

This information follows the *Credit History* section of the Trans Union report. Like the reports of the other credit reporting agencies, the *Inquiries* section tells who has received a copy of your credit report with the date of each inquiry. In the sample, the only inquiry shown is noted as a *CONSM DISCL,* meaning that the consumer requested a copy of the report.

Also listed in this section are the names of companies to whom Trans Union provided your name and address so that the company could offer credit to the consumer or so that the company could review the consumer's account. As the sample report shows, six companies asked Trans Union for this information in 1995 with Sears doing so twice.

The TRW Credit Report

A sample of TRW's credit report is shown in Figure 3.3. This report is easier to use than those of Equifax and Trans Union because of its straightforward narrative format. The TRW report comes with a dispute form called *Research Request* for consumers who find problems in their credit reports.

Consumer ID Number

TRW assigns each consumer an ID number. This number, listed at the top of the first page of a TRW credit report, should be used if you have to call or write the company about your credit report.

Credit History

Like the credit reports of Trans Union and Equifax, TRW's begins with *Credit History.* TRW, however, has reduced the number of columns with headings here to a mere four.

Account information in this section is presented under three different headings from far left to far right: *Account Name, Description* and *Status/Payments.* Each account is assigned an *Item Number* beginning with *1* and is listed in alphabetical order. The *Item Number* appears to the immediate left of each account. The information listed under *Account Name* includes the name and address of a consumer's creditor and its account or reference number.

Information under the *Description* column is presented in narrative form. In the case of loans, this information includes the date the loan was taken out, the terms of the loan, the consumer's responsibility for the loan payments and the original amount of the loan. The descriptive information for accounts like bankcards and retail charges tells how long the consumer has had the account, who is responsible for the account and the type of account as well as the credit limit on the account.

Information in the *Status/Payments* column of TRW's report summarizes an account's payment history, including whether account payments are current; whether all payments have been made on time; the account balance as of a specified date; and the date the creditor last reported account payment information to TRW.

This section of TRW's credit report may also indicate your payment history on an account for up to 24 months prior to the balance date. It should be read from left to right with the first entry representing the month just prior to the balance date. The codes *C, N, 1, 2,* etc., indicate the status of the account. *C* indicates that the

FIGURE 3.3 Sample TRW Credit Report

TRW

This is your TRW consumer identification number. Please refer to this number when you call or write TRW.

ID #

HOW TO READ THIS REPORT:

AN EXPLANATORY ENCLOSURE ACCOMPANIES THIS REPORT. IT DESCRIBES YOUR CREDIT RIGHTS AND OTHER HELPFUL INFORMATION. IF THE ENCLOSURE IS MISSING, OR YOU HAVE QUESTIONS ABOUT THIS REPORT, PLEASE CONTACT THE OFFICE LISTED ON THE LAST PAGE.

YOUR CREDIT HISTORY:

THIS INFORMATION COMES FROM PUBLIC RECORDS OR ORGANIZATIONS THAT HAVE GRANTED CREDIT TO YOU. AN ASTERISK BY AN ACCOUNT INDICATES THAT THIS ITEM MAY REQUIRE FURTHER REVIEW BY A PROSPECTIVE CREDITOR WHEN CHECKING YOUR CREDIT HISTORY. IF YOU BELIEVE ANY OF THE INFORMATION IS INCORRECT, PLEASE LET US KNOW. FOR YOUR CONVENIENCE, A DISPUTE FORM AND INSTRUCTIONS ARE INCLUDED ON THE LAST PAGE OF THIS REPORT.

ITEM	ACCOUNT NAME	DESCRIPTION	STATUS/PAYMENTS
1	* TRAVIS COUNTY COURT P O BOX 1748 AUSTIN,TX 78767 REFERENCE # 00000000	THE ORIGINAL AMOUNT OF THIS COURT ITEM IS $2,000. THE PARTY THAT BROUGHT THIS ACTION AGAINST YOU OR THE COURT REFERENCE NUMBER IS	THIS FEDERAL TAX LIEN WAS FILED IN AND RELEASED ON
2	AMERICAN EXPRESS CO P O BOX 7871 SROC FORT LAUDERDALE,FL 33329 NATL CREDIT CARDS ACCT #	THIS CREDIT CARD ACCOUNT WAS OPENED 04/75 AND HAS 1 MONTH REPAYMENT TERMS. YOU HAVE CONTRACTUAL RESPONSIBILITY FOR THIS ACCOUNT AND ARE PRIMARILY RESPONSIBLE FOR ITS PAYMENT. THE HIGH BALANCE OF THIS ACCOUNT IS $559.	AS OF 07/95 THIS ACCOUNT IS CURRENT AND ALL PAYMENTS HAVE BEEN PAID ON TIME. YOUR BALANCE AS OF 07/05/95 IS $129. PAYMENT HISTORY: -CCCCCCCCCCC/CCCCCCCCCCCC

COMPLIMENTARY CREDIT REPORT (CCR)   08 10 95 23:43   PAGE 1

Note: This is a copy of an actual credit file. Identifying information (i.e., name, address, Social Security number, date of birth, account numbers, etc.) has been removed to protect consumer's identity.

Source: Reprinted by permission of TRW.

FIGURE 3.3 *(continued)*

ITEM	ACCOUNT NAME	DESCRIPTION	STATUS/PAYMENTS
3	AMERICAN EXPRESS OPTIMA P O BOX 7871/SROC FORT LAUDERDALE,FL 33329 BANKING ACCT #	THIS CREDIT CARD ACCOUNT WAS OPENED 12/89 AND HAS REVOLVING REPAYMENT TERMS. YOU HAVE CONTRACTUAL RESPONSIBILITY FOR THIS ACCOUNT AND ARE PRIMARILY RESPONSIBLE FOR ITS PAYMENT. THE CREDIT LIMIT OF THIS ACCOUNT IS $5,500. THE HIGH BALANCE OF THIS ACCOUNT IS $1,693.	AS OF 07/95 THIS ACCOUNT IS CURRENT AND ALL PAYMENTS HAVE BEEN PAID ON TIME. YOUR BALANCE AS OF 07/24/95 IS $1,562. PAYMENT HISTORY: -CCCCCCCCCCC/CCCC----CCCC
4	ANBCC P O BOX 15687 WILMINGTON,DE 19850 BANKING ACCT #	THIS CREDIT CARD ACCOUNT WAS OPENED 04/84 AND HAS REVOLVING REPAYMENT TERMS. YOU HAVE CONTRACTUAL RESPONSIBILITY FOR THIS ACCOUNT AND ARE PRIMARILY RESPONSIBLE FOR ITS PAYMENT. THE CREDIT LIMIT OF THIS ACCOUNT IS $2,200. THE HIGH BALANCE OF THIS ACCOUNT IS $751.	AS OF 03/95 THIS ACCOUNT IS CURRENT AND ALL PAYMENTS HAVE BEEN PAID ON TIME. YOUR BALANCE AS OF 03/31/95 IS $0. THE LAST PAYMENT REPORTED TO TRW WAS MADE ON 05/16/94. PAYMENT HISTORY: NNNNNNNNNNCC/CCCCCCCCCCCC
5	ANN TAYLOR P O BOX 1304 NEW HAVEN,CT 06505 UNDEFINED FIRM TYPE ACCT #	THIS CHARGE ACCOUNT WAS OPENED 09/87 AND HAS REVOLVING REPAYMENT TERMS. YOU HAVE CONTRACTUAL RESPONSIBILITY FOR THIS ACCOUNT AND ARE PRIMARILY RESPONSIBLE FOR ITS PAYMENT. THE CREDIT LIMIT OF THIS ACCOUNT IS $700.	AS OF 05/93 THIS ACCOUNT IS CURRENT AND ALL PAYMENTS HAVE BEEN PAID ON TIME. YOUR BALANCE AS OF 07/31/95 IS $0. PAYMENT HISTORY: NNNNNNNNN---/NNNNNNNNNNNN
6	BANK OF AMERICA 1825 EAST BUCKEYE ROAD PHOENIX,AZ 85034 BANKING ACCT #	THIS CREDIT CARD ACCOUNT WAS OPENED 11/83 AND HAS REVOLVING REPAYMENT TERMS. YOU HAVE CONTRACTUAL RESPONSIBILITY FOR THIS ACCOUNT AND ARE PRIMARILY RESPONSIBLE FOR ITS PAYMENT. THE CREDIT LIMIT OF THIS ACCOUNT IS $6,000. THE HIGH BALANCE OF THIS ACCOUNT IS $1,667.	AS OF 04/93 THIS ACCOUNT IS PAID IN FULL AND ALL PAYMENTS HAVE BEEN PAID ON TIME.

COMPLIMENTARY CREDIT REPORT (CCR)   08 10 95 23:43   PAGE 2

Note: This is a copy of an actual credit file. Identifying information (i.e., name, address, Social Security number, date of birth, account numbers, etc.) has been removed to protect consumer's identity.

FIGURE 3.3   Sample TRW Credit Report *(continued)*

TRW

This is your TRW consumer identification number. Please refer to this number when you call or write TRW.

 ID #

ITEM	ACCOUNT NAME	DESCRIPTION	STATUS/PAYMENTS
7	BLOOMINGDALE BROTHERS 9111 DUKE DRIVE MASON,OH 45040 UNDEFINED FIRM TYPE ACCT #	THIS CHARGE ACCOUNT WAS OPENED 01/74 AND HAS REVOLVING REPAYMENT TERMS. YOU HAVE CONTRACTUAL RESPONSIBILITY FOR THIS ACCOUNT AND ARE PRIMARILY RESPONSIBLE FOR ITS PAYMENT. THE CREDIT LIMIT OF THIS ACCOUNT IS $501. THE HIGH BALANCE OF THIS ACCOUNT IS $153.	AS OF 07/95 THIS ACCOUNT IS CURRENT AND ALL PAYMENTS HAVE BEEN PAID ON TIME. YOUR BALANCE AS OF 07/07/95 IS $0. THE LAST PAYMENT REPORTED TO TRW WAS MADE ON 06/28/93. PAYMENT HISTORY: NNNNNNNNNNNNN/NNNN-NNNNNNN
8	CHASE MANHATTAN BANK 802 DELAWARE AVENUE WILMINGTON,DE 19801 BANKING ACCT #	THIS CREDIT CARD ACCOUNT WAS OPENED 04/84 AND HAS REVOLVING REPAYMENT TERMS. YOU HAVE CONTRACTUAL RESPONSIBILITY FOR THIS ACCOUNT AND ARE PRIMARILY RESPONSIBLE FOR ITS PAYMENT. THE CREDIT LIMIT OF THIS ACCOUNT IS $1,200. THE HIGH BALANCE OF THIS ACCOUNT IS $696.	AS OF 07/95 THIS ACCOUNT IS CURRENT AND ALL PAYMENTS HAVE BEEN PAID ON TIME. YOUR BALANCE AS OF 07/02/95 IS $10. YOUR SCHEDULED MONTHLY PAYMENT IS $10. THE LAST PAYMENT REPORTED TO TRW WAS MADE ON 06/19/95. PAYMENT HISTORY: -CCCCCCCCCCCC/CCC-CCCCCCCC
9	* CHEVRON U S A P O BOX 5010 CONCORD,CA 94524 NATL CREDIT CARDS ACCT #	THIS CREDIT CARD ACCOUNT WAS OPENED 09/66 AND HAS REVOLVING REPAYMENT TERMS. YOUR ASSOCIATION WITH THIS ACCOUNT IS UNSPECIFIED. THE HIGH BALANCE OF THIS ACCOUNT IS $217.	AS OF 04/92 THIS ACCOUNT IS CURRENT AND PAYMENTS ARE BEING PAID ON TIME BUT WAS PAST DUE 60 DAYS IN 04/30/92. YOUR BALANCE AS OF 07/31/95 IS $50. PAYMENT HISTORY: CCCCCCCCCCCCC/CCCCCCCCNNCCC

Note: This is a copy of an actual credit file. Identifying information (i.e., name, address, Social Security number, date of birth, account numbers, etc.) has been removed to protect consumer's identity.

FIGURE 3.3   *(continued)*

ITEM	ACCOUNT NAME	DESCRIPTION	STATUS/PAYMENTS
10	CITIBANK MASTERCHARGE PO BOX 6500 SIOUX FALLS,SD 57117 BANKING ACCT #	THIS CREDIT CARD ACCOUNT WAS OPENED 07/83 AND HAS REVOLVING REPAYMENT TERMS. YOU HAVE CONTRACTUAL RESPONSIBILITY FOR THIS ACCOUNT AND ARE PRIMARILY RESPONSIBLE FOR ITS PAYMENT.	AS OF 05/92 THIS ACCOUNT IS CURRENT AND ALL PAYMENTS HAVE BEEN PAID ON TIME. YOUR BALANCE AS OF 07/06/95 IS $0. THE LAST PAYMENT REPORTED TO TRW WAS MADE ON 04/06/92. PAYMENT HISTORY: NNNNNNNNNNNN/NNNNNNNNNNNN

***CREDIT LINE CLOSED - CONSUMER'S REQUEST - REPORTED BY SUBSCRIBER

ITEM	ACCOUNT NAME	DESCRIPTION	STATUS/PAYMENTS
11	COMMERCIAL CREDIT CORP 5775 AIRPORT #600 AUSTIN,TX 78752 FINANCE ACCT #	THIS NOTE LOAN WAS OPENED 07/86 AND HAS 36 MONTH REPAYMENT TERMS. YOU HAVE CONTRACTUAL RESPONSIBILITY FOR THIS ACCOUNT AND ARE PRIMARILY RESPONSIBLE FOR ITS PAYMENT. THE ORIGINAL AMOUNT OF THIS ACCOUNT IS $6,900.	AS OF 08/89 THIS ACCOUNT IS PAID IN FULL AND ALL PAYMENTS HAVE BEEN PAID ON TIME.
12	FCNB PRF CH P O BOX 2650 PORTLAND,OR 97208 BANKING ACCT #	THIS CHARGE ACCOUNT WAS OPENED 04/84 AND HAS REVOLVING REPAYMENT TERMS. YOU HAVE CONTRACTUAL RESPONSIBILITY FOR THIS ACCOUNT AND ARE PRIMARILY RESPONSIBLE FOR ITS PAYMENT. THE CREDIT LIMIT OF THIS ACCOUNT IS $400.	AS OF 12/89 THIS ACCOUNT IS CURRENT AND ALL PAYMENTS HAVE BEEN PAID ON TIME. YOUR BALANCE AS OF 07/31/95 IS $0. THE LAST PAYMENT REPORTED TO TRW WAS MADE ON 05/30/87. PAYMENT HISTORY: NNNNNN-NNN-N/NNNNNNNNNNNN
13	FFB MORTGAGE CAPITAL COR P O BOX 684366 AUSTIN,TX 78768 FINANCE ACCT #	THIS CONVENTIONAL REAL ESTATE LOAN WAS OPENED 1981 AND HAS 30 YEAR REPAYMENT TERMS. YOU ARE OBLIGATED TO REPAY THIS JOINT ACCOUNT. THE ORIGINAL AMOUNT OF THIS ACCOUNT IS $30,500.	AS OF 01/95 THIS ACCOUNT IS CURRENT AND ALL PAYMENTS HAVE BEEN PAID ON TIME. YOUR BALANCE AS OF 07/21/95 IS $25,981. YOUR SCHEDULED MONTHLY PAYMENT IS $417. THE LAST PAYMENT REPORTED TO TRW WAS MADE ON 07/01/95. PAYMENT HISTORY: CCCCCCCCCCCC/CCCCCCCCCCCC

COMPLIMENTARY CREDIT REPORT (CCR)   08 10 95 23:43   PAGE 4

Note: This is a copy of an actual credit file. Identifying information (i.e., name, address, Social Security number, date of birth, account numbers, etc.) has been removed to protect consumer's identity.

FIGURE 3.3   Sample TRW Credit Report *(continued)*

TRW

This is your TRW consumer identification
number. Please refer to this number when
you call or write TRW.

ID#

ITEM	ACCOUNT NAME	DESCRIPTION	STATUS/PAYMENTS
14	FIRST OMNI BANK P O BOX 825 MILLSBORO,DE 19966 BANKING ACCT #	THIS CREDIT CARD ACCOUNT WAS OPENED 07/80 AND HAS REVOLVING REPAYMENT TERMS. YOU HAVE CONTRACTUAL RESPONSIBILITY FOR THIS ACCOUNT AND ARE PRIMARILY RESPONSIBLE FOR ITS PAYMENT. THE CREDIT LIMIT OF THIS ACCOUNT IS $1,000. THE HIGH BALANCE OF THIS ACCOUNT IS $1,211.	AS OF 05/91 THIS ACCOUNT IS PAID IN FULL AND ALL PAYMENTS HAVE BEEN PAID ON TIME.
15	FROST NATIONAL BANK P O BOX 1600 SAN ANTONIO,TX 78296 BANKING ACCT #	THIS CREDIT EXTENSION, REVIEW OR OTHER PERMISSIBLE PURPOSE WAS OPENED 07/93 AND HAS 180 MONTH REPAYMENT TERMS. YOU ARE OBLIGATED TO REPAY THIS JOINT ACCOUNT. THE ORIGINAL AMOUNT OF THIS ACCOUNT IS $25,000.	AS OF 11/93 THIS ACCOUNT IS PAID IN FULL AND ALL PAYMENTS HAVE BEEN PAID ON TIME. YOUR BALANCE AS OF 11/25/93 IS $0. PAYMENT HISTORY: C-C
16	FROST NATIONAL BANK P O BOX 1600 SAN ANTONIO,TX 78296 BANKING ACCT #	THIS CREDIT EXTENSION, REVIEW OR OTHER PERMISSIBLE PURPOSE WAS OPENED 04/94 AND HAS 180 MONTH REPAYMENT TERMS. YOU ARE OBLIGATED TO REPAY THIS JOINT ACCOUNT. THE ORIGINAL AMOUNT OF THIS ACCOUNT IS $14,436.	AS OF 06/95 THIS ACCOUNT IS CURRENT AND ALL PAYMENTS HAVE BEEN PAID ON TIME. YOUR BALANCE AS OF 06/25/95 IS $13,759. YOUR SCHEDULED MONTHLY PAYMENT IS $137. THE LAST PAYMENT REPORTED TO TRW WAS MADE ON 06/06/95. PAYMENT HISTORY: CCCCCCCCCCCC/CC

COMPLIMENTARY CREDIT REPORT (CCR)   08 10 95 23:43   PAGE 5

Note: This is a copy of an actual credit file. Identifying information (i.e., name, address, Social Security number, date of birth, account numbers, etc.) has been removed to protect consumer's identity.

FIGURE 3.3 *(continued)*

ITEM	ACCOUNT NAME	DESCRIPTION	STATUS/PAYMENTS
17	FROST NATIONAL BANK P O BOX 1600 SAN ANTONIO,TX 78296 BANKING ACCT #	THIS CREDIT EXTENSION, REVIEW OR OTHER PERMISSIBLE PURPOSE WAS OPENED 08/94 AND HAS 36 MONTH REPAYMENT TERMS. YOU ARE OBLIGATED TO REPAY THIS JOINT ACCOUNT. THE ORIGINAL AMOUNT OF THIS ACCOUNT IS $5,000.	AS OF 06/95 THIS ACCOUNT IS CURRENT AND ALL PAYMENTS HAVE BEEN PAID ON TIME. YOUR BALANCE AS OF 06/25/95 IS $3,756. YOUR SCHEDULED MONTHLY PAYMENT IS $163. THE LAST PAYMENT REPORTED TO TRW WAS MADE ON 06/15/95. PAYMENT HISTORY: CCCCCCCCC
18	LORD & TAYLOR 424 5TH AVENUE NEW YORK,NY 10018 UNDEFINED FIRM TYPE ACCT #	THIS CHARGE ACCOUNT WAS OPENED 06/72 AND HAS REVOLVING REPAYMENT TERMS. YOU HAVE CONTRACTUAL RESPONSIBILITY FOR THIS ACCOUNT AND ARE PRIMARILY RESPONSIBLE FOR ITS PAYMENT. THE CREDIT LIMIT OF THIS ACCOUNT IS $400. THE HIGH BALANCE OF THIS ACCOUNT IS $502.	AS OF 06/95 THIS ACCOUNT IS PAID IN FULL AND ALL PAYMENTS HAVE BEEN PAID ON TIME. YOUR BALANCE AS OF 06/05/95 IS $0. PAYMENT HISTORY: N-NNNNNNNNNN/NNNNNNNNNNNN
19	NEIMAN MARCUS 1201 ELM ST 27TH FLR DALLAS,TX 75270 DEPARTMENT STORES ACCT #	THIS CHARGE ACCOUNT WAS OPENED 04/88 AND HAS REVOLVING REPAYMENT TERMS. YOU HAVE CONTRACTUAL RESPONSIBILITY FOR THIS ACCOUNT AND ARE PRIMARILY RESPONSIBLE FOR ITS PAYMENT. THE HIGH BALANCE OF THIS ACCOUNT IS $180.	AS OF 07/95 THIS ACCOUNT IS CURRENT AND ALL PAYMENTS HAVE BEEN PAID ON TIME. YOUR BALANCE AS OF 07/30/95 IS $0. THE LAST PAYMENT REPORTED TO TRW WAS MADE ON 08/16/94. PAYMENT HISTORY: NNNNNNNNNNNC/CCNNNCCCCCNN
20	PHILLIPS PETROLEUM CO PO BOX 77 BARTLESVILLE,OK 74004 NATL CREDIT CARDS ACCT #	THIS CREDIT CARD ACCOUNT WAS OPENED 12/87 AND HAS REVOLVING REPAYMENT TERMS. YOU HAVE CONTRACTUAL RESPONSIBILITY FOR THIS ACCOUNT AND ARE PRIMARILY RESPONSIBLE FOR ITS PAYMENT. THE HIGH BALANCE OF THIS ACCOUNT IS $166.	AS OF 06/95 THIS ACCOUNT IS CURRENT AND ALL PAYMENTS HAVE BEEN PAID ON TIME. YOUR BALANCE AS OF 06/05/95 IS $0. THE LAST PAYMENT REPORTED TO TRW WAS MADE ON 09/14/94. PAYMENT HISTORY: NNNNNNNNCNCC/CNNNNNNNNNN

COMPLIMENTARY CREDIT REPORT (CCR)   08 10 95 23:43   PAGE 6

Note: This is a copy of an actual credit file. Identifying information (i.e., name, address, Social Security number, date of birth, account numbers, etc.) has been removed to protect consumer's identity.

FIGURE 3.3 Sample TRW Credit Report *(continued)*

TRW

This is your TRW consumer identification number. Please refer to this number when you call or write TRW.

ID #

ITEM	ACCOUNT NAME	DESCRIPTION	STATUS/PAYMENTS
21	SEARS ROEBUCK & CO P O BOX 5000 RANCHO CUCAMONGA, CA 91730 DEPARTMENT STORES ACCT #	THIS CHARGE ACCOUNT WAS OPENED 09/81 AND HAS REVOLVING REPAYMENT TERMS. YOU HAVE CONTRACTUAL RESPONSIBILITY FOR THIS ACCOUNT AND ARE PRIMARILY RESPONSIBLE FOR ITS PAYMENT. THE CREDIT LIMIT OF THIS ACCOUNT IS $3,240.	AS OF 03/92 THIS ACCOUNT IS CURRENT AND ALL PAYMENTS HAVE BEEN PAID ON TIME. YOUR BALANCE AS OF 07/13/95 IS $0. PAYMENT HISTORY: NNN-NNNNNNNN/NNNNNNNNNNNN
22	* WELLS FARGO BANK P O BOX 4051 CONCORD, CA 94524 BANKING ACCT #	THIS CREDIT CARD ACCOUNT WAS OPENED 04/84 AND HAS REVOLVING REPAYMENT TERMS. YOU HAVE CONTRACTUAL RESPONSIBILITY FOR THIS ACCOUNT AND ARE PRIMARILY RESPONSIBLE FOR ITS PAYMENT. THE CREDIT LIMIT OF THIS ACCOUNT IS $3,000. THE HIGH BALANCE OF THIS ACCOUNT IS $871.	AS OF 07/91 THIS ACCOUNT IS CURRENT AND PAYMENTS ARE BEING PAID ON TIME BUT WAS PAST DUE 60 DAYS IN 07/31/91. YOUR BALANCE AS OF 06/30/95 IS $0. PAYMENT HISTORY: NNNNNNNNNNNNN/NCCCCCCCCCCCC

***CREDIT LINE CLOSED - REPORTED BY SUBSCRIBER

YOUR CREDIT HISTORY WAS REVIEWED BY:

THE FOLLOWING INQUIRIES ARE NOT REPORTED TO THOSE WHO ASK TO REVIEW YOUR CREDIT HISTORY. THEY ARE INCLUDED SO THAT YOU HAVE A COMPLETE LIST OF INQUIRIES.

ITEM	ACCOUNT NAME	DATE	REMARKS
23	CITICORP CREDIT SVCS INC PO BOX 6000 SIOUX FALLS, SD 57117 BANKING	10/14/94	INQUIRY MADE FOR PRESCREEN PROGRAM. YOUR FILE WAS MATCHED AGAINST THIS CREDITOR'S CRITERIA TO DEVELOP A LIST OF NAMES FOR A CREDIT OFFER OR SERVICE.

COMPLIMENTARY CREDIT REPORT (CCR)   08 10 95 23:43   PAGE 7

Note: This is a copy of an actual credit file. Identifying information (i.e., name, address, Social Security number, date of birth, account numbers, etc.) has been removed to protect consumer's identity. *Please note that the inquiries section on this sample report does not reflect any inquiries related to getting new or additional credit.*

FIGURE 3.3 *(continued)*

ITEM	ACCOUNT NAME	DATE	REMARKS
24	NEIMAN MARCUS 1201 ELM STR 27TH FLR DALLAS,TX 75270 DEPARTMENT STORES	03/14/95	INQUIRY MADE FOR REVIEW OF YOUR CREDIT HISTORY BY YOUR CREDITOR.
25	TEXACO CREDIT CARD BK NA P O BOX 2000 BELLAIRE,TX 77402 OIL COMPANIES	02/13/95	INQUIRY MADE FOR PRESCREEN PROGRAM. YOUR FILE WAS MATCHED AGAINST THIS CREDITOR'S CRITERIA TO DEVELOP A LIST OF NAMES FOR A CREDIT OFFER OR SERVICE.
26	CITICORP CREDIT SVCS INC PO BOX 6000 SIOUX FALLS,SD 57117 BANKING	01/06/95	INQUIRY MADE FOR PRESCREEN PROGRAM. YOUR FILE WAS MATCHED AGAINST THIS CREDITOR'S CRITERIA TO DEVELOP A LIST OF NAMES FOR A CREDIT OFFER OR SERVICE.

PLEASE HELP US HELP YOU:

AT TRW WE KNOW HOW IMPORTANT YOUR GOOD CREDIT IS TO YOU. IT'S EQUALLY IMPORTANT TO US THAT OUR INFORMATION BE ACCURATE AND UP TO DATE. LISTED BELOW IS THE INFORMATION YOU GAVE US WHEN YOU ASKED FOR THIS REPORT. IF THIS INFORMATION IS NOT CORRECT, OR YOU DID NOT SUPPLY US WITH YOUR FULL NAME, ADDRESS FOR THE PAST 5 YEARS, SOCIAL SECURITY NUMBER AND YEAR OF BIRTH, THIS REPORT MAY NOT BE COMPLETE. IF THIS INFORMATION IS INCOMPLETE OR NOT ACCURATE, PLEASE LET US KNOW.

YOUR NAME   SOCIAL SECURITY #

ADDRESS

                                             YEAR OF BIRTH

IDENTIFICATION INFORMATION:

THE FOLLOWING ADDITIONAL INFORMATION HAS BEEN PROVIDED TO US BY ORGANIZATIONS THAT REPORT INFORMATION TO US.

ADDRESS

          REPORTED 01/90 BY A TRW MEMBER   REPORTED 09/90 BY A TRW MEMBER

          REPORTED 10/87 BY A TRW MEMBER   REPORTED 01/10 BY A TRW MEMBER

EMPLOYERS

FROM 5/1/95 THE NUMBER OF INQUIRIES WITH THIS SOCIAL SECURITY # = 0

Social Security Number You Gave Was Issued: 1963 - 1965

COMPLIMENTARY CREDIT REPORT (CCR)   08 10 95 23:43   PAGE 8

Note: This is a copy of an actual credit file. Identifying information (i.e., name, address, Social Security number, date of birth, account numbers, etc.) has been removed to protect consumer's identity.

FIGURE 3.3   Sample TRW Credit Report *(continued)*

Note: This is a copy of an actual credit file. Identifying information (i.e., name, address, Social Security number, date of birth, account numbers, etc.) has been removed to protect consumer's identity.

account is current, *N* that it's current with a zero balance, *1* that the account is 30 days past due, etc. A dash means that no information was reported for that month.

Other Account-Related Information

Additional account-related information, such as whether an account was closed by the consumer or by the subscriber reporting the information to TRW, is listed at the bottom of each block of account information. In the sample report, for example, the consumer closed the Citibank MasterCard, but the credit line with Wells Fargo Bank was closed by the subscriber.

Public Record Information

TRW, alone among the big three, presents *Public Record* information in the *Credit History* section of its report. In fact, public record items are listed before any of a consumer's credit accounts.

Inquiries

The *Inquiries* section of the TRW credit report, *Your Credit History Was Reviewed By*, follows the *Credit History* section. It lists the name and address of companies that ask to review your credit history and the date of the request. In addition, TRW indicates why the report was requested.

Identification Information

The last part of the TRW credit report presents *Identification Information* about a consumer. First, the report lists the information—name, address, Social Security number and year of birth—that the consumer provided TRW when requesting a copy of the credit report. Then it presents other identifying information about a consumer provided by TRW's subscribers and the date that information was reported. As illustrated by the sample TRW report, this information includes former addresses and the names and addresses of employers.

Confidential Credit (CREDCO)

The Confidential Credit (CREDCO) report combines the consumer credit information found in the big three's files to create a single, comprehensive credit report with a common format. CREDCO is the only credit reporting agency with the big three's authorization to access credit data for a direct-to-consumer product.

By eliminating the need to contact three different companies and to pay numerous fees, CREDCO's product makes it easier for you to find out what is in your credit files. You will, however, pay a premium for this convenience. The report costs $26.00, plus $4.95 for handling and shipping, for a total cost of $30.95, which is more than the combined cost of ordering a credit report from each of the big three.

To obtain a copy of your CREDCO report, call 800-443-9342. You will receive an application or order form and once you return that with your payment, you can expect to receive your report in ten days. If you pay for your report with a credit card, you may want to fax your credit report application to 619-637-3728. If you need your report ASAP, you can take advantage of the company's express overnight service by paying $49.95.

The report comes with an easy-to-understand explanation of how to read the report and three *Credit Report Dispute Forms*—one for each of the big three. The company also maintains a consumer assistance line that can be reached by calling 800-443-9342.

How To Read Your Confidential Credit Report

Figure 3.4 shows a sample Confidential Credit report. CREDCO's report format is relatively easy to understand; however, because it retains some of the codes and symbols used by Equifax and Trans Union but does not provide an explanation, it is not as useful as it might be.

The report is organized into three basic sections: *Identifying Information, Report Summary* and *Detailed Account Information*. It also includes a *Reference Number* for each consumer.

Reference Number

Located on each page of the CREDCO report in the upper right-hand corner, the *Reference Number* should be mentioned when contacting the agency about your report.

Identifying Information

This section provides consumer identification information, including name, current address, former address, Social Security number and age. Like Equifax, CREDCO provides additional identifying information at the end of the report.

FIGURE 3.4　Sample Confidential Credit Report

CONFIDENTIAL CREDIT

REPORT DATE: 09/06/95

Reference Number :
Membership Number:

NAME(S):　　　　　　　　　　　　　　　　　　Social Security Nbr:　　　AGE:

CURR ADDR:
FRMR ADDR:

REPORT SUMMARY:

							Public	Collection
Oldest Account	09/66	Real Estate Bal	$25,927	Current Accts.	26			
Credit Accounts	26	Installment Bal	$17,332	Revolving Credit Avail.	85%		Records	Accounts
Closed Accts.	9	Revolving Bal	$2,461	Was Delq/Derog	4	EFX	1	0
Inquiries	6	Total R/E Pmt	$417	Now Delq/Derog	0	TRW	1	0
Inqs/6 mos	0	Total Other Pmt	$325	Past Due Amt	$0	TUC	1	0

```
Account Name/Number/Type of Account
Credit Bureau Date  High/  Mthly  Account  Last  Account Past      Last  Past Due Hist
(Id) Bur Code Open  Limit  Pymt   Balance  Rptd  Status  Due Amt  Delnq 30 60 90+ Date  Historical Acct Status


AMERICAN EXPRESS CO /           30 DAY ACCOUNT
(01) EFX  I  04-75   234   N/A    234      08-95 CURRENT                00 00 00  08-95 11111111111111111111111
(02) TRW  I  10-YR   500   N/A    234      08-95 CURRENT                00 00 00  08-95 1-1-11111111111111111111
(03) TUC  I  04-75   234   N/A    234      08-95 CURRENT                00 00 00  08-95 1111111111


ANB CC /                        REVOLVING
(01) EFX  I  04-84  2200    15    139      07-95 CURRENT                00 00 00  07-95 11111111111111111111111111
(03) TUC  I  04-84  1935    15    -0-      05-95 CURRENT                01 00 00  05-95 1-----------111111111111
     COMMENTS: EFX: SECURED LOAN.


ANBCC /                         REVOLVING
(02) TRW  I  10-YR  2200   N/A    -0-      03-95 CURRENT                00 00 00  03-95 11111111111111111111111111


ANN TAYLOR /           REVOLVING
(01) EFX  I  09-87   700   N/A    -0-      05-93 CURRENT                00 00 00  05-93 11111111111111111111111
(02) TRW  I  09-87   700   N/A    -0-      07-95 CURRENT                00 00 00  07-95 1111111111---11111111111
     COMMENTS: EFX: CHARGE.
```

Continued on page Two

Note: This is a copy of an actual credit file. Identifying information (i.e., name, address, Social Security number, date of birth, account numbers, etc.) has been removed to protect consumer's identity.

Source: © 1991 CREDCO, Inc. Reprinted with permission.

FIGURE 3.4 Sample Confidential Credit Report *(continued)*

CONFIDENTIAL CREDIT

Page Two

Reference number :
Membership number:

```
Account Name/Number/Type of Account
Credit Bureau Date  High/  Mthly  Account  Last  Account Past  Last  Past Due  Hist
(Id) Bur Code  Open  Limit  Pymt   Balance  Rptd  Status  Due Amt  Delnq  30 60 90+ Date  Historical Acct Status
---------------------------------------------------------------------------------------------------------------
```

Account	Bur	Code	Date Open	High/Limit	Mthly Pymt	Account Balance	Last Rptd	Account Status	Past Due Amt	Last Delnq	Past Due 30 60 90+	Hist Date	Historical Acct Status
BK OF AMER /					REVOLVING								
(01) EFX	I		11-83	6000	N/A	-0-	03-93	CURRENT			00 00 00	03-93	1111111111111111111111
(02) TRW	I		10-YR	6000	N/A	CLOSED	04-93	CURRENT			00 00 00	04-93	1
(03) TUC	I		11-83	6000	N/A	-0-	03-93	CURRENT			00 00 00	03-93	11111111111
BLOOMINGDALE BROTHERS /					REVOLVING								
(01) EFX	I		01-74	153	N/A	-0-	08-95	CURRENT			00 00 00	08-95	1111111111111111111111111
(02) TRW	I		10-YR	500	N/A	-0-	08-95	CURRENT			00 00 00	08-95	11111111111111111-11111
(03) TUC	I		01-74	153	20	-0-	08-95	CURRENT			00 00 00	08-95	11111111111111111111111
COMMENTS: EFX: CHARGE.													
CENTURIONS&T /					REVOLVING								
(01) EFX	I		12-89	5500	N/A	1562	07-95	CURRENT			00 00 00	07-95	1111111111111111111111111
(02) TRW	I		12-89	5500	N/A	1484	08-95	CURRENT			00 00 00	08-95	11-1111111111111111----11
(03) TUC	I		12-89	1484	N/A	1484	08-95	CURRENT			00 00 00	08-95	11-111111111
CHASE VISA /					REVOLVING								
(01) EFX	I		04-84	200	10	10	08-95	CURRENT			00 00 00	08-95	1111111111111111111111111
(02) TRW	I		10-YR	700	10	554	09-95	CURRENT			00 00 00	09-95	111-11111111111111-11111
(03) TUC	I		04-84	200	10	10	08-95	CURRENT			00 00 00	08-95	1-1111111-11
CHEVRON U S A /					REVOLVING								
(01) EFX	U		09-66	217	N/A	50	07-95	CURRENT			00 00 00	07-95	1111111111111111111111111
(02) TRW	U		10-YR	200	N/A	50	07-95	CURRENT			00 01 00	07-95	11111111111111111111111111
(03) TUC	I		09-66	217	N/A	50	08-95	CURRENT			00 00 00	08-95	1111111111
CITIBANK MASTERCHARGE /					REVOLVING								
(02) TRW	I		10-YR	N/A	N/A	CLOSED	08-95	CURRENT			00 00 00	05-92	1111111111111111111111111
(03) TUC	I		07-83	2300	20	N/A	03-92	UNRATED			00 00 00	03-92	-11111111111
COMMENTS: TRW: CLOSED BY CONSUMER. TUC: CREDIT LINE CLOSED.													
COMMERICAL /					INSTALLMENT								
(01) EFX	I		07-86	6951	193	-0-	09-89	CURRENT			00 00 00	09-89	1111111111111111111111111
(02) TRW	I		07-86	6900	N/A	CLOSED	08-89	CURRENT			00 00 00	08-89	1
(03) TUC	I		07-86	6951	N/A	-0-	07-89	CURRENT			00 00 00	07-89	1

Continued on page Three

Note: This is a copy of an actual credit file. Identifying information (i.e., name, address, Social Security number, date of birth, account numbers, etc.) has been removed to protect consumer's identity.

FIGURE 3.4   (continued)

CONFIDENTIAL CREDIT

Page Three   Reference number :
                                                          Membership number:

```
Account Name/Number/Type of Account
Credit Bureau Date  High/  Mthly  Account  Last  Account  Past   Last   Past Due  Hist
(Id) Bur Code Open  Limit  Pymt   Balance  Rptd  Status   Due Amt Delnq  30 60 90+ Date  Historical Acct Status
-------------------------------------------------------------------------------------------------------------------

COOLIDGE BK /                CREDIT LINE
(03) TUC  I  10-76   -0-     38     N/A    10-91  CURRENT                 00 00 00  10-91  111111-1111---1111
         COMMENTS: TUC: CLOSED.

FCNB PRF CH /                REVOLVING
(02) TRW  I  10-YR   400     N/A    -0-    07-95  CURRENT                 00 00 00  07-95  1111111-111-111111111111

FFB MORTGAGE CAPITAL CO /         REAL ESTATE
(01) EFX  J  03-81  31000   417   26000    08-95  CURRENT                 00 00 00  08-95  11111111111111111111111111
(02) TRW  J  19-81  30000   417   25927    08-95  CURRENT                 00 00 00  08-95  11111111111111111111111111
(03) TUC  J  03-81  30500   417   25981    07-95  CURRENT                 00 00 00  07-95  11111111--11
         COMMENTS: EFX: REAL ESTATE MORTGAGE.

FI BANCARD /                 REVOLVING
(01) EFX  I  04-84  1935     N/A  CLOSED   01-90  CURRENT                 00 00 00  01-90  111111111111111111111111
(03) TUC  I  04-84  1900     N/A  CLOSED   02-90  CURRENT                 00 00 00  02-90  1111
         COMMENTS: EFX: ACCOUNT TRANSFERRED. TUC: ACCOUNT
                   TRANSFERRED.

FIRST OMNI BANK /            REVOLVING
(01) EFX  I  07-80  1211     N/A   -0-     04-91  CURRENT                 00 00 00  04-91  111111111111111111111111
(02) TRW  I  10-YR  1000     N/A  CLOSED   05-91  CURRENT                 00 00 00  05-91  1
(03) TUC  I  07-80  1211     N/A   -0-     05-91  CURRENT                 00 00 00  05-91  1111111111111111111

FRANKLIN SAV /               REAL ESTATE
(01) EFX  J  03-81  31000   347   CLOSED   01-93  CURRENT                 00 00 00  01-93  111111111111111111111111
(03) TUC  J  03-81  30500   347    -0-     01-93  CURRENT                 00 00 00  01-93  1111111-11-1
         COMMENTS: EFX: CLOSED. EFX: REAL ESTATE MORTGAGE.

FROST BROS /                 REVOLVING
(01) EFX  I  11-83   396     N/A   -0-     09-90  CURRENT      01-90      00 03 00  09-90  11111111311111131111311113111
(03) TUC  I  11-83   396     15    -0-     09-90  CURRENT      01-90      00 02 00  09-90  1----1-1311----3

FROST NATIONAL BANK /              INSTALLMENT
(01) EFX  J  08-94  5000    163   3624     07-95  CURRENT                 00 00 00  07-95  1111111111
(02) TRW  J  08-94  5000    163   3624     07-95  CURRENT                 00 00 00  07-95  11111111111
(03) TUC  J  08-94  5000    163   3624     07-95  CURRENT                 00 00 00  07-95  111111111
```

Continued on page Four

Note: This is a copy of an actual credit file. Identifying information (i.e., name, address, Social Security number, date of birth, account numbers, etc.) has been removed to protect consumer's identity.

FIGURE 3.4 Sample Confidential Credit Report *(continued)*

CONFIDENTIAL CREDIT

Page Four

Reference number :
Membership number:

```
Account Name/Number/Type of Account
Credit Bureau  Date  High/  Mthly  Account  Last  Account  Past    Last   Past Due  Hist
(Id) Bur Code  Open  Limit  Pymt   Balance  Rptd  Status   Due Amt Delnq  30 60 90+ Date   Historical Acct Status
```

Account / Bureau	Date Open	High/ Limit	Mthly Pymt	Account Balance	Last Rptd	Account Status	Past Due Amt	Last Delnq	Past Due 30 60 90+	Hist Date	Historical Acct Status
FROST NATIONAL BANK /				INSTALLMENT							
(01) EFX J	04-94	14000	137	14000	07-95	CURRENT			00 00 00	07-95	11111111111111
(02) TRW J	04-94	14400	137	13708	07-95	CURRENT			00 00 00	07-95	111111111111111
(03) TUC J	04-94	14436	137	13708	07-95	CURRENT			00 00 00	07-95	11111111111
FROST NATIONAL BANK /				INSTALLMENT							
(01) EFX J	07-93	25000	231	-0-	11-94	CURRENT			00 00 00	11-94	111111111111111
(02) TRW J	07-93	25000	N/A	CLOSED	11-93	CURRENT			00 00 00	11-93	11-1
(03) TUC J	07-93	25000	231	CLOSED	11-94	CURRENT			00 00 00	12-93	1-1
LORD & TAYLOR /			REVOLVING								
(01) EFX I	06-72	502	N/A	-0-	07-94	CURRENT			00 00 00	07-94	1111111111111111111111111
(02) TRW I	10-YR	400	N/A	CLOSED	06-95	CURRENT			00 00 00	06-95	11-11111111111111111111
(03) TUC I	06-72	502	N/A	-0-	07-94	CURRENT			00 00 00	07-94	1111111111111111111111111
NEIMAN MARCUS /			REVOLVING								
(01) EFX I	04-88	180	N/A	-0-	07-95	CURRENT			00 00 00	07-95	11111111111111111111111
(02) TRW I	04-88	100	N/A	-0-	07-95	CURRENT			00 00 00	07-95	11111111111111111111111
(03) TUC I	04-88	180	N/A	-0-	08-95	CURRENT			00 00 00	08-95	111111111111111---11111
PHILLIPS PETROLEUM CO /			REVOLVING								
(01) EFX I	12-87	166	N/A	-0-	08-95	CURRENT			00 00 00	08-95	111111111111111111111111
(02) TRW I	12-87	100	N/A	-0-	07-95	CURRENT			00 00 00	07-95	111111111111111111111111
(03) TUC I	12-87	166	N/A	-0-	08-95	CURRENT			00 00 00	08-95	111111111111111111111111
SEARS /			REVOLVING								
(01) EFX I	09-81	3240	N/A	-0-	03-92	CURRENT			00 00 00	03-92	1111111111111111111111111
(02) TRW I	10-YR	3200	N/A	-0-	08-95	CURRENT			00 00 00	08-95	11111-11111111111111111111
(03) TUC I	09-81	1300	10	-0-	03-92	CURRENT			00 00 00	03-92	1111111111111
WELLS FARGO BANK /			REVOLVING								
(01) EFX I	04-84	3000	N/A	CLOSED	04-95	CURRENT	06-91		04 01 00	04-95	1-----------------------
(02) TRW I	10-YR	3000	N/A	CLOSED	07-95	CURRENT			00 01 00	07-91	111111111111111111111111
(03) TUC I	04-84	3000	N/A	CLOSED	04-95	CURRENT	05-91		03 01 00	07-93	1-1-1-111111------------

COMMENTS: EFX: CLOSED. TRW: CREDIT LINE CLOSED. TUC: CREDIT LINE CLOSED.

Continued on page Five

Note: This is a copy of an actual credit file. Identifying information (i.e., name, address, Social Security number, date of birth, account numbers, etc.) has been removed to protect consumer's identity.

FIGURE 3.4 *(continued)*

CONFIDENTIAL CREDIT

Page Five   Reference number :
                                                   Membership number:

RECENT INQUIRIES INTO YOUR CREDIT FILE

(Id) Bur   Date   Abbreviated Company Name:
----

(01) EFX 08-17-94 FROST BK L
(03) TUC 08-17-94 FROST BK-CON
(01) EFX 12-28-93 1ST USA BK
(02) TRW 04-13-92 TRW
(02) TRW 03-18-92 TRW
(02) TRW 09-23-91 TRW

PUBLIC RECORD INFORMATION

(Id) Bur Court and Tax Recordings:
----

(01) EFX FEDERAL TAX LIEN FILED IN   FOR   RELEASED   (DK: , CC: , CN:
(02) TRW FEDERAL TAX LIEN FILED FOR $; RELEASED   . (DK: , PL: , CC: , CN:
(03) TUC FEDERAL TAX LIEN FILED IN   FOR $; STATUS UNKNOWN 04-90. (DK: , PL: TAX LIEN, AT:
          CC: CN: COUNTY CLERK)

CURRENT NAMES AND ADDRESSES ASSOCIATED WITH YOUR CREDIT HISTORY

(Id) Bur Names and Current Addresses:
----

(01) EFX
(02) TRW
(03) TUC

PREVIOUS ADDRESSES ASSOCIATED WITH YOUR CREDIT HISTORY

(Id) Bur As of Previous Addresses:
----

(01) EFX 08-94

Continued on page Six

Note: This is a copy of an actual credit file. Identifying information (i.e., name, address, Social Security number, date of birth, account numbers, etc.) has been removed to protect consumer's identity.

FIGURE 3.4   Sample Confidential Credit Report *(continued)*

CONFIDENTIAL CREDIT

Page Six   Reference number :
                                                  Membership number:

PREVIOUS ADDRESSES ASSOCIATED WITH YOUR CREDIT HISTORY

(Id) Bur As of Previous Addresses:
----

(01) EFX 04-91
(02) TRW 09-90
(03) TUC 09-86
(02) TRW 10-87

OTHER INFORMATION ASSOCIATED WITH YOUR CREDIT HISTORY

(Id) Bur Type   Content:
----

(01) EFX EMPLOYMENT   EMPLOYER:
(01) EFX EMPLOYMENT   OCCUPATION:
                        EMPLOYER:
(01) EFX EMPLOYMENT   OCCUPATION:
                        EMPLOYER:
(02) TRW EMPLOYMENT   EMPLOYER:
(02) TRW EMPLOYMENT   EMPLOYER:

CONSUMER REFERRAL INFORMATION

Bur Credit Bureau Name, Address and Phone Numbers:

EFX - EQUIFAX INFORMATION SVCS, PHONE: (800) 378-2732
        P.O. BOX 740256, ATLANTA, GA 30374

TRW - TRW CREDIT DATA, PHONE: (800) 422-4879
        P.O. BOX 2106, ALLEN, TX 75002

TUC - TRANS UNION CORPORATION, PHONE: (800) 851-2674
        P.O. BOX 390, SPRINGFIELD, PA 19064

Continued on page Seven

Note: This is a copy of an actual credit file. Identifying information (i.e., name, address, Social Security number, date of birth, account numbers, etc.) has been removed to protect consumer's identity.

FIGURE 3.4 *(continued)*

CONFIDENTIAL CREDIT

Page Seven   Reference number :
                                                              Membership number:

On behalf of CONFIDENTIAL CREDIT this report is furnished at your request. This credit report is
issued to permissible users as defined by the Fair Credit Reporting Act (Public Law 91-508) and is
done in the strictest of confidence. Good faith effort has been made to obtain information from
sources deemed as reliable, but the accuracy of this information is not guaranteed. (First
American CREDCO, 9444 Balboa Avenue, Suite 500 X3 Dept., San Diego, CA 92123.)

Note: This is a copy of an actual credit file. Identifying information (i.e., name, address, Social Security number, date of birth, account numbers, etc.) has been removed to protect consumer's identity.

Report Summary

A unique feature of CREDCO's report, the *Report Summary,* is an overview of the information provided. Reading from left to right over five lines of information, the summary highlights such information as the number of current and closed accounts; the total real estate balance and the total installment account balance; and the amount past due. The report does not provide specific details about individual accounts; all of the information is in the aggregate.

Credit History

This section of CREDCO's *Credit History* is organized into vertical columns that should be read from left to right. Under each creditor/account listing, there are up to three lines of information—one line of account-related data for each of the credit bureaus reporting information on the account. In reporting this information, the report uses abbreviations for both Trans Union (TUC) and Equifax (EFX).

Account Name/Number/Type of Account

The *Account Name/Number/Type of Account* section of the report straight-forwardly provides the name of each creditor, a number for each account and a definition of the type of account. For example, the sample report shows that the first American Express account listed is a 30-day account and the second is a re-volving account. Later in the report, the Coolidge Bank account is shown to be a credit line and the FFB Mortgage Capital Co. is a real estate loan.

Date Open

The *Date Open* column reports the date when you are reported to have opened an account. The sample report shows that according to both Equifax and Trans Union, the consumer opened a 30-day American Express account on 4/75. TRW reports that the account was opened "10-YR" or 10 years prior to the date that the account history was reported by TRW. This is an example of a small short-coming in the report as there is nothing in CREDCO's report or the explanatory material explaining what the abbreviation means. However, a call to CREDCO's toll-free customer service office will explain what it means.

High/Limit

Information in the *High/Limit* column indicates the amount of your credit limit on an account or the most you have ever charged to an account.

Mthly Pymt

This column of information reflects the amount of your monthly payments on a revolving or installment account. *NA* means that the information was not avail-able or does not apply.

Account Balance

This is the amount you owe on an account as of the date the information was reported by the applicable creditor. For example, the sample report shows all three credit bureaus reporting a balance of $234 on the consumer's American Express card (30-day account).

Last Rptd

Information in the *Last Rptd* column reflects the last date that a creditor updated the account information in your file. That date is not necessarily the last date that you made a payment on the account.

Account Status

Account Status information indicates whether, as of the date the information was reported, an account was current, delinquent, in collection, etc. All of the accounts on the sample report are current.

Past Due Amt, Last Delnq and Past Due 30/60/90

Should an account be past due, that information will be indicated in the *Past Due Amt* column. Next to that is *Last Delnq*, a column that shows the last date on which an account was past due, followed by a series of three columns indicating the number of times an account was past due—30 days, 60 days or 90 days plus. On the sample report, the consumer's Frost Bros. revolving account was last delinquent on 1/90 according to Equifax and Trans Union.

Historical (Date) and Account Status

This section of the report uses number codes to provide a month-by-month payment history of up to 24 months for each account listed. A *1* means the account is current; a *2* means that it is 30 days late; a *5* means that it is 120 days late, etc. A complete explanation of the number codes comes with each report.

Other Information Provided in the Confidential Credit Report

The Confidential Credit report provides four additional types of information at the end of each credit report—recent inquiries (the credit bureau to which the inquiry was made, the date of the inquiry and the company making the inquiry), public record information, current names and addresses as well as previous addresses and other information associated with your credit history such as your employment history. The names, addresses and telephone numbers of the big three also are included.

CHAPTER

FOUR

Correcting Credit Report Problems

Years ago, when Robert and Sylvia were newlyweds, they went through rough times and had trouble paying their bills. They received many credit card offers and quickly succumbed to the love of easy credit. Robert and Sylvia wanted so many things, and charging was an easy way to get them.

About a year into their marriage, Robert's employer announced that all employees would have to take a pay cut. With too much credit card debt and a lower monthly income, Robert and Sylvia again experienced difficulty paying their bills. Soon, they were in serious financial trouble.

Eventually, with the help of Consumer Credit Counseling (CCC) Service, Robert and Sylvia recovered from their money problems and paid off their debts. CCC is a national nonprofit organization with local chapters around the country that helps consumers in financial difficulty.

During the bad times, Robert and Sylvia's credit histories were seriously damaged. Later, they tried to clean up their credit histories so that they might be eligible for new credit. However, they quickly became frustrated with the process. By the time they came to see me, they wanted to sue one of the credit bureaus they had been dealing with—an option available to them under the FCRA.

Robert and Sylvia felt frustrated because they had spent an entire year following all of the steps necessary to get inaccurate information deleted from their credit record. Yet, one month their credit record would be free of the misinformation; the next month it would reappear. When contacted about the problem, the credit bureau blamed the creditors who were supplying account information each month.

Robert and Sylvia's situation is not unusual. Many consumers ruin their credit by taking on more debt than they can handle. These people face years without credit followed by years of credit rebuilding. Robert and Sylvia discovered during the rebuilding process what many other consumers have learned—that sometimes, dealing with credit bureaus requires patience and perseverance. In this chapter you will learn how to deal with credit record omissions and correct credit record errors and inaccuracies.

Credit Record Problems

Although there is no firm number regarding the percentage of credit files that have problems, estimates during the early 1990s ran as high as 50 percent. Given recent industry efforts to reduce that rate, the percentage is probably lower today. However, given that the industry collects more than 2 billion pieces of credit-related information each month and generates more than 550 million credit reports on 180 million consumers every year, there are bound to be errors in some credit files from mistakes by credit bureaus themselves as well as from errors in the information they receive. Because, like Robert and Sylvia, you too may find errors and omissions, it is important that you read your credit report carefully.

As you read it, be on the alert for the credit record problems summarized in Figure 4.1.

 HOT TIP

One way you can help reduce the potential for error in your credit file is to use the same name every time you fill out a credit application. For example, if you have a middle name, use it consistently or not at all. If you are a junior or a senior, always specify so.

Correcting Problems in Your Credit Record

If you find information that you believe is inaccurate in your record, complete the special form that came with your report. The TRW and Equifax forms are both called *Research Request;* Trans Union's *Investigation Request.* Follow all instructions for completing the form.

You can also attach a letter or additional explanatory information to your completed form as well as any evidence that helps prove the error in your report. This information could include copies of canceled checks, receipts, account statements or previous correspondence between you and the creditor. Providing

FIGURE 4.1   Common Credit Record Errors

Common credit record errors include the following:

- Information is commingled. Your credit record includes credit information for someone with a name similar or identical to yours.

- The name of a former spouse appears on your credit record.

- Your name is misspelled, your address is wrong or your Social Security number is incorrect.

- Duplicate accounts show up.

- Account information is inaccurate or incomplete. For example, information for an account shows that you were delinquent for several months a year ago, but it fails to show that you caught up and have paid on time for the past nine months. Other problems could include incorrect account balances and reporting paid-off or closed accounts as open.

- Outdated information is included. In most cases, a credit reporting agency is legally permitted to maintain and report negative account information on a consumer for seven years and bankruptcies for ten years.

- Account information does not relate to you.

- Unauthorized inquiries are listed.

- There is a failure to show that a tax lien has been released.

If you discover these or other problems, correct them as soon as possible to minimize any possible damage to your credit record. Regardless of which credit reporting agency you are dealing with, the process for correcting errors is always the same under the terms of the FCRA.

this type of backup information is a good idea if you do not feel that the credit bureau's form allows you adequate space.

Although the FCRA does not require that you put your concerns in writing, doing so gives you several important benefits. First, you will have a record of what you said and when you said it. Second, you will know when to follow up with a phone call if you have not heard from the credit bureau within a reasonable amount of time. (The big three try to respond within 30 days.) Third, if legal action should become necessary, the letters will help create a written record of the steps you took to resolve your problem.

Send your completed *Research/Investigation Form,* and your letter if you prepare one, to the indicated address via certified mail. Ask for a signed receipt to guarantee that the right person sees it. File the signed receipt with a copy of your completed form, letter and documentation.

> ### 💰 HOT TIP
>
> In some parts of the country you may not get a form to complete when you receive your credit report but instead will be given a phone number to call. When you call that number you will get instructions for initiating an investigation into your problem.

What To Include in Your Letter

When writing your letter, be as succinct as possible. Explain clearly the problems you've found in your credit report, and attach a copy of the report to your letter. Highlight or mark clearly each of the problems you are writing about. See Figure 4.2 for a sample letter.

Any documentation you can provide to substantiate your claim that your record contains errors will strengthen your case and may also speed up the investigation process. For example, if the IRS placed a lien on your property because of back taxes and if the fact that you have since paid those taxes and gotten the lien released is not reflected in your credit report, you should enclose a copy of the document releasing the lien.

Another way to support your case with a credit bureau is to ask the creditor involved to write a letter for you that substantiates your claim. Send a copy of that letter to the credit bureau along with a note from you.

Also include in your letter the ID number from the top of your credit report and all of the same identification information you are required to include in a credit report request letter, such as your full name, current addresses for the past five years, Social Security number and so forth. For a review of the information that must be included in your credit report request letter, return to Chapter 2.

Recordkeeping

Set up a simple recordkeeping system to help monitor the status of your dealings with a credit bureau and/or creditor and to help organize materials related to the credit record problem.

Make copies of all correspondence related to the problem that you send and receive, and keep them in a folder. Whenever you have a telephone conversation regarding the credit record problem, keep a record of that discussion, including the date and time of the call as well as to whom you spoke and what was said.

Other things to keep in your recordkeeping system include receipts related to any costs you may have incurred trying to resolve the credit record problem, account statements and your credit report. In addition, whenever you have to take

FIGURE 4.2   Letter to Credit Bureau Regarding a Credit Record Problem

---

Date

Address of Credit Bureau

Dear Sir or Madam:

I recently reviewed a copy of the credit file your company is maintaining on me. In doing so, I identified the following problem(s): *(Clearly describe each problem using as few words as possible.)*

I have enclosed the following documentation to support my claim. *(Itemize the documentation you are enclosing.)*

I would like you to investigate this problem as quickly as possible, correct it and provide me with a corrected copy of my credit report. Please send my copy to: *(your complete mailing address)*

Also, please send a corrected credit report to anyone who has reviewed my credit history over the past six months for credit purposes. *(You also may request that a corrected credit report be sent to anyone who has reviewed it for employment purposes over the past two years.)* Please send me written confirmation that this request has been honored.

If you need to reach me by phone, call *(area code/telephone number)*.

Thank you for your prompt attention to this request.

Sincerely,

Signature

Consumer ID # _____
Full Name _____
Social Security Number _____
Birthdate _____
Spouse's Name _____
Current Address _____
_____

Previous Addresses for the Past Five Years
_____
_____
_____
_____
_____

time off from work to do something related to the credit record problem, make a note of the date, the purpose of the errand and the amount of time you took off.

Good recordkeeping not only helps you monitor what is happening with a credit bureau's investigation into your complaint; it also creates a written record that may be useful if you have to pursue legal action against a credit bureau or file a formal complaint with the FTC.

The Credit Bureau's Response

Once the credit bureau receives your letter, it will ask the creditor involved to verify the disputed information. If the item in dispute is a matter of public record, the credit reporting agency will contact the appropriate agency or office. The credit bureau will mail the creditor or agency a dispute form or will contact it via e-mail. E-mail allows erroneous information to be confirmed and deleted from your records more quickly than in the past.

If the creditor or agency indicates that the reported information is in error or if the correctness of the item cannot be verified, the credit reporting agency—by law—must delete the information from your credit record.

 HOT TIP

Although the FCRA says only that credit bureaus must complete an investigation into a consumer inquiry and get an answer back to the consumer within a "reasonable period of time," the policy of Associated Credit Bureau, Inc. members is that they will do so within 30 days. Further, any information not verified or updated within 30 days will be removed from the credit files. Therefore, if a month goes by and you have not received a response from the credit bureau you contacted, it is probably time to pick up the phone and request that the information be deleted from your file.

Unfortunately, the FCRA is vague about how thoroughly a credit bureau must investigate a complaint about an item in a consumer's credit report. Therefore, although most bureaus claim that they thoroughly research consumer complaints, their investigations are often superficial.

If a creditor says that the information you are disputing is correct, for example, the credit bureau typically will not pursue its investigation by doing its own research into your complaint or questioning the creditor's response. Credit bureaus tend to give more weight to what a creditor says than to what the consumer contends. Therefore, if the creditor involved contends that the information is correct, the credit bureau is likely to accept the creditor's word, not yours, even if you provide strong evidence.

Aside from the vague wording of the FCRA, there are several other reasons why credit bureaus tend to favor creditors and others who provide them with information about consumers. Perhaps the most important reason is that the creditor, not the consumer, is the credit reporting agency's customer.

Credit bureaus are protected by law from financial responsibility in the case of "honest mistakes" in a consumer's record. Also, in most cases credit bureau subscribers are not legally liable for the accuracy of the consumer-related information they report to credit bureaus—a weakness in the FCRA.

If Your Problem Is Resolved

After a credit record problem is resolved, the credit bureau involved should send you a copy of your corrected report. Review it carefully to make certain that the problem has been resolved and then file it together with the rest of your credit bureau correspondence.

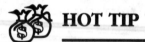 **HOT TIP**

Because the big three have begun sharing information that needs to be changed in a consumer's credit record, any error in your file will be corrected simultaneously in the files of these three credit reporting agencies.

After you receive your corrected report, it is always a good idea to wait a couple of months and request another copy of the report. This is because it is possible, as the result of a computer glitch or human error, that the problem you thought had been corrected may reappear in your record.

If the problem was in a file maintained by TRW or Equifax, at your request the company will send a corrected version of your credit report to all creditors who have checked your file over the past 6 months (If you are a resident of Maryland, New York or Vermont, it's 12 months.) and to any potential employer who has seen it over the past 2 years. When you send your request letter, send it by certified mail and ask for a signed receipt.

If the credit bureau you are dealing with is Trans Union, be certain that when you fill out the *Investigation Request Form,* you complete the bottom section of the form. This section asks you to list the creditors, employers and others that you want to receive an updated copy of your report should the company's investigation result in a change in your credit file. Because there is limited room, on the bottom of the form you may need to attach a sheet with additional names. Although the form does not ask you to list employers' addresses, include them if you can.

If you ask that a corrected report be sent to creditors and employers, be sure to ask the credit bureau for a written confirmation that all of those who saw your report before it was corrected have received the revised report.

If a Credit Bureau's Investigation Does Not Correct a Credit Record Problem

After completing its investigation, it is possible the credit bureau will determine that the credit record information you are disputing is correct. If so, you will receive correspondence from the credit bureau to that effect.

If you receive such a notice, you have several options. You can attempt to locate new or additional documentation to support your assertion that your credit record is in error. If you are able to locate new documentation, make copies of it, write the credit reporting agency and attach copies of the new documentation to the letter. Be sure to make a copy of the letter for your files, and send the materials via certified mail, return receipt requested.

If you have not already done so, you should contact the creditor involved and ask that it correct the problem. Prepare a letter similar to the one you mailed to the credit bureau and include with it copies of any supportive documentation you may have. In your letter, ask that the creditor send a correction to all of the credit bureaus it reports to as well as to you. Also ask that the creditor direct the credit bureaus involved to correct the file they are maintaining on you. See Figure 4.3 for a sample letter.

To make certain that the creditor follows your instructions, ask to receive a copy of the letter(s) that will be sent to each of the major credit reporting agencies.

If the creditor confirms that there is a problem in your credit record, you should also write each of the credit bureaus it reports to once you have received written confirmation of the problem, and ask them to correct your file. This new round of letters is in addition to the letters you have asked your creditor to write and is recommended to ensure that the necessary credit record changes actually get made.

Include with your letter a copy of the creditor's letter that acknowledges the problem and outlines how the creditor intends to correct your account history. Ask each credit bureau to send a corrected credit report to you and to anyone who requested a copy of your report over the past six months (and over the past two years for employment purposes).

Another option for resolving a credit record problem is to call your state attorney general's office or office of consumer affairs to see if they can help you. Many states have consumer protection laws that supplement the provisions of the FCRA. Also, consider contacting your local Better Business Bureau. Contact each of these offices in writing, copy the name of the credit bureau on each letter and follow up with a phone call.

FIGURE 4.3   Letter to a Creditor Regarding a Credit Record Problem

---

Date

Address of Creditor

Dear Sir or Madam *(Direct your letter to the credit manager.)*:

Recently, I requested a copy of my credit report from *(name of credit bureau)*. In reviewing the report, I discovered a problem(s) relating to the account I have with you. My account number is _____ *(Provide account number.)*.

The problem(s) is: _____
(Describe the problem(s) as clearly and succinctly as possible.) I have enclosed documentation that supports my case.

I would appreciate if you would check into this problem and advise me of your findings. If you determine that you have not been reporting accurate, complete information on my account to the credit bureaus you work with, please provide the correct information to those credit bureaus and direct them to make the appropriate change(s) in the files that they are maintaining on me.

In addition, I would like to receive a copy of whatever you send the credit bureaus in response to this letter. Please send that correspondence to me at *(Give your complete mailing address.)*.

If you need to reach me by phone, call *(area code/telephone number)*.

Thank you for your prompt attention to this request.

Sincerely,

Signature

A Written Statement

If you are still unable to get the error corrected, the FCRA gives you a fourth option. The law provides that in situations where a credit bureau's investigation fails to resolve your complaint, you may prepare a written statement of up to 100 words explaining your side of the issue. The law also requires that the credit bureau must make the statement a permanent part of your credit record and that it must be included whenever there is a request for a copy of your credit report.

💰 HOT TIP

If you need help writing your statement, the FCRA requires credit reporting agencies to provide someone to assist you.

Limitations of a Written Statement

Although it is always a good idea to insert a written statement when you cannot get a credit record problem resolved, you need to be aware that such statements are of limited impact. *First,* there is no guarantee that anyone who subsequently reviews the information in your credit file will actually read your written statement.

Second, changes in the way the credit reporting industry operates weakens the force of written statements. For example, most credit applications are now read by computer, which means that your written statement may never be viewed by the individual who makes the credit decision.

Third, an increasing number of creditors now use the big three's automated credit rating systems rather than reviewing a consumer's entire file. Once again, the person making the credit decision will not see the written statement because decisions are based on ratings derived from the information in your credit record rather than on a review of the information in the record itself.

For these reasons, it is always a good idea when applying for credit to let the creditor know that your file includes a written statement and that you would like the creditor to read it. Also, consider providing potential creditors (and anyone else you know who will be reviewing your credit record) a copy of your statement as it appears in your file.

Other Actions

If you take all of the steps outlined here to resolve a credit record problem and the problem remains, you may want to consider a number of other actions. These include formal complaints, mediation and legal action. You may also want to contact the organizations listed in Figure 4.4.

FIGURE 4.4   Helpful Organizations

The following organizations are willing to help consumers who take all of the standard steps for correcting a credit record problem and have no success:

National Foundation for Consumer Credit
Consumer Credit Counseling (CCC) Service
8611 2nd Ave., Ste. 100
Silver Spring, MD 20910
301-589-5600
(National Foundation for Consumer Credit) 800-388-2227
(This number automatically gives you the phone number for the CCC office nearest you.)

Bankcard Holders of America
524 Branch Dr.
Salem, VA 24153
800-638-6407

Public Interest Research Group
218 D St., S.E.
Washington, DC 20003
202-546-9707

Formal Complaints

Filing a complaint with the FTC is one option available to consumers who have trouble with a credit reporting agency. In fact, credit bureau problems currently comprise one of the *biggest* categories of consumer complaints received by the FTC. In the recent past, such problems have been the number one category. Although the FTC will not take action on behalf of an individual consumer, it will move against a credit reporting agency if it receives a sufficient number of complaints about a particular agency.

To contact the FTC, write Federal Trade Commission, Bureau of Consumer Protection (Washington, DC 20580). In your letter, explain your credit record problem and provide a chronological account of all that you have done to try to resolve the problem and the results of your efforts. Provide copies of all correspondence and any documentation you may have that supports your side of the dispute. For a sample letter, see Figure 4.5.

You should also file a complaint with your local Better Business Bureau and your state's office of consumer affairs or attorney general's office. These offices will be able to advise you of your legal rights and of any law that may apply in your state.

FIGURE 4.5   Letter to the Federal Trade Commission

Date

Federal Trade Commission
Bureau of Consumer Protection
Washington, DC 20580

Dear Sir or Madam:

I am writing to register a complaint about *(name of company)*, located at *(address of company)*. A description of my problem with this company follows.

(Succinctly describe the problem you have been trying to resolve and how the problem has affected your ability to get credit, employment, insurance or other. Include a chronology of events that illustrates how long you have been working to resolve the problem, the various steps you have taken and people you have spoken with. Detail the response of company representatives, and when possible, include the names and titles of the persons you have spoken with.)

While I understand that you do not take action on behalf of an individual consumer, I want you to be aware of the troubles I have been experiencing with *(name of company)*. I hope that if you receive enough complaints, you will do what you can to make sure that this company cannot harm other consumers as it has harmed me.

Sincerely,

Signature

Mediation

Mediation is an increasingly popular dispute resolution technique that may be helpful in solving a problem with a credit reporting agency or creditor. Generally, it is less expensive, less stressful and less time-consuming than going to court.

Many communities have dispute resolution centers where trained volunteers or staff work with the parties in a dispute to identify an acceptable compromise. The goal is to create a win/win situation for all the parties.

To find out if there is a dispute resolution center in your community, call your local, county or state bar association, or look in your telephone book under "Mediation Services." Call your local bar association to get the names of attorneys who also offer mediation services.

Legal Options

The FCRA gives you the option of pursuing legal action if you are unable to resolve a credit record problem. It says that you may sue a credit reporting agency or the creditor—whoever is at fault—and that the suit can be for actual and punitive damages. And if the court decides in your favor, you may collect attorney fees and court costs. To win a case, however, you will have to prove that the credit bureau or creditor acted negligently, something that is difficult to do.

Because some states have their own credit reporting laws, be sure to contact your state's office of consumer affairs or the attorney general's office to find out if your state has such laws and to determine if you should use state law rather than the FCRA to sue over a credit record problem.

Small Claims Court

Depending on the laws of your state, you may be able use the FCRA or your own state's credit reporting law to sue in small claims court—*the people's court.*

Small claims courts are designed to allow you to present your case before a judge without the assistance of a lawyer for relatively little cost and a minimum of paperwork. These courts have the advantage of being relatively inexpensive and are appropriate when the legal problem is straightforward and you feel comfortable organizing your own case and speaking on your own behalf.

Small claims courts do have limitations, however. Only certain types of cases may be heard, and you can sue only up to the maximum dollar value set by the state. Furthermore, winning a judgment against a firm does not guarantee that you will be able to collect on that judgment. For a discussion of when small claims court is appropriate and how to use it to resolve credit-related problems, see Chapter 6.

Traditional Civil Court

In instances when small claims court is not an option, you may want to explore the feasibility of using the traditional civil court system. Remember, however, that you will probably need an attorney's assistance if you pursue this legal route and that such legal help can be costly.

If you need legal help, it is always a good idea to explore sources of free or low-cost legal assistance in your community. These are discussed in the following section. If none exists in your area, or if none meets your needs and you are considering working with a private attorney, here are suggestions to help keep costs down:

Call your local, county or state bar association for names of attorneys who can help you. Look for lawyers who are establishing their practices since they may have lower fees. Contact each of these attorneys to find out if any of them offer an initial free consultation session. It is possible that you will get all the legal advice you need during this session.

During these calls you also should find out how much each lawyer charges on an hourly basis. That way, if you cannot find an attorney who will provide a free consultation, you will know which lawyers charge the least.

If you are going to pay for legal advice, schedule an hour's appointment with the attorney you select. At the start of your meeting, indicate that you only want this initial meeting to last one hour and during that hour you would like to get an assessment of what your legal position is, how strong a case you have, what your options are, how the lawyer would recommend proceeding and how the attorney would want to be paid. If the lawyer says your chances of winning are slim to none, don't pursue legal action. If the lawyer feels that you have a strong case, you will have to weigh the costs and the benefits of legal action for yourself when deciding whether to hire an attorney.

When talking fees with a lawyer, find out if your case can be handled on a contingency basis. This means that the lawyer would get paid a percentage of whatever is won for you but gets nothing if the case is lost.

Low-Cost/No-Cost Sources of Legal Assistance

Many communities offer sources of low-cost/no-cost legal assistance. These may include Legal Aid, law school clinics and clinics run by your area's bar association.

Legal Aid

Approximately 300 Legal Aid offices are available across the country; however, that number may decrease as a result of congressional budget cuts. Funded in part by the federal Legal Services Corporation, these offices offer free legal services to anyone who qualifies on the basis of income. Although each office sets its own eligibility criteria, Legal Aid services are not available to anyone whose household income is greater than 125 percent of the federal poverty guidelines. In addition, Legal Aid offers assistance with credit-related problems, but each office sets its own priorities for the types of cases it will take. To determine whether Legal Aid can help you, call the office nearest you or call the Legal Services Corporation in Washington, D.C., at 202-336-8800.

Legal Clinics

If there is a law school in your area, it may sponsor a legal clinic where consumers can get free legal advice. These clinics not only offer law students on-the-job training, but they also provide a service to the community.

Your local or county bar association may sponsor a low-cost/no-cost legal clinic. Call for information.

Negative but Accurate Account Information

When you review your credit record, you may find that it contains negative but accurate information. According to the FCRA, most negative information may be reported for up to seven years; bankruptcies may be reported for up to ten years although it is the policy of members of Associated Credit Bureaus to delete Chapter 13 bankruptcies after seven years. Therefore, you may have to live with negative information in your credit record for a while. In such situations, however, the FCRA says that you may insert a statement in your credit record explaining the reason for the negative information.

Inserting a Statement

If circumstances such as sudden illness, costly medical bills, loss of a job or an unexpected decrease in income affect your ability to meet your credit obligations, consider preparing a short statement for inclusion in your credit file that explains the problem, how it affected your finances and what you are doing to get your finances back on track. However, it is important to remember that in some instances those who evaluate your credit-worthiness will not actually see your complete file but will instead base their decision on credit risk scores derived from the information in your file. In such situations, those creditors will never see the explanatory statement in your file.

To counter this problem, it is a good idea to provide a copy of your explanatory statement to anyone who you know will be using information in your credit record to make a decision about you.

Negotiating with a Taxing Entity

If your credit record has been damaged because a taxing entity has placed a lien on your property as a result of unpaid back taxes, the sooner you can pay off that debt and get the lien removed the better. If you can't pay your tax debt in full, there are a couple of strategies to try depending on to whom you owe money. If it is the IRS or a state income taxing authority, you may be able to negotiate a deal whereby the taxing entity accepts an amount less than the total amount you owe and begins reporting to credit reporting agencies that the lien has been removed.

If you owe property taxes, the taxing authority is not going to accept less than what you owe, but it may be willing to work out a payment plan for you, allowing you to wipe out your debt with installment payments rather than making you come up with one lump sum. In turn, the taxing authority may be willing to lift the lien; if not, you'll at least be working toward the time when it will be.

To initiate negotiations, contact the appropriate office of the taxing entity involved, tell them what you want to accomplish and find out whom you need to talk with, the paperwork you need to complete and so forth. If the first person you speak with is unwilling to work with you, go to the next level of decision making within the organizational structure of the taxing authority. And remember, you are working with a bureaucracy, so decisions may come slowly.

One final note on negotiating. If you decide to seek a negotiated compromise with the IRS, you may want to get the assistance of a lawyer or a CPA familiar with IRS or state/local tax negotiations and the tax code. These people will know whether your tax liability is likely to be compromised, how best to approach the negotiations and which laws and forms apply.

The IRS

If the IRS has a lien on your property, it is important that you know about Form 656, *Offers in Compromise*. The Internal Revenue Code allows the IRS to negotiate a compromise of a tax liability that is not in a lawsuit if one or both of the following criteria are met. First, there must be grounds for doubting liability for the amount owed; second, there must be a question as to whether the full amount owed, plus penalty and interest, will ever be collected. It is up to consumers to provide evidence that they are not liable for all or part of the tax liability. Such evidence might include canceled checks, copies of tax forms, correspondence and signed agreements. If you can prove there is doubt about your liability, the amount by which your unpaid back taxes are reduced will depend on the IRS's degree of doubt.

To determine your ability to pay, the IRS will use a set of standard guidelines, which will examine the value of all your assets and your current and future earnings potential. The IRS will also determine whether you are up-to-date on your other tax payments.

If the IRS is willing to negotiate a compromise with you, it may involve your paying a percentage of your future earnings.

Handling Omissions

As discussed in Chapter 2, not all creditors report account information to credit bureaus, and some do so only under special circumstances. If, in reviewing your credit report, you notice that an account with a good payment history is missing from your file, and if you feel that your chances of getting future credit would be improved if that account information were a part of your credit history, you can take steps to get it added to your file. You may also want to have missing account information added to your credit record if you are denied credit because of an *insufficient credit file* or *no credit file,* and the missing information would help create a more complete picture of your ability to manage credit.

 HOT TIP

_____

Creditors like to see a responsible use of credit over time. Therefore, if a creditor does not report regularly to a credit reporting agency and you feel that the missing account information is important to your credit file, you will have to update your credit report periodically to develop a pattern of timely payments on that account.

Adding Information

If you find important omissions in your credit record, contact the credit bureau in writing. Specify exactly what you would like to have included in your file, and provide the name, address and telephone number of the creditor with the appropriate account number. In addition, enclose any relevant documentation that helps substantiate your payment history. Figure 4.6 shows a sample letter. Be sure that you provide all of the identifying information specified in Figure 4.1.

The following is a list of the types of information you may want to add to your credit file to create a more complete picture of yourself as a credit manager:

- Details on loans for which you have a good history

- Active accounts with good payment histories that are not mentioned

- Information related to your mortgage, especially if you have paid it in full

- Settlements on tax liens, judgments or disputed bills

Although credit reporting agencies are not required to add information to a file at the request of a consumer, they may do so for a fee. However, they will want to verify your information before doing so.

FIGURE 4.6   Letter To Add Information to Your Credit Record

Date

Address

Dear Sir or Madam:

In reviewing the credit file you maintain on me, I noted that my credit record does not include certain information that I feel is important to a complete portrait of me as a credit-using consumer. Therefore, I request that you add the following account information to my credit file:

(Include a copy of your credit report, and specify the account information you would like added to it. Note relevant account numbers, and provide the complete name(s) and address(es) of applicable creditor(s).)

If you need additional information from me, you can reach me at *(area code/telephone number and mailing address).* Please let me know if there will be a fee involved.

Thank you for your assistance.

Sincerely,

Signature

Consumer ID # _____

Full Name _____

Social Security Number _____

Birthdate _____

Spouse's Name _____

Current Address _____

_____

Previous Addresses for the Past Five Years

_____

_____

_____

_____

CHAPTER
FIVE

Rebuilding Your Credit

As Sam V. sat in my office telling me about the new book he had bought that explained "the secret" of rebuilding credit, I kept thinking how easy it is for people desperate to rebuild their credit to be victimized. Sam's "book" was actually a mere 37 pages long, including copies of standard forms. For that, Sam had paid $49.95! The book discussed a clever way for a consumer to create a new credit identity, including substituting federal identification numbers used for tax purposes for Social Security numbers.

"So what do you think?" Sam asked.

"First of all, some of the things suggested by this book are illegal," I responded. "Plus, I'd be suspicious of any publication that doesn't include the name of the person who wrote it or how to get in touch with the author."

Sam looked at the book as if for the first time. "You're right. Whoever wrote this didn't put their name on it."

"Sam", I said, "this book is suggesting that you participate in a fraud. When it comes to rebuilding credit, the best advice I can give you is that there are no quick fixes despite what that book says. Rebuilding credit requires hard work; it takes time; and it takes diligence. And I might also add that it can take a tough hide to withstand the initial rejections you'll probably get from potential creditors.

I then shared with Sam the same philosophy and practical advice about rebuilding credit that I am going to share with you in this chapter.

A Credit-Wise Philosophy

A lot changes when you lose your credit. The most noticeable change is that you have to live on a cash basis, which usually means making difficult choices about how to spend your limited dollars. When you lose your credit, you cannot turn to credit cards when you've used up your paycheck!

Often, people who no longer have credit and who have to rely on themselves begin to reassess their values and priorities. They ask themselves what they really want out of life, how important spending and material possessions are to them, and whether those things are so important that they will use credit to get these possessions. They also begin thinking about sacrificing and saving for things they really need or want.

This is an important conversation to have with yourself if your credit history has been seriously damaged and you can now begin to rebuild your credit. From my experience some people who file for bankruptcy or get into serious financial difficulty shared a common pattern: their desires for things exceeded their ability to pay and they began using credit to immediately fulfill their every desire. These people failed to distinguish between what they needed and what they wanted and between what they could save for future purchases and what had to be purchased with credit. Many of them tried to get as much credit as possible and then used it, whether they could meet the payments or not.

As a rule, those who can distinguish between needs and desires, who can delay using credit except when absolutely necessary and who are willing to sacrifice to get what they want are less apt to develop serious money problems. Credit is not something you use to make all your dreams come true. Credit is a tool to obtain something really important when there is no other practical way of paying for it.

Why Having Credit May Be Necessary

Although there are arguments for living without credit and it can certainly be done, in today's world that's not always practical. Not having credit will make buying a house or another major purchase more difficult, and it can also mean that you won't be able to obtain a loan to help finance your children's college education. This may not be a problem for those of you who don't consider owning a house or buying a new car a desire or even a necessity. And some of you will also decide that you're going to place most of the financial burden for your children's education on them, not on yourself. But those of you who don't share these views will probably want new credit.

A Sound Approach to Credit Rebuilding

To prevent yourself from getting into trouble again, strictly limit the amount of credit you apply for and get credit only for a specific purpose. In other words, don't get credit just to have credit. That means no more multiple bankcards—one will do—or multiple bank credit lines. You don't need them and having them will only tempt you.

If you want to buy a home, then focus on rebuilding and obtaining credit for that purpose. The same holds true for cars and other big-ticket items. The key to successful credit rebuilding is gaining the trust of your creditors, and you'll have to do that the old fashioned way—earn it. You need to prove to potential creditors that despite your past money troubles and regardless of why they developed, you will manage your money wisely and pay all of your debts on time in the future.

I recommend that you begin rebuilding trust at the local level, in your own community. That is where you should focus your efforts to get new credit. You have a better chance of rebuilding if potential creditors can meet you face-to-face, are familiar with where you work, may know your family or attend your same church. Now let's talk about *how* to rebuild your credit.

When To Start Rebuilding Your Credit

Once the financial difficulties that contributed to your credit history problems are behind you, you can start rebuilding your credit. Usually, however, if you filed for bankruptcy, you must wait until your bankruptcy has been concluded. Even though your bankrutpcy will be a part of your credit history for a number of years, you can start rebuilding 18 to 20 months after its conclusion.

To prepare for getting new credit, the following are some things you need to do first.

- Review your credit record with each of the big three credit bureaus to spot errors and missing information.

- Correct any errors you find and add written statements as necessary.

- Begin saving each month, even if it's only a small amount. Having a financial cushion will help you resist the temptation to use credit in the future.

- Keep trouble-free any credit accounts you may still have.

- Develop good money management skills. Your local Consumer Credit Counseling Service office, a nearby college or university, a county extension service and the like are all possible sources of help.

The Credit Rebuilding Process

To start, you should remember a few credit rebuilding rules of thumb. First, it's going to take time so don't get impatient. Be prepared to spend at least two to three years or longer to rebuild. Second, don't be fooled into thinking that you can speed up the process with the help of a credit repair firm. As Chapter 6 makes clear, spending money with these firms is a waste; they can't do anything you can't do for yourself for free. Third, keep to a minimum the amount of credit you get. One national bankcard is all you need as most restaurants, retailers and other consumer-oriented businesses accept either MasterCard or Visa. Having multiple bankcards can be too much temptation for some and will not be viewed favorably by potential creditors. Incidentally, you will probably have to start with a secured national bankcard, described later in this chapter.

You should set a goal of paying off your bankcard in full each month. If that is sometimes not possible, don't charge more to the card until the previous charges are paid off. And, as I've already suggested, concentrate on building credit in your own community. Saving money with a local bank will greatly help your rebuilding effort.

The best way to initiate the credit rebuilding process is to obtain a small cash-secured loan with a friendly local bank. After you've paid off the first bank loan, apply for a second small loan that is not cash secured. You may also want to apply to your bank for a secured national bankcard.

 HOT TIP

Credit cards issued by local retailers usually come with relatively high interest rates. However, because most local retailers accept national bankcards, store charge cards are usually an unnecessary option.

The process I've just described is not the only way to rebuild a damaged credit history, but it is one that has worked well for many of my clients. What is best for you will depend on your previous credit history and your present circumstances. Remember, however, regardless of how you rebuild your credit, your goal is not to get all the credit you can but to get only the credit you need.

Getting a Bank Loan

After you've begun saving and have between $500 and $1,000 in your account, call the bank and schedule an appointment with a consumer loan officer. Explain over the phone that you have had money troubles and damaged your credit and that you would like to discuss in person the possibility of getting a cash-secured loan. This is a loan that you guarantee by depositing money with the bank making the loan.

It's possible that the loan officer will tell you over the phone that he or she is not interested in talking with you because of your credit history. If so, call another bank in your community and continue calling banks until you find a loan officer willing to meet with you.

It's usually best to start with the bank where you already have your savings and/or checking accounts, but if that bank isn't interested in working with you, then you should try banks that are actively promoting debt consolidation loans or the bank where your employer banks. If your employer has banked there for a long time and is an important customer, and if you are a valued employee, the bank may be willing to work with you, especially if your employer provides a reference letter. Try credit unions too.

Banks and Loan Officers

Banks are highly regulated businesses. They are expected to minimize the risks they take lending and investing money to safeguard their depositors' funds. In fact, if a bank makes too many high-risk loans, it may lose its charter and be out of business.

The career of a successful loan officer is in large part influenced by the success of the loans the officer makes. A loan officer who makes lots of loans that perform well—loans that are paid off on schedule—is much more likely to have a successful career at a bank than one who makes lots of loans that perform poorly.

It's understandable therefore that with a damaged credit history, you are not going to be as attractive to a loan officer as someone with an unblemished record. As a result, it may take you a while to locate a loan officer willing to work with you.

If you can't find any loan officers willing to do business with you, recontact those who seemed most sympathetic or with whom you had the best rapport and ask each of them what you should do to get a loan. You may have to save more money as tangible proof of how serious you are about getting your finances back on track; you may have to increase your income; or you may simply have to wait until there is more distance between you and your financial problems.

When You Meet with a Loan Officer

When you find a loan officer willing to meet with you, ask the officer to mail you a loan application. Complete it and bring it to your meeting to save time. Also bring along a copy of your current credit report so you can discuss it, provide any necessary explanations and show that you have not had any recent problems with credit.

 HOT TIP

Dress conservatively for your meeting and don't wear a lot of jewelry. Above all, be sure to show up on time!

At the start of this chapter I talked about how credit rebuilding is all about building trust. This meeting with a loan officer provides you an opportunity to begin doing just that. Therefore, do whatever you can to assure the officer that your financial problems will not reoccur and that today you're a good candidate for a loan. Explain how your life has changed since you got into financial trouble and/or what you have done to stabilize your financial situation. Remember, because loan officers are inherently conservative and risk-averse, they need to be convinced that you are a good risk. If your credit problems were the result of poor money management skills, tell the loan officer about the steps you've taken to develop better skills. If your money troubles developed because of problems in your life—your spouse was laid off; you got divorced; you were ill and unable to work—explain how things have changed. Also, be ready to talk about why you need credit again: you're a businessperson who must travel or entertain a lot; your children are approaching college age and you need to borrow money to help pay for their education; you and your spouse would like to buy a house and start a family.

Should your first meeting go well, the loan officer will probably want to schedule a second meeting after ordering and reviewing another copy of your credit record. The officer will need assurance there are no reoccuring credit problems, you have been forthcoming about all aspects of your financial history and you've not begun applying for a lot of new credit. If the officer seems reluctant to make the loan, even on a secured basis, ask what you can do.

If the loan officer approves you for a cash-secured loan, it will probably be for an amount close to what you have in your savings account. The officer will probably ask you to put the proceeds of the loan in a certificate of deposit (CD) at the bank and will expect you to begin paying off the loan according to your agreement. You will probably have a year or so to complete your payments. Be sure to make each payment on time to convince the loan officer that you are serious about rebuilding your credit so the officer will be open to making you a second loan that is not cash secured. A second loan can be important because a positive payment history on just one loan is usually not enough to rebuild your credit history.

Getting a Second Loan

After you have paid off your first loan, contact each of the big three credit bureaus to request a copy of your credit report. Make sure that each report accurately reflects the history of your payment on your cash-secured loan. If one or more of the reports do not, talk to your loan officer about reporting your payment history to those credit bureaus. If the officer doesn't report, then you should ask the credit bureau to add the information.

After your first loan has been paid in full, let your loan officer know that you want to apply for a second loan that is not cash secured. If you had no trouble paying off the first loan, you should not have trouble getting a second small loan. If you do, go to another bank. Once you get a second loan, pay it off just like the first one, and after it's paid off, once again check your credit history with each of the big three.

Shopping for a National Bankcard

Before applying for a national secured bankcard—Visa or MasterCard—take some time to understand the terminology and features of bankcards. There are a lot of offers out there, and your goal should be to get the best deal. The "best deal" is not simply the bankcard with the highest credit limit; in fact, the credit limit should be one of the least important factors for you. And because the bankcard you apply for will probably be secured, as explained below, your credit limit will depend on how much money you put up as security. Factors more important to consider include the card's annual fee, interest rate, late payment fee and grace period. For a short definition of these and other bankcard terms, refer to Figure 5.1.

Secured or Collateralized Bankcards

Using a secured bankcard responsibly is an excellent way to build creditors' trust in the ability of someone with a damaged credit history to use new credit and

FIGURE 5.1   National Bankcard Features

When evaluating the best national bankcard to apply for, the criteria to consider are listed below.

- *Annual fee.* This is the amount you pay each year for use of your bankcard; it can range from $15 to $35 to as much as $50 for gold or premium cards. Some cards have no annual fee, but if you are considering applying for one of these, be sure the card company isn't substituting a monthly fee or a very high rate of interest for the annual fee.

- *Credit limit.* This is the maximum you can charge on your bankcard.

- *Grace period.* This is the amount of time allowed you to pay your bankcard balance in full each month before you are assessed a finance charge or interest. Not all cards have a grace period, but if you are not going to pay off your account balance each month, the longer the grace period the better.

- *Interest rate.* All bankcard issuers charge interest on an account's unpaid balance. The interest rate you pay will depend on the issuer's terms of credit and the laws of the state where the card issuer is located. If you don't pay off your card balance every month, find a card with the lowest possible rate of interest.

- *Late charge.* Some card issuers charge a late fee, which can be as high as $20, if you do not pay your bill on time.

- *Penalty for exceeding your credit limit.* Some card issuers charge users if they charge more on their account than their credit limit allows.

 HOT TIP

Don't apply for a lot of bankcards. Not only is there no reason for multiple bankcards, but every time you apply for one, the potential creditor's inquiry into your credit history will show up on your report and make future creditors less interested in working with you.

---

eventually get an unsecured card. Banks that issue secured cards require cardholders to *secure* the purchases they make with their cards by opening a savings account or by purchasing a CD from them. If you are unable to pay your secured bankcard debt, the issuer will still be able to obtain the money you owe by withdrawing it from your savings account or cashing in your CD. On the other hand, if you make your payments in full and on time each month, the issuer will have no need to tap your collateral, and your payment history will gradually improve. Eventually, depending on your payment history, you may be able to obtain a regular bankcard.

For a list of banks that offer secured bankcards, write Bankcard Holders of America (524 Brach Dr., Salem, VA 24153; 800-638-6407). The list costs $4; the organization also publishes lists of national bankcards with low interest rates and no annual fees.

Don't take at face value any bankcard's promotional literature—it's primarily a sales pitch. Read the fine print and comparison shop! Don't take shopping for and choosing a bankcard any less seriously than buying a car or a major appliance. It's an important decision.

Once You've Obtained a Secured Bankcard

Once you obtain a national secured bankcard, use it to charge only necessities, not something frivolous that you would normally buy with cash. Put aside the cash amount of your charged purchase for paying your bankcard bill when it arrives. After you have used your card for six months or so, get a copy of your credit record from each of the big three to make certain your account payments are now a part of your credit history.

 HOT TIP

Be wary of bankcards that allow you to carry over your account balance from month to month. Doing so can make it easy to run up a big balance that you may be unable to pay.

> ### 💰 HOT TIP
>
> Credit unions tend to offer national bankcards with low annual rates, so you may want to check these out if you're eligible.

When evaluating secured bankcards, your first concern should be whether the issuer reports to one or more of the big three. If not, you will not achieve the major benefit you are seeking by applying for a national bankcard—rebuilding a positive credit history. During the evaluation process you also need to ask questions that you would not typically ask if you were shopping for a regular national bankcard. These questions include the following:

- Do I have to pay an application fee? If I do and fail to qualify, can I get the fee back?

- How much money do I have to deposit as collateral for the bankcard? This is important because you will not have access to that money, which can range from a few hundred dollars to a few thousand.

- What rate of interest will my deposit earn?

- Do I have the option of putting my deposit in a CD or money market account rather than in a lower-yielding savings account?

- What percent of my deposit will my credit line be? It could range from 50 to 100 percent. Obviously, the higher the percent the better.

- Can I increase my credit limit without increasing my deposit, assuming that the account has a good payment history?

- How soon after I've had use of the card can I increase my credit limit?

- Can I convert a secured card to an unsecured card? If so, under what conditions?

- How soon after an account is past due will the issuer tap into my collateral?

- If I close my account, when can I get my collateral back?

- Are there fees associated with closing the account?

Beware of Bankcard Scams

Some companies deceptively advertise secured and unsecured Visa bankcards and MasterCards. They may use television, newspapers or postcards to market their offers. Typically, the ads lead you to believe that simply by calling an 800 or 900 telephone number, you will be able to get a national bankcard. Getting a bankcard is rarely as easy as that and if it is, you can be sure the card will not be a good deal. Therefore, before responding to one of these ads, it is important that you know the problems associated with them and that you realize they promise a lot more than you will actually get. Here are some of the problems:

- If you call a 900 number, you will be charged for the call and the company you are calling will get a percentage of that fee.

- You may have to pay an application fee for the bankcard.

- The ads may not tell you what the cost of the call will be despite the fact that a 900 call can be quite expensive, ranging from 50¢ to $50 or more.

- Often, the ads are not clear about the terms of credit, including the amount of the security deposit required, if any, the application cost, processing fees, annual fees and the like.

- The ads do not always inform you about such requirements as age and income

Alternative Ways To Buy on Credit

As I have already made clear, rebuilding your credit is not going to happen overnight. For some consumers it will take years to get a conventional bank loan. Therefore, it's important for those of you with credit problems to be aware of alternative credit sources. Most of these will cost more than conventional credit, but if you need a car for work or if owning a house now is really important to you, the following information should be helpful.

Buying a Home

It's unlikely that any bank will be willing to grant you a home mortgage until your financial problems have been over for at least two to three years; and any bankruptcy proceeding will have to be concluded before you can apply for a bank loan. When a bank does lend you money for a home, you'll probably have to put up a larger-than-average down payment and you may be charged a higher rate of interest than someone without your credit history. With this information in mind, alternative sources of credit for buying a home include the following:

- *HUD (Department of Housing and Urban Development) homes.* These are foreclosed homes originally financed with an insured mortgage from the Federal Housing Administration (FHA). They can be an excellent source of well-priced real estate in your community and can include single-family homes, condominiums and town houses. Although they are sold "as is," you can get some especially good bargains if you are willing to buy a "fixer upper." To find out about the HUD homes for sale in your area, look in your local paper's real estate classified section or call an area REALTOR®. Real estate brokers who sell HUD homes maintain a complete list of available HUD properties.

- *Owner-financed homes.* Some homesellers are willing to finance the purchase of their home to generate a steady stream of income, perhaps for retirement. Frequently, the seller will have less stringent credit requirements than a lending institution, but will probably require a larger down payment than a bank and may charge a relatively high rate of interest.

- *Rent to purchase.* If you've rented a home for a while and the owner has come to like and trust you, the owner may be willing to allow you a lease agreement with an option to buy.

- *Loan brokers.* Loan brokers make their money by linking people who want to borrow money to buy a home or make some other significant purchase with investors, including mortgage companies, that will loan them money. The money a loan broker may find for you will be "high-risk" money, which means it comes at a relatively high rate of interest. You will also be required to put up a larger-than-average down payment.

    The loan broker is paid from the loan the broker arranged for you. Obviously, you would not have to incur this cost if you had a good credit history and could get a loan in the conventional way.

    Be wary of any loan broker who asks for money before a loan has been secured. That's not how a reputable loan broker does business. An honest broker gets paid only if a loan goes through, so if you pay money in advance, you may lose it.

Buying a Car

The biggest and most important purchase most people make is a car. Consider yourself lucky if you live in a community with good public transportation because you are in a minority.

What follows are some ways to buy a car when your credit has been damaged.

- *Contact your friendly banker.* One reason to start cultivating a good relationship with a banker in your area is so you can get a car loan when it is a necessity. If you've done this according to the credit rebuilding advice in this chapter, schedule an appointment with your banker to find out the conditions the bank would set to finance your purchase. Your discussion with the banker will probably focus on how big a down payment you can afford to pay—the bigger the better—and the age of the car you want to buy. Banks do not like to loan money for old, used cars because of fear they will not be able to get their money back if the car has to be repossessed.

Your banker may also want to know if you can find a cosigner for the car loan. The cosigner would have to be someone who has good credit, is willing to sign the loan agreement and will promise to pay off the debt if you default. Friends, family and employers are often cosigners.

- *Look for "bad credit no problem" ads.* In most major cities, some of the larger car dealerships offer "high-risk" loan programs similar to those loan brokers offer. Typically, these car dealers will sell you a car no matter what your past credit history so long as your job is stable, your down payment is big enough and you don't mind the high interest rate.

- *Used-car dealers.* Many used-car dealers will finance the purchase of a car if you have a stable job and can make an appropriate down payment. Be aware however, that you're not going to get a bargain and that these dealers can be dangerous to deal with. Often, a used-car dealer will not know the history of the car you're considering or whether it's mechanically sound. Most sell their cars "as is," which means that you could end up buying someone else's problems.

- *Check out friends and relatives.* Sometimes a friend or relative has a car they don't need anymore. They may be willing to sell it to you at reasonable terms rather than trading it in or selling it to someone else.

CHAPTER SIX

Avoiding Credit Repair Company Rip-Offs

I first met Carlos S. several years ago when he came to my office to file for bankruptcy as a result of a failed business. His business troubles and a divorce had left Carlos's credit history in a shambles. Recently, he returned to see me with his new wife, Michelle.

Michelle had her own financial problems as the result of a divorce. Despite the fact that her former husband had agreed, as part of their divorce settlement, to pay off the bills that had accumulated during their marriage, he had not done so. Consequently, Michelle was left with many of them. Although it had taken a long time, she had finally managed to pay everyone she owed. However, in reviewing her credit record she discovered that it did not reflect those payments, showing instead that she still owed money to her creditors.

Understandably, Carlos and Michelle were concerned that the misinformation in Michelle's credit record, combined with Carlos's bankruptcy, would prevent them from building the life they had envisioned. Michelle especially was feeling frustrated because she had worked very hard and made many sacrifices to pay off the debts from her former marriage.

When Carlos and Michelle arrived for their appointment, they showed me a newspaper advertisement for a company that claimed it could clear a consumer's credit history of all negative information, even a bankruptcy. Carlos and Michelle asked if I had ever heard of the company as they were considering hiring it to take care of the problems in Michelle's credit record.

"It looks pretty good," Carlos told me.

"Too good to be true," I replied.

I explained to both Michelle and Carlos that the ad was for a credit repair or credit fix-it company. I talked with them about the dangers of dealing with such a company, how they could correct their own credit records and how long the FCRA allowed credit bureaus to report certain negative information.

Nearly everyone who has had problems with their credit wants to have a clean credit record, free of damaging information. However, the desire for a problem-free record can sometimes cause people to pay for the assistance of a credit repair company rather than follow the advice in Chapters 4 and 5.

Credit repair companies make big promises but rarely give consumers the results they expect and pay for. In this chapter I will explain what credit repair companies are, how they work and how they rip off consumers.

What Is a Credit Repair Company?

Credit repair or *fix-it* companies are businesses that charge exorbitant amounts of money to "clean up" a consumer's credit record. For fees that range from $50 to as much as $2,000, these companies claim they can erase bad credit and even make bankruptcies disappear from a consumer's credit record. Some of these firms will move into a locale, charge unsuspecting consumers a hefty up-front fee and then skip town, leaving the consumers poorer and without the credit record improvements they were promised.

Despite their claims, credit repair companies cannot do anything you can't do yourself for little or no cost under the terms of the FCRA. That law gives you the right to have inaccurate or outdated information deleted from your credit records as well as the right to have inaccuracies corrected.

Furthermore, there are certain types of information that neither you nor a credit repair firm can remove from your credit record until the law says it can be deleted. As indicated in Chapter 1, the FCRA says that most negative information in your credit record is legally reportable for seven years, but bankruptcies may be reported for up to ten years. Credit repair companies *do not* have the authority to change the law for their clients. Generally, only time can erase negative information from your credit record unless the information is erroneous. In that case you should follow the advice in Chapter 4, and you should *not* hire a credit repair company.

How To Spot a Credit Repair Company

Some credit repair firms are easy to spot; others can be more difficult to identify because they may market themselves as financial counseling and advice companies. To prevent you from getting duped, the following are some sure signs of a credit repair company:

- The company's advertising and literature make impossibly extravagant promises, such as: "We can wipe out bankruptcies and other negative information, no matter how bad your credit history."

- The company says it will use "little-known loopholes" in the FCRA to rid your credit record of negative information.

- The company claims that it can get you a major bankcard despite your credit record.

Credit repair firms use a wide variety of techniques to market their services to consumers. These techniques can include fliers distributed in parking lots and posted on telephone poles, television advertising, direct mail and telemarketing. Some firms have even marketed their services on cyberspace although once discovered, they were shut down by the FTC. Credit repair firms that use direct mail or telemarketing techniques often develop target lists of consumers from court records of people who have filed for bankruptcy.

Regardless of the specific technique(s) a credit repair firm uses to interest a consumer in its services, its goal is to get you to either call a telephone number to learn more about its services or schedule an appointment with a representative of the firm.

For consumers anxious to get rid of adverse information in their credit files, the message they hear on the telephone or in the credit repair company office can have a lot of appeal. Therefore, to help you separate fact from fiction so that you will not fall for empty promises, here are some claims frequently used when these firms market their services to desperate consumers . . . and the real story behind each claim.

1. **Credit repair company myth:** "If you are bankrupt, you won't be able to get credit for ten years."
   Fact: Although bankruptcies do stay on a consumer's credit record for ten years, each creditor has its own standards for granting credit and not all creditors refuse to work with bankrupt consumers. This is especially true if consumers can demonstrate that the cause of their bankruptcies was not misuse of credit but rather circumstances beyond their control, such as unexpected job loss or serious illness. Furthermore, members of Associated Credit Bureaus, Inc., including the big three, will report Chapter 13 bankruptcies for no longer than seven years.

2. **Credit repair company myth:** The credit repair company is affiliated with the federal government in some way.
   Fact: Such claims are simply not true.

3. **Credit repair company myth:** File segregation, a technique used by credit repair firms to create a new, problem-free credit identity for a consumer and explained later in this chapter is legal.
   Fact: It is a federal crime to make false statements on a credit or loan application, something the credit repair company may ask you to do as part

of the file segregation process. It is also a federal crime to misrepresent your Social Security number and to obtain an Employee Identification Number (EIN) number from the IRS under false pretenses.

Also, if as part of the file segregation process you use the mail or the telephone to apply for credit and provide false information, you put yourself at risk of being accused of mail or wire fraud. In addition, in certain states file segregation may constitute civil fraud.

Products and Services of Credit Repair Companies

In addition to their credit repair services, some credit repair companies also offer debt consolidation loans, debt counseling services and national bankcards. Frequently, credit fix-it company loans come with very high interest rates and substantial up-front fees. Some companies also require that borrowers post their homes as collateral. Often the credit repair company will misrepresent the terms of the collateralized loan, making consumers vulnerable to the loss of their homes.

The debt counseling services of credit repair companies are often no more than referrals to a bankruptcy attorney. Typically, their offers for a national bankcard are no more than an application for a secured bankcard, something consumers can obtain on their own, as explained in Chapter 5. You don't need to pay a fee to a credit repair firm to apply for a secured bankcard.

State Restrictions

Credit repair firms tend to operate in states that do not have legislation controlling their activities. However, given the unscrupulous tactics of these firms and that they often prey on vulnerable consumers, some 34 states have passed legislation regulating credit repair firms. A list of these states appears in Figure 6.1.

Among other things, state laws may require credit repair firms to

- buy insurance (bonding) to protect consumers who sue them if the credit repair firm requires money up front;

- inform consumers of their rights under the FCRA;

- provide consumers with a written contract;

- offer consumers a cancellation period during which they can change their minds before signing a contract with the credit repair firm.

In addition, some states provide remedies for consumers who are "ripped off" by credit repair firms.

FIGURE 6.1 States with Legislation Controlling the Actions of Credit Repair Firms

States that have passed legislation to control the activities and business practices of credit repair firms include the following:

Arkansas	Michigan
Arizona	Nebraska
California	Nevada
Colorado	New Hampshire
Connecticut	New York
District of Columbia	North Carolina
Florida	Ohio
Georgia	Oklahoma
Hawaii	Oregon
Illinois	Pennsylvania
Indiana	Tennessee
Iowa	Texas
Kansas	Utah
Louisiana	Virginia
Maine	Washington
Maryland	West Virginia
Massachusetts	Wisconsin

Credit Repair Company Tactics

To fix problems in a credit record, credit repair companies use some fairly standard tactics that frequently operate at the edge of the law. In fact, one credit repair technique explained earlier, *file segregation*, is illegal and could result in fines and even imprisonment for you. Thus, it is important that you are aware of credit repair tactics so that if a company's advertising does not alert you to the fact that it is a credit fix-it firm, its tactics will.

The Use of "Loopholes"

The FCRA includes a section entitled "Procedure in Case of Disputed Accuracy" that gives you the right to challenge any information in your credit record you do not believe is accurate. As explained in Chapter 4, if a credit reporting agency is unable to verify contested credit record information within a "reasonable period of time," by law it must delete the contested information from your credit record.

Credit repair companies abuse this provision of the FCRA by inundating credit reporting agencies with numerous and repeated requests to delete negative information in a consumer's record. It doesn't matter if all of the information being contested is correct or not. The repair company's strategy is to overwhelm a reporting agency with so many requests that it cannot possibly verify all of them within a "reasonable period of time." The credit repair firm knows that under the FCRA the credit reporting agency has to delete the adverse credit information it was unable to verify.

As a defense against this credit repair tactic, credit reporting agencies will often use a provision of the FCRA that allows them to dismiss those requests that appear "frivolous." Also, credit bureaus have taken steps to decrease the amount of time it takes them to respond to verification requests. A quicker response time has helped undermine the tactics of credit reporting agencies. Credit repair companies, however, continue to manipulate the FCRA at the expense of consumers.

Quick-Fix Methods

A popular approach to credit repair used by many firms is to create a new, problem-free credit identity for you. Although a credit repair firm may employ various methods to create this new identity, its objective is consistent—to hide the negative information in a file by "tricking" the credit bureau's computer.

One commonly used method for accomplishing this is called *file segregation* or *skin-shedding*. As mentioned earlier, this is an illegal technique that involves altering a consumer's credit file.

Typically, consumers who are in financial trouble receive a letter or phone call from a credit repair firm telling them that for a fee the firm can help hide the negatives in their credit records and establish new credit identities to be used when applying for future credit. Once consumers pay the fee, the credit repair firm will direct them to apply to the IRS for an Employee Identification Number (EIN) and to use it rather than their Social Security number whenever they apply for credit. An EIN resembles a Social Security number and is used by businesses to report information to the IRS and the Social Security Administration. Consumers will also be instructed to use a new mailing address on the credit application.

Some credit repair firms advise their clients to send a check for partial payment of an account and to write on the check that in cashing it the creditor agrees to cease all collection activity and delete negative information related to the account from the consumer's credit file. However, creditors are not obligated to honor such terms of payment. Furthermore, if a creditor indicated that it accepted the terms, consumers would need to take additional steps to ensure that the terms were actually met. It is unlikely that the credit repair firm would do the necessary follow-up, thereby leaving the consumers poorer—since they would have paid both the creditor and the credit repair firm—with the problem they were trying to erase still in their records.

Quick-fix credit repair methods are not recommended. Not only are they morally questionable, in some cases they are illegal too. Such methods allow consumers who may have gotten into serious financial trouble because of poor money management techniques and the abuse of credit to get new credit before they have had the opportunity to put their money problems in perspective, understand the reasons for their problems and acquire better money management skills. These consumers are apt to repeat past mistakes and end up in serious financial trouble sometime in the future.

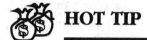 **HOT TIP**

If a credit repair company refuses to provide you with a written statement of services before you agree to work with it, consider it a clear sign that the company intends to rip you off.

If You Still Want To Work with a Credit Repair Firm

If, despite the information and warnings in this chapter, you decide you still want to work with a credit repair company, below are several steps you can take to make it more likely you will get the assistance you need and are paying for.

- Call your state attorney general's office or office of consumer affairs to find out if there have been any complaints or legal actions taken against the credit repair company you are considering.

- Contact the Better Business Bureau for the same information.

- Meet with a company representative and obtain a detailed written statement explaining exactly what the company will do for you and what its services will cost. Also, find out what the company *cannot* do to improve your credit record. Ask the representative to base the plan of action on your credit report and provide a copy that can be used in preparing a written statement. Having a written statement of services from the credit repair company will help you distinguish a company that is making promises it cannot keep from one that is being realistic about what it can do to help you. A written statement will also help should legal action become necessary in the future.

- Don't give a credit repair company any money up front.

- Avoid companies that promise money-back guarantees. These guarantees are often nothing more than ploys by credit repair firms to get your money. Once enough money has been collected from unsuspecting consumers, these credit repair firms will leave town or go out of business before any or all of its promised services are provided.

What To Do if You Get Ripped Off by a Credit Repair Company

If you become the victim of a credit repair company, the following are steps you should take right away:

- Contact your state attorney general or state office of consumer affairs. Your state may be one of those that has passed legislation to regulate credit repair companies. If so, you may be able to get all or some of your money back.

- Tell your local Better Business Bureau about the problems you've had with the credit repair company.

- File a complaint with the FTC. Although this agency will not take action against a company as a result of an individual complaint, it may do so if it receives enough complaints to establish a pattern of abuse. To contact the FTC about a problem with a credit repair company, write: Federal Trade Commission, Credit Practices Division, Washington, DC 20580.

 HOT TIP

If you get ripped off by a credit repair firm, it's always a good idea to complain to the FTC because your complaint just could be the one that triggers the agency to take action. Your effort may help prevent other consumers from being victimized.

Bringing Your Case to Small Claims Court

Tim and Sylvia G. were as frustrated as any two people I had ever seen. They had spent eight months trying to clear their credit record of incorrect information that had caused them problems in trying to obtain a home remodeling loan. Although they had finally gotten a loan, it was for a smaller amount and at a higher rate of interest than if their record had contained correct information. Tim and Sylvia were so mad that they wanted to sue the credit reporting agency they had been dealing with.

Listening to the couple recount all that they had done to get their credit record corrected, it was obvious to me that they had pursued all options. I concluded, therefore, that legal action was definitely in order and talked with Tim and Sylvia about using small claims court.

I explained that they did not have to use a lawyer in small claims court. This appealed to Tim and Sylvia since they didn't have a lot of money to spend on legal assistance. I also talked to the couple about the advantages and disadvantages of using this court and provided them with an overview of the small claims court process in their state.

Sometimes, dealing with credit record problems can be both time-consuming and frustrating. Consequently, you may find that you have exhausted all noncourt options for resolving a problem and yet your credit record problem remains.

In this chapter we will review the circumstances under which small claims court may be appropriate, as well as the factors to consider when determining whether you should take a credit bureau or creditor to small claims court. We will also outline how to prepare for small claims court along with an overview of the court process. However, since this process varies from state to state, you should contact the small claims court in your city or county to learn about specifics.

Option of Last Resort

Before you turn to small claims court, you should exhaust all noncourt means for resolving your problem. Going to court should be your option of last resort. Also, the judge will want to be assured that you have made every effort to work out the problem.

A good way to make certain that you have made every effort to resolve your problem is to review Chapter 4, which discusses how to deal with credit record problems. If you have overlooked one of the options available to you, now is the time to pursue it. Those options include

- writing a letter to the credit reporting agency;

- writing a letter to your creditors requesting that they correct the problem and notify the credit reporting agency;

- contacting the office of your state attorney general or your state's office of consumer affairs;

- seeking help from your area's Consumer Credit Counseling office, Bankcard Holders of America or the Public Interest Research Group in Washington, D.C.;

- filing a complaint with the Better Business Bureau;

- filing a complaint with the FTC; and

- using mediation.

What Is Small Claims Court?

Small claims court is a civil court where ordinary consumers can settle noncriminal disputes without a lawyer for relatively little money. In essence, it is a *do-it-yourself court* for people with straightforward legal problems.

Small claims court has several advantages for consumers who want to resolve a legal problem as cheaply as possible and who feel comfortable preparing and presenting their own cases in a low-key environment.

These advantages include the following:

- There is no need for an attorney. Although many states allow consumers to bring a lawyer with them, it is neither expected nor is it is usually necessary.

- Legal mumbo jumbo, paperwork and forms are kept to a minimum.

- Legal problems can be settled quickly. Generally, there is only a short delay between the time consumers file their paperwork with the court and the date their cases are heard. Once in court, the actual hearing before a judge may not last longer than 15 minutes, and the judge's decision may be rendered in person soon after the hearing ends or by mail a short time later.

Small claims court also has a number of significant limitations, including the types of problems and solutions that can be pursued and the maximum amount of money for which consumers can sue.

Cases Heard in Small Claims Court

Because small claims courts hear only cases that involve monetary damages, you cannot use one of these courts to force a credit bureau to correct an error in your credit record. However, through the small claims court process you may be able to put additional pressure on a company to resolve your problem. This is most likely to happen if you are dealing with a local or a regional business rather than with one of the big three or another national company.

Through a suit in small claims court you may also be able to recoup some of the damages you have suffered as a result of your credit record problem. Because of the problem in their credit record, for example, Sylvia and Tim were forced to take a smaller home-remodeling loan than they wanted at a higher rate of interest than they otherwise would have paid. Their credit record problem cost them money. The couple might consider suing the credit bureau for the difference between what the loan would have cost if the inaccurate information were not in their record and what the loan actually cost.

If you were denied a job promotion because of inaccurate information in the credit report your employer reviewed, small claims court might also be appropriate. In such a situation, you might sue for the lost opportunity to earn an additional $3,000 a year.

Suits for mental anguish/emotional stress are also allowed in some small claims courts. Winning this type of suit is problematic, however, because you must prove that the emotional stress or mental anguish you suffered was intentionally produced by the party you are suing. And because there is no rule of thumb covering the amount of money to sue for in cases that involve mental anguish and emotional distress, it can be difficult to justify the amount you are asking.

Consumer Lawsuits Against Credit Bureaus

The cases summarized below represent situations in which consumers sued credit bureaus and won. It is important to note, however, that cases with the highest monetary awards were not pursued in small claims court and that attorneys were hired.

- *Millstone v. O'Hanlon Reports, Inc. (Missouri).* The court awarded $2,500 in actual damages for loss of sleep, nervousness, frustration and mental anguish over a consumer report.

- *Jones v. Credit Bureau of Garden City (Kansas).* A consumer received $500 from the court for expenses, lost wages, mental anguish and embarrassment.

- *Thompson v. San Antonio Retail Merchants Ass'n* (Texas). $10,000 in actual damages was awarded a consumer for humiliation and mental distress resulting from credit bureau errors. (The consumer had incurred no out-of-pocket expenses.)

- *Morris v. Credit Bureaus of Cincinnati (Ohio).* The court awarded $10,000 in damages resulting from inaccurate information about the consumer. The court stated the amount was reasonable compensation for injuries to the consumer's reputation, family, work and sense of well-being as a result of the agency's negligence.

Maximum Claims

Each state sets its own maximum dollar amount (in legal terms called *the jurisdictional amount*) for claims in small claims court. Presently, maximums range from a high of $15,000 in some Tennessee counties to a low of $1,000 in Mississippi. Most maximums, however, are in the $2,000 to $3,000 range. The small claims court clerk in your area can tell you the maximum in your state. If the amount you would sue for is substantially higher than your state's maximum, small claims court may not be appropriate.

 **HOT TIP**

It may encourage you to know that state maximum amounts allowed in small claims courts are on the rise nationally.

The Law

When considering the possibility of small claims court, an essential first step is to determine what law you will use as the basis of your legal action. Some of these courts do not allow consumers to file claims based on the federal FCRA, and others allow only the use of a state credit reporting law if one exists.

To find out if your state has a credit reporting law and your rights under that law, call your state attorney general's office or state consumer affairs office and request a copy if there is a law. In addition, ask for any consumer brochures or other information related to the law.

A copy of the FCRA is located in Appendix A. For a consumer-oriented discussion of this law, contact the FTC in Washington, D.C., or the applicable FTC regional office. The addresses and phone numbers of these offices can be found in Appendix B. If you have questions about the FCRA, call the FTC's Office of Consumer and Business Protection Bureau (202-326-3650).

If you have questions about your state's law or how it might apply to your situation, call your attorney general's office, your state office of consumer affairs or the small claims court clerk in your area. The listing for your area's small claims court clerk can be found in the municipal, city or county pages of your telephone directory under "Justice of the Peace" or "Conciliation."

Other avenues for help are a low-cost/no-cost source of legal assistance or an attorney—options covered in Chapter 4.

Deciding on Small Claims Court

If, after reading the law(s) and talking to experts, you decide that your problem and the solution you seek fit small claims court, your next step is to determine whether to pursue a remedy in that court. This determination should be based on an objective review of a series of factors, including: the statute of limitations; likely costs, including your own time and energy; the amount of your claim; the strength of your case; and the likelihood of collecting once you win.

When analyzing these factors, put aside all anger and frustration; do not get caught up in a spirit of revenge. Use small claims court only if you are confident that you have a good case, only if the potential gain outweighs the potential costs and only if you feel that you have at least a good chance of collecting from the defendant should you win a judgment.

The Statute of Limitations

Before analyzing any of the decision-making factors, make sure that the statute of limitations—the amount of time you have to file in small claims court—has not run out on your case. The statute of limitations, which is generally at least a year, varies from state to state. To find out what the statute of limitations is in your state, call the small claims court clerk.

Likely Costs

Out-of-pocket costs for using small claims court will be relatively low. At a minimum you will probably have to pay a filing fee, which can range from as little as $10 to as much as $50, and a fee to serve papers on the company you are filing a claim against. In some courts these fees can be added to the final judgment should you win.

 HOT TIP

Even though some small claims courts allow you to use an attorney, professional legal assistance is generally not advisable, given the relative simplicity of the typical case and the relatively low dollar value of judgments.

Call your area's small claims court clerk for specific cost information. The clerk should be able to provide you with a printed fee schedule. Don't forget to factor into your cost estimate the amount of time and energy you will have to spend preparing your case for small claims court. For instance, you may have to take time off from work to pick up and file papers and to appear in court among other things. It is important that you consider whether the potential gain from an action in small claims court is worth your time and energy.

 HOT TIP

Contact the small claims court clerk in your area to find out if you qualify for a waiver of filing fees for low-income people that many small claims courts grant.

In addition to court costs, there will likely be other costs involved in preparing a case for small claims court. These may include copying, facsimiles, overnight deliveries and long distance calls.

Once you have projected all of your expenses—the cost of time away from work, court costs, such miscellaneous costs as copying and long distance calls—compare them to the amount of your claim.

When you conduct your analysis, remember that it is possible the judge will award you less than the amount you sue for if you win—or decide in favor of the defendant. Therefore, create best-case/worst-case scenarios.

The Amount of Your Claim

If the dollar amount of your claim is slightly greater than your state's maximum, you can reduce it to the maximum amount. For example, if you live in New

York where the maximum is $3,000 and your total claim is $3,500, it will benefit you to reduce your claim to $3,000 so that you can use the small claims process rather than pursuing the more expensive civil court process.

If the amount of your claim is significantly greater than your state's maximum, however, you may want to consider using the civil court process and hiring an attorney on a *contingency* basis—that is, if the attorney wins for you, the attorney gets paid a percentage of the judgment, but if the suit is lost, the attorney gets nothing.

The Strength of Your Case

Your chances of winning in small claims court will be determined in large part by the strength of your case and how well you present it. Therefore, it is important to objectively evaluate all of your documentation in deciding whether you can make a strong argument and show that you have made a good faith effort to deal with your problem through all available channels. If you can't, forget small claims court.

Good supporting documentation might include: copies of all correspondence related to the credit record inaccuracy and the problems it has caused you; your telephone log of conversations regarding the credit problem; receipts and account statements; your credit records; and medical bills plus a statement from your doctor if you are claiming mental anguish and emotional stress.

Collecting

The likelihood that you will actually be able to collect on a judgment if you win must be a key factor in deciding whether to use small claims court. Nothing is more frustrating than to spend time, energy and money getting a judgment against a business and then have difficulty collecting because the company simply won't or can't pay.

Although small claims courts have collection tools, it will be up to you to pursue collection—the court won't do it for you. Therefore, after getting a judgment, you may have to spend additional time, energy and possibly money to get what you have been awarded by the court.

One way to assess the likelihood of collecting is to do some research into a company's financial situation and its past behavior vis-à-vis lawsuits. Call your area's small claims court to find out if there have been other judgments against the company and how the court responded to them. Find out if the company you are going to sue has gone bankrupt. That information will be available through the federal bankruptcy court in your area. If the company has filed for bankruptcy, small claims court will be a waste of your time.

Other possible sources of information about a company include the office of your state's attorney general or your state's office of consumer affairs. Find out if they have received complaints about the company and the nature of the complaints. Do the same with your area's Better Business Bureau. If you are considering suing a local credit bureau or creditor, area business people may be able to tell you about the company.

Using Small Claims Court

If after a review of all the decision-making factors just discussed you decide that you have a good case, that the likelihood of a win and the amount of that win outweigh the time and expense involved and that you have a reasonable chance of collecting on the judgment, it is time to start preparing for court. Preparation will involve completing all necessary paperwork, organizing your evidence, contacting witnesses (if any) and setting a court date.

Researching and Organizing Your Case

Your odds of winning in small claims court will increase if you take the time to research and organize your case. Start by identifying and highlighting the sections of the law you will be using to address your problem so you can easily refer to them.

Next, write down the heart of your case—what the creditor or credit bureau did or didn't do that you feel is a violation of the law; why the creditor or credit bureau is legally liable and the applicable section(s) of the law; what you have done to try to resolve your problem; and the defendant's response to your actions. Whenever possible, present your information in chronological order with applicable dates cited.

Although the use of witnesses is not common in cases involving a dispute between a consumer and a credit bureau or creditor, there are instances when they can help. For example, there may be people who are familiar with your problem and the steps you have taken to resolve it. Perhaps one of them went with you to visit a creditor or to review your credit record with a credit bureau employee.

Therefore, if you have people whose testimony you believe could help strengthen your case, make sure they are willing and able to appear in court on your behalf. Once you know who can appear, list them in writing, noting what specific points they can make to support your case.

Finally, establish the specific amount of damages you will ask for, and write down a rationale for that amount.

 **HOT TIP**

When deciding how much to sue for, it is always a good idea to ask for a little extra because the judge has the authority to award less.

Legal Assistance

As you organize your case, it is possible you will need legal assistance. If so, review Chapter 4 for sources of legal help.

A few states are experimenting with the use of paralegals or legal advisors in small claims court who can help you prepare your case. Call the small claims court clerk to find out if your state offers this assistance.

Small Claims Court Forms

Although the names of the forms and their formats vary from state to state, the types of forms are fairly standard. As an example, sample forms for the municipality and county of San Francisco, California, have been included in Appendix D. Typical forms include the following:

- *General claim or plaintiff's claim.* This form allows you to present the particulars of your claim and should be completed at the office of the clerk of small claims court or mailed to that office. Once the form is received, the court clerk will assign a number to your case. Depending on your state, the clerk will either file your claim or retype it and give you a case number. If it is retyped, you will be asked to sign it. One copy of the signed form will go to the judge; the other will be provided to the defendant when papers are served.

- *Written evidence.* Some states require that at the time you file your initial paperwork with the court, you also provide the evidence on which you base your case.

Setting a Court Date

When you file your claim, talk with the clerk about setting a court date. Be sure to schedule your hearing for a date that is convenient, and do not feel obligated to take the first date offered.

If you need to change your hearing date once it has been set, contact the defendant to see if together you can work out an acceptable new date. If you can agree on a new date, inform the clerk in writing of your mutual decision and formally request the date you have selected. This approach usually will save time as the clerk won't have to go back and forth between you and the defendant trying out different dates.

If you cannot make the scheduled date, be sure to alert the court ahead of time. If you simply don't show up, you risk having the judge dismiss your case or decide it on the basis of the defendant's testimony. If your case is dismissed, you may lose the right to reschedule (depending on the state you are in).

If you and the defendant cannot agree on a new court date, write the clerk to explain why you need the date changed and that your efforts to work with the defendant have been unsuccessful. Indicate the next dates you would be available for court.

How To Behave in Court

Be sure to get sufficient sleep the night before your hearing. Dress tastefully and conservatively. Know what you are going to tell the judge and have your evidence organized.

When you arrive in court, put aside all stereotypes you have about courtrooms and proper court behavior. You are not Perry Mason. No one expects that you will act like him or that you will act like a lawyer at all. That is the point of small claims court; it is a court for nonlawyers!

 HOT TIP

To help reduce any courtroom jitters, it is a good idea to visit small claims court before your day in court to listen to a couple of cases. You will see firsthand how the process works, and you will have a better sense of what to expect when the date of your hearing arrives.

Courtroom Proceedings

You will present your case to a judge. There will probably be a clerk and a bailiff who will sit in front of the judge. The clerk will make certain that the judge has all the necessary papers and files.

Until you are called to present your case, you will stay seated on a bench behind a low wooden "fence" that divides the courtroom. When your case is called by the clerk, you should come forward and sit at the counsel table just on the other side of the fence. If you have any witnesses, they should join you at the table.

Before you present your case, provide the judge with a packet of backup information, including copies of the evidence you will be citing and a chronology of events (if appropriate). As you present your story, speak slowly and deliberately, and try to stay unemotional. Do not be accusatory; simply lay out the facts.

After you have finished speaking, the judge may ask you some questions, or the defendant—if present—may be called to speak. After the judge has gotten all the necessary information, you will usually be notified by mail of the court's decision. If the defendant does not appear in court, however, you will probably win by default; and this will be announced in the courtroom.

HOT TIP

The appropriate time to ask to be awarded court costs is at the end of your statement.

If You Win Your Case

As mentioned earlier, if you win in small claims court, there is no guarantee that you will see the money you are awarded. However, using one or more of the collection tools available in your court and coupling them with patience and persistence, you may be able to get the money you are due. Although available collection tools vary from state to state, they usually include

- a letter;

- removal of cash receipts; and

- seizure of the assets of a business.

Check with the small claims clerk in your area to find out about the tools available to you, how they work and how to use them.

HOT TIP

In most states, the defendant in a small claims court suit may appeal the court's decision, generally within a 10-day to 30-day period. If an appeal is filed and accepted, not only must you delay initiating collection efforts but you may also have to spend more time, energy and money dealing with the appeal.

Requesting Payment

Generally, the first step in the collection process is a letter from you asking the defendant to pay the judgment. Keep a copy and send the original via certified mail with a return receipt requested so you can be certain the defendant received the letter. See Figure 7.1 for a sample letter.

FIGURE 7.1   Sample Letter Requesting Payment of Judgment

Date

Address of Defendant

Dear *(name of business owner):*

On *(date that judgment was rendered),* the small claims court in *(city, town, county)* found that you owe me *($ amount of judgment).* I therefore request payment of that amount within ten days of the date of this letter. Please contact me at *(address and/or telephone number)* if you anticipate a problem with this request. Thank you for your cooperation.

Sincerely,

Signature

 HOT TIP

   Don't send your letter until after the time limit for an appeal of the judge's decision has passed. Otherwise you risk having it serve as a reminder to the defendant that the judge's decision can be appealed.

Should your letter result in a check from the defendant, make a copy of the check and put it in your file. If the check bounces, the defendant may owe you additional money. If this happens, check with the small claims court in your area.

Cash Collection Seizure of Assets

Frequently, it is possible to file a formal request for someone from the office of your local sheriff, constable or marshall to visit the business you sued and collect cash in payment of the judgment.

Another option is to request that the defendant's assets be seized and sold. However, if the company has no assets, such a seizure may be impossible. Furthermore, seizures can be expensive so small claims courts are reluctant to initiate them for relatively small amounts of money.

Your small claims court clerk can explain the process for both these collection tools and their associated costs.

Property Liens

Putting a lien on a company's property means that you have a legal interest in that property. To put a lien on a company's property, you file the judgment in the deed of records in any county where you suspect the defendant owns property. This is called *abstracting the judgment*. Putting a lien on a company's property offers you as lien-holder two basic collection options. First, you may be able to have the sheriff in your jurisdiction seize some of the defendant's property and liquidate it in a public sale with all or part of the sale proceeds going to pay the judgment in your case. However, this particular use of a lien is relatively unusual because it is expensive and time-consuming to organize a public sale, and small claims settlements are small.

 HOT TIP

Judgments expire after a certain number of years; the exact number varies from state to state. However, judgments as well as any relevant liens may be renewed before their expiration dates.

Second, you can wait until the business tries to sell the property you have a lien on or tries to refinance it. Typically, you will be notified if the property is going to be sold and you will be paid out of the sale proceeds. If the property holders are trying to refinance the property you have a lien on, they probably will be required to pay off that lien before the refinancing can go through.

Levying on or Seizing Property

Levying means seizing through legal process. Before pursuing this approach, get advice about what types of business property you can levy against as this varies from state to state. If the small claims court clerk in your jurisdiction cannot help you, contact one of the low-cost/no-cost sources of legal assistance mentioned earlier in this chapter. You also should talk to the clerk about the levying process in your locale.

It is always a good idea to write a final demand letter before levying. In your letter, review what you have done to collect your judgment, and let the business know that you are prepared to levy its property if you do not receive your money.

Be sure to indicate that payment must be made with a money order, cash or a cashier's check only. See Figure 7.2 for a sample letter.

If you get no response by the date stated in your letter, follow the levy process as outlined by the small claims court clerk in your area.

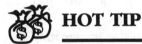 **HOT TIP**

Because you are allowed to collect interest on an uncollected judgment, check with your small claims court to find out what annual rate you can apply to the judgment in your case.

FIGURE 7.2 Sample Demand Letter

Date

Address of Defendant

Dear *(name of business owner):*

On _____ *(date that judgment was rendered)*, the small claims court in _____ *(city, town, county)* found that your company owes me *($ amount of judgment)*. Since that date I have contacted you by letter requesting payment in full; a copy of that letter is attached. To date I have received no money from you and no response to my letter. *(If you have done anything else to try to collect, review those steps and their outcomes.)*

I am ready to pursue additional measures to collect the judgment and have been informed by the small claims court that I may levy against your property. I am prepared to do this if I have not received payment in full by _____ *(date by which you want to receive payment; specify day, month and year)*. Payment should be in the form of cash, a money order or a cashier's check; I do not want a company check.

Thank you for your cooperation.

Sincerely,

Signature

The Pros and Cons of Small Claims Court

Small claims court is the option of last resort for trying to solve credit record problems. It should be used only if you feel that its potential benefits outweigh its potential drawbacks, including the amount of your time and energy it will require plus other costs. Therefore, it is important that you remove all emotion and frustration from your decision making before you pursue a claim in small claims court and that you objectively review all the information in this chapter. To help you decide whether to use small claims court, here is a short summary of the court's pros and cons.

Pros of Using Small Claims Court

- You don't need an attorney.

- A case can be settled quickly.

- Minimal paperwork and forms are involved.

- Minimal costs are involved.

Cons of Using Small Claims Court

- Only claims that involve monetary damages can be pursued.

- Relatively low judgments are awarded.

- It can be difficult to collect on a judgment.

CHAPTER
EIGHT

Establishing Credit
for Women

The daughter of a long-time client came to me for advice. Sandra C. had just started college and had received several credit card offers through the mail. In talking with her college friends, Sandra had learned how easy it was to get credit, but she was a bright young woman who had seen her parents go through difficult financial times.

Sandra was living away from home for the first time, and she wanted to avoid getting into financial trouble—in college and after graduation. Sandra's parents had suggested that she talk with me for advice to get her started on the right foot. This was a pleasant and refreshing experience for me because most people want to know what to do about their troubles either during or after a financial crisis.

Sandra had many questions. She wanted to know how to build her credit and—just as important—how to manage it. She also wanted to know whether she would have to make any changes in her credit accounts if she married. Sandra wanted me to tell her about the mistakes I had seen other women make and how to avoid them. She also asked about the credit-related laws that give women special protection and rights.

Sandra is unique in seeking information about credit during her first days as an adult consumer. Unfortunately, most of my female clients wait too long. As a result, many of them face serious problems with credit after finding themselves alone—sometimes very unexpectedly as the result of divorce or the death of a spouse—and financially unprepared. To avoid such problems, it is imperative that all women educate themselves about credit and money management, and establish and maintain their own credit separate from their husbands'. Single women with an established credit history should maintain their separate credit identity if they marry. Similarly, married women who share their husbands' credit should build a credit file in their own names with as few ties as possible to their husbands' credit.

In this chapter I will discuss the reasons women often have difficulty developing their own credit histories, provide an overview of some of the special credit-related issues commonly faced by women and talk about how best to deal with those issues. Special issues related to credit and divorce are discussed in Chapter 8.

Why Many Women Have Problems with Credit

Without a credit identity of their own, women who experience changes in their marital status are likely to have problems with credit. Women's credit-related problems tend to be the result of a number of factors that include:

- the role women traditionally have played in the American economy, their tendency to take their husbands' names and their reliance on their husbands to handle such money matters as credit applications and loans;

- women's general lack of knowledge about credit reporting and how credit information is reported to credit bureaus;

- a lack of understanding on the part of both men and women about the importance of a woman's having a credit history completely separate from her husband's.

In the past, most women did not work outside the home, and consumer credit was acquired and maintained in their husbands' names rather than in their own or in both names. Although many women helped manage their households' finances—and in some cases even helped pay for their families' use of credit—most never developed their own credit identities. These women were financial nonentities in the eyes of creditors and the credit reporting industry.

Today, increasing numbers of women have moved into the workplace, and two-income households are the norm rather than the exception. Also, the federal Equal Credit Opportunity Act, explained in detail later, now makes it easier for women to obtain credit.

Despite these important changes, many women, like consumers in general, remain relatively uninformed about credit, credit bureaus and the credit reporting process. Women also tend not to understand the critical importance of having credit in their own names, and consequently they do not.

In a society in which many women delay marriage to establish their careers and wives tend to outlive their husbands, however, women cannot afford to remain financially naive and vulnerable. Women need to know how to manage their own money and credit whether they are single, married, widowed or divorced. Married women in particular need to actively participate in the management of their families' finances and maintain or develop their own credit identities.

Learning about Credit and Money Management

There are a number of ways by which women can educate themselves about money matters. This could include taking courses at a local community college or university, contacting the local Consumer Credit Counseling office to find out if they offer any courses in money management and understanding credit, and reading books and magazines on these subjects.

Another educational resource is the *American Association of Retired Persons* (AARP) that sponsors the *Women's Financial Information Program* (WFIP), a seven-week program specifically designed for middle-aged and older women. WFIP teaches money management skills and helps women develop the confidence to make decisions about money matters. The WFIP is offered though local groups like YMCAs and community colleges. For more information, write AARP (601 E St., N.W., Washington, DC 20049; 202-434-2277). A banker, the family's financial advisor and/or a CPA may also be able to advise a woman about sources of basic information about credit and money management.

The Significance of Account-User Status Designations

An important but often overlooked part of credit education is understanding the meaning of common account-user status designations and why some user status designations are better for building credit than others. This knowledge is invaluable to the woman who wants to build a credit history in her own name.

Account-user status designations indicate to creditors and potential creditors the persons who can use an account and the degree to which each user is legally responsible for managing the account and making payments. Generally, the person who can use an account and the person who has payment responsibility are established at the time credit is applied for.

Many women do not understand that being listed as an authorized user on their husbands' accounts does little to build their own credit identity. Nor do they understand that if all of their accounts are joint accounts—shared with their husbands— these women risk losing that credit if they become separated, divorced or widowed.

Different account designations convey different messages about a user's responsibility for an account. Therefore, various designations will be of greater or lesser help to the woman who is trying to establish her own credit identity.

The most common account-user designations and their effects on a woman's credit building efforts are summarized below.

- *Authorized user status.* A woman who is listed as an *authorized user* on her husband's account has permission to use the account but has no legal responsibility for it. In other words, authorized user status indicates that a woman is relying on her spouse's earning power to pay. Accounts with this status are of minimal value to women who want to establish their own credit identities.

- *Joint-user status.* If a woman has *joint-user status* on an account, she and her husband can both use the account—and they legally have equal responsibility for account payments. Because there is shared responsibility, joint-user accounts can help women build their own credit histories. However, these accounts also link a woman's credit history to her husband's. This means that if a woman's husband abuses a joint credit account, the adverse account information will appear in her credit history as well as his.

- *Individual.* If a woman's accounts are designated as *individual*, she has sole responsibility for payments and is the only person authorized to use the account. Women with individual accounts qualified for that credit without their husbands. Individual accounts place women in the strongest financial position if their marital status changes because individual accounts do not link women's use of credit or ability to obtain credit to their spouses' incomes and credit histories.

Women Living in Community Property States

It is important for women living in a community property state to realize that they will not necessarily enjoy the benefits of separate credit and will be less able to insulate themselves from any money troubles that their husbands or former husbands may have. Community property states are:

Arizona	New Mexico
California	Texas
Idaho	Washington
Louisiana	Wisconsin
Nevada	

(The Commonwealth of Puerto Rico also has community property laws.)

In community property states, husbands and wives are viewed as economic partners, and the earnings and property of each spouse are considered to be jointly held and controlled. Thus, a husband and wife are equally liable for one another's debt, and credit grantors may take legal action against all the community property to collect a debt her spouse incurs and does not pay, and vice versa.

When a woman applies for credit in her own name in a community property state, the creditor may ask her marital status and request information about her husband—if he is going to be contractually liable for a debt or if she is relying on his income to help make the payments. However, if half of a woman's community property and income qualifies her for the credit she's applying for, her husband does not have to cosign even though the creditor still has the right to collect information about him.

If a woman living in a community property state uses property that is jointly owned by her husband and herself as collateral, a creditor may require her husband to sign the note on the mortgage or deed of trust even if the woman will be solely responsible for repayment. However, a woman's husband cannot be required to cosign the bank note unless he is going to be specifically obligated to help repay the debt.

Women and Credit in Separate Property States

Most states are separate property states where the credit history of a woman's husband is irrelevant to her request for credit because by law she alone is responsible for making payments on any debt she incurs in her name. In these states, a husband is not required to cosign a credit application, and creditors are barred from asking about a woman's marital status.

Exceptions do apply when property is involved. When a woman wants to finance the purchase of property in her own name and she posts collateral, the creditor may require that her spouse cosign the note. (The same would hold true if the husband purchased property in his own name.) By having the spouse cosign, the creditor is ensuring that the property can be taken back and sold to recover its costs if one spouse defaults. A creditor may also require a spouse to sign a security agreement so that it can repossess the property should the owner spouse default.

For specific information about marital property rights in your state, contact the office of your state's attorney general or your state's office of consumer affairs.

The Advantage of Individual Credit

Having good individual credit provides women several important benefits both in and out of marriage. First, if a woman's husband experiences financial difficulty and has trouble paying his bills or if he is a poor money manager and doesn't make account payments on time, her good credit will remain unblemished although his is damaged. This would not be the case if the woman and her husband shared the accounts he was not paying on time.

Second, a woman with her own credit is better able to maximize her family's financial options and opportunities. This ability can be especially important if a woman's spouse gets into financial trouble, loses his job or becomes seriously ill and has to stop working. In such situations, a woman with her own credit will be able to provide her family with more alternatives for dealing with difficult financial problems.

Third, as discussed earlier, women with their own credit identities will be better able to create a positive life for themselves after separation, divorce or widowhood.

If you are a married woman who is building credit, your ultimate goal should be to obtain individual credit in your own name, keeping joint credit to an absolute minimum. Realistically, however, if you have little or no individual credit to start with, initially you may need to apply for joint credit as a means of building your file and then, once a good payment history is established on those accounts, use them to get individual credit. However, this approach should be pursued only if you feel absolutely confident that your husband will not abuse the credit and thus damage your credit history and his at the same time. Shared credit should be viewed only as a means to an end—individual credit.

How To Build Your Own Credit History

There is no single, surefire way to develop a credit history for yourself, but the approach outlined in this section is an excellent way to begin. It starts with the easiest-to-get forms of credit and builds to types of credit that are more difficult to obtain.

Before you begin the credit building process, make sure that any assets owned by you and your husband are listed in both of your names. Such assets might include property, cars, boats, stock and bank accounts. These assets should be listed every time you apply for credit.

You should also request a copy of both your credit files and your husband's from each of the big three credit bureaus before you begin to apply for credit. That way you will know which—if any—credit reporting agencies are maintaining a credit file on you and what is in any file. When you receive the credit reports, review them carefully for accuracy. If you find any errors, correct them by following the steps outlined in Chapter 5.

If you have a credit file in your own name and you need to use joint accounts to help build your history, make sure those accounts are part of your credit record, assuming they have a good payment history. Also, make sure that any credit you had in your maiden name or in another town is part of your credit record. If you find that certain accounts are missing, write to the appropriate credit bureau and ask that it add the information. Most will, although they may charge a small fee.

Once you have reviewed your credit records and those of your husband and dealt with any problems that they may contain, it is time to initiate the credit building process. If you have little or no credit, the best approach is to obtain a small cash-secured loan from your bank. This is an important first step. If your marital situation changes and you need to borrow money, you will already have a positive relationship established with a lender.

Schedule an appointment with a loan officer and explain what you want to accomplish. If the first bank you talk with is unwilling to work with you, go to another bank. When you find a bank that is willing to work with you, open a checking account or a savings account in your own name at that bank.

The bank you are working with will make you either an unsecured or a secured loan. It may ask that you secure the loan with an asset, or it may want to make a cash-secured loan. If it makes you a cash-secured loan, the bank will probably ask that you put the loan proceeds in a certificate of deposit (CD) at the bank. In other words, you will not have the use of the loan money. This is all right, however, as the purpose of the loan is to build a strong credit history in your own name, not to purchase things. If you default on the loan, the certificate of deposit or the asset you have posted as collateral allows the bank to recover its losses.

💰 **HOT TIP**

_____

If the bank requires you to have a cosigner to get a loan, do not ask your husband to cosign. Instead, ask a close friend or relative.

Once you have paid off your loan, request a copy of your credit record to make sure that it reflects your loan payments. If it does not, ask your loan officer to report the payment history.

Depending on your situation, you may now be ready to obtain a credit card in your own name. Or you may need to apply to your bank for a second, this time unsecured, loan or for a loan without a cosignator.

If you apply for a credit card, begin by applying for credit that is relatively easy to obtain. This type of credit includes retail store charge cards and oil and gas cards. Charge a small amount and make your payments on time.

After you have demonstrated that you can manage this new credit, apply for a national bankcard. Having one can help make other forms of credit more available to you. If your own bank offers a bankcard and if its terms are competitive, apply for it.

If all of your credit is in your husband's name, you can request each applicable credit reporting agency to open a file in your name. This file will include: any accounts you set up in your own name; accounts in your husband's name that you use; and accounts in your husband's name that you are contractually liable for. (These accounts only apply to you if you live in a community property state.) At the same time, contact all applicable creditors and ask them to begin reporting credit information in your name as well as your husband's. Then you will be ready to follow the steps already outlined to build your credit history.

Secured Bankcards

If you are unable to obtain a national bankcard, apply for a secured bankcard. These are cards designed for people who want a bankcard but cannot qualify for an unsecured MasterCard or Visa. You may be able to use your secured bankcard as a stepping stone to an unsecured bankcard if you demonstrate that you are able to use your secured credit wisely and if you make all account payments on time.

If you are approved for a secured card, you will be required to collateralize your credit purchases by either opening a savings account with the issuing bank or purchasing a CD from it. Then if you default on your payments, the card issuer can withdraw money from your account—or cash in your CD—to pay your account balance.

When shopping for a secured bankcard, there are several factors you should consider: the amount of the deposit you will be required to put up and the rate of interest you will be earning on that money; what your credit line will be as a percentage of your deposit; whether you can convert your secured card to an unsecured card, assuming a positive payment history; and the fee for an application or processing.

HOT TIP

For an up-to-date list of banks offering secured and unsecured bankcards and the terms of those cards, call Bankcard Holders of America (800-638-6407).

If you already have some credit in your name, or if you and your husband have some long-standing, well-performing joint credit accounts, you may shorten the credit building process. This is especially true if you have a well-paying, relatively secure job. Credit building may be a matter of simply making sure that you have a bank account, at least one oil and gas card, a national bankcard, and a travel and entertainment card in your name.

During the credit building process, be sure to use your full name rather than your husband's name when applying for new credit—for example, Ms. or Mrs. Susan J. Smith and not Mrs. John Smith. Also, review the credit cards that you have now to see if any of them are in your husband's name.

If a credit card is not in your name, information for that account is being reported in your husband's name only. In that case you have two options—assuming the account is in good standing. You can ask your husband to contact the creditor and request that you be listed as a joint user on the account and have a new card issued in your own name. Or you can apply for individual credit from the creditor, depending on at what stage you are in the credit building process.

Additional Credit Building Advice

As you build your personal credit history, be sure to limit the amount of credit you obtain. Future potential creditors will not look favorably upon a consumer who has a lot of credit, even if most of that credit represents inactive accounts. This is because creditors have no way of knowing when you might begin using an inactive account, how much additional debt you might assume, and if additional debt will jeopardize your ability to make future payments on already active accounts.

Remember, too, that credit bureaus maintain a record of the number of creditors who make inquiries about your credit history. If creditors feel that you are applying for too much credit and possibly going beyond your ability to pay, they may view you as a credit risk.

Finally, use your credit to purchase necessities only, not frivolous items, and keep account balances as low as possible. Be sure to make all account payments on time so that the credit history you build will be a positive one.

The Equal Credit Opportunity Act

When building your own credit, it is important to know about the federal *Equal Credit Opportunity Act* (ECOA). Enacted in 1974, the ECOA was written to help ensure that—among other things—women are not denied access to credit simply because of their sex. The ECOA also helps married women develop their own credit histories.

Prior to its passage, most women—regardless of their marital status—had a difficult time obtaining credit and therefore found it hard, if not impossible, to establish a credit file in their own names. This situation existed because, as indicated earlier in this chapter, until quite recently, men were the traditional bread-winners in our society. Credit and money management were not viewed as subjects that most women needed to be concerned about. Even in the case of women who chose to work after marriage, the credit industry assumed that ultimately marriage, childbirth and family would interrupt their careers and affect their ability to pay their bills if they were allowed to have credit of their own. Women, therefore, were considered poor credit risks, and most credit accounts were established in their husbands' names. Furthermore, even if a woman's name was on an account that she actively used, payment history information was traditionally reported to credit bureaus in her husband's name only.

To help women develop their own credit histories, the ECOA requires creditors to report account payment data in the names of both spouses on any accounts that a married couple both use or are both liable for. Therefore, if you are a joint user or an authorized user on an account, that account should appear in both your husband's credit file and your credit file. However, this requirement does not apply to accounts opened before June 1, 1977.

Some creditors might disregard this requirement of the ECOA. If you feel that having shared account information—joint-user account information especially—in your credit record will be helpful to you in obtaining individual credit, write to each of the major credit bureaus and ask if it is maintaining a file in your name. If it is, request a copy of your record as well as a copy of your husband's. Then compare both sets of credit reports to determine if there are any creditors who are reporting information on accounts opened after June 1, 1977, in your husband's name only.

If you discover that an account with a positive payment history is being reported in your husband's name only, write to the creditor. Explain that the account is a shared account that was opened after June 1, 1977. Ask that the creditor begin reporting account information in your name as well as your husband's. See the sample letter in Figure 8.1 and ECOA provisions of special interest to women in Figure 8.2.

FIGURE 8.1 Sample Letter to Creditor Asking It To Begin Reporting Account Information in Both Spouses' Names

---

Date

Name and Address of Creditor

Dear *(name of credit manager):*

As of June 1, 1977, according to the provisions of the federal ECOA, creditors were to begin reporting account information on authorized user and joint accounts in the names of both spouses. In reviewing the credit files maintained on myself and my husband by *(name of the credit bureau),* I noted that you are not reporting information in my name for account #_____ that we have with you. That account was opened after June 1, 1977.

I am writing to ask that you begin reporting account information in my husband's name and in my name. I also ask that you make my file reflect the current status of my husband's file as reported by you.

Thank you for your assistance. If you have any questions, you may call me at *(area code/telephone number).*

Sincerely,

Signature

Attach to the letter a copy of your credit reports and your husband's, and highlight the relevant account name(s) and number(s).

After a few months request another copy of your credit report, and check to make certain that the creditor honored your request.

If you and your husband share accounts that were opened before June 1, 1977, and you would like those accounts reflected in your credit report, you will have to write to each creditor and ask that they start doing so. Although creditors are not required to, most will probably honor your request.

Credit bureaus that comply with the ECOA will report negative as well as positive account information on authorized users and joint accounts. Therefore, although one of the goals of the ECOA is to make it easier for women to establish their own credit histories, the law can also harm those women whose husbands misused authorized or joint-user accounts.

In such situations, a woman can try to distance herself from her husband's mismanagement by preparing a written statement for her credit file explaining the reason for the negative account information. This statement also should be attached to any application a woman completes for credit in her own name.

FIGURE 8.2   Provisions of the ECOA of Special Interest to Women

- Creditors may not discriminate on the basis of race, color, religion, sex, national origin or marital status.

- A woman may apply for credit under her married name, maiden name or a combination.

- Creditors must judge the merits of a woman's request for credit based on her earnings and her credit history. Creditors cannot require a husband to cosign an unsecured note. If a woman applies for a secured loan—for a car or a home for example—the lender may require the woman's spouse to sign the legal document that describes legal ownership of the property. The lender may not require the woman's spouse to cosign the bank note, assuming the woman qualifies on her own. This provision of the ECOA, however, does not apply in community property states.

- When a woman applies for credit, the creditor may not ask for information about her husband. An important exception to this provision applies to women who rely on alimony or child support to qualify or to help qualify for credit.

- All of a woman's income—including income from part-time work, public assistance, child support and alimony—must be considered when a creditor evaluates her application for credit. However, the creditor may consider the reliability of this income when judging a woman's creditworthiness.

- Women who are applying for secured credit can be required to indicate whether they are married, separated or single. A woman's marital status, however, cannot be used to deny her credit or limit the amount of credit she may obtain.

- Creditors may not ask a woman to indicate her sex on a credit application unless it is an application for a home loan. In such instances, gender information is to be used only for government-reporting purposes.

- If a woman is applying for unsecured credit in her own name, a creditor may not ask her to indicate her marital status. Exceptions apply to women living in community property states.

- Creditors may not ask about a woman's birth control practices or if she plans to have children nor may the creditors make assumptions about such matters.

- Although creditors may ask a woman if she has a phone at home, they may not ask whether the phone is in her name. This is because many household telephones are listed in the man's name.

Advice for Women Who Are Getting Married and Have Credit

If you are one of countless single women who work and have a positive credit history in your own name, it is important to preserve that good history after you marry. When you marry, therefore, do not cancel your credit accounts and continue to maintain at least one bank account—checking or savings—in your own name. There is no reason to merge your accounts and your money with your husband's; it is far easier to maintain an already-positive credit identity that is separate from a spouse's than it is to lose that identity and have to reestablish it later. Furthermore, as indicated earlier, having your own credit when married can greatly benefit your family during difficult financial times.

If you change your name upon marriage, immediately notify your creditors of the name change. Ask them to begin reporting account information to credit bureaus in your married name. A few months later, request a copy of your credit report from each of the credit reporting agencies the creditors report to, and review the reports to make sure that your creditors followed your instructions.

If you marry and have no credit history in your own name, begin immediately to establish one following the credit building steps outlined earlier in this chapter.

Credit Advice for Women Who Were Married before the ECOA Went into Effect

If you were married before the ECOA went into effect, if all of your credit is shared with your husband, and if most of that credit was established before June 1, 1977, it is very likely that the big three credit reporting agencies are not maintaining credit files in your name. As a result, establishing your own credit identity will be somewhat more difficult than for married women who are listed as authorized or joint users on accounts that were opened after 1977. Nonetheless, it can be done.

Your first step should be to contact each of the big three to confirm that, indeed, none of them is maintaining a file in your name. If you find one that is, request a copy of your credit report so you will know what's in it. If the report contains errors, get them corrected.

Request copies of your husband's reports, too. Because you may need to open one or more joint accounts as part of the credit building process, you need to make certain that your husband's record is problem-free.

Talk with your husband about what you are trying to accomplish and why it is important for you to have your own credit. If he doesn't understand why it is important and is reluctant to do what he can to help you get started, suggest that he read this chapter and talk to Consumer Credit Counseling, a financial adviser or a banker.

Once your husband understands the importance of your establishing credit, suggest that you apply for some new joint credit. Because payment information on this new credit must be reported to credit bureaus in both your names, it will get the credit building process started.

Don't forget that your ultimate goal is to establish credit in your name only; a credit history based on joint accounts is not enough.

Widows and Credit

If your husband is ill and death is on the horizon, it is important that you prepare fiscally for widowhood. This includes building a credit history for yourself; correcting problems in your credit file if you already have one (Do the same for your husband's credit file.); preparing written explanations for any adverse information in your credit record that is the result of events beyond your control—your husband's financial troubles or his mismanagement of money; and talking with a trusted financial advisor.

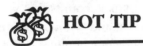 **HOT TIP**

An excellent book about the financial and psychological issues that widows face is *On Your Own: A Widow's Passage to Emotional and Financial Well-Being,* 2nd edition, by Alexandra Armstrong and Mary Donahue (Dearborn Financial Publishing).

If widowhood happens suddenly and you haven't been able to prepare yourself credit-wise, you will face a number of financial obstacles that may impede your ability to build a happy and satisfying life on your own. Without your own credit history, you may find yourself without access to ready credit. If you were an authorized user on your husband's accounts, those accounts can be canceled by his creditors. In addition, a creditor has the right to request that you reapply for credit on joint accounts if an account was based on your spouse's income. If a joint account was based on your income, however, or if either of you could have qualified for the credit at the time of application, you will probably not be required to reapply.

To postpone dealing with a loss of credit right away, you often can delay reporting your husband's death to his creditors. Use this time to get your financial situation in order. It is not always advisable, however, to delay reporting your husband's death for an extended period of time because in some instances, if creditors learn about your husband's death before you tell them, the information may prejudice them in the reapplication process.

Generally, how you deal with this situation is a judgment call. There are many women who continue to use their husbands' credit cards long after their spouses have died, but this may lead women to delay establishing credit in their own names. And this in turn may cause women trouble later on if they wish to buy a new car, a smaller home, go back to school or do home remodeling.

When you apply for credit after your husband's death (and during any credit reapplication process), potential creditors cannot discount or ignore such income as annuities, pensions, Social Security or disability payments. However, they are allowed to evaluate the reliability of these payments when making their credit granting decisions.

If at the time of your husband's death you have little or no credit history of your own, it is essential that you do what you can to build one. As you begin the credit building process, don't forget that the ECOA requires the creditor to consider information in your husband's file when you apply for credit if you can prove that his credit history reflects yours. Although this is a long shot, it may be worth the effort depending upon your particular credit situation.

Other Considerations

Once your husband dies, any bank accounts that you held jointly with a right of survivorship will go directly to you and will not be tied up in the probate process. The same holds true for life insurance benefits. To receive these monies, however, you will need to file a claim, and it could take as long as six weeks after filing before you actually see the money. This is another reason why it is a good idea to have your own credit and your own bank account as you may need ready and adequate access to cash and possibly credit immediately after your husband's death.

If your husband dies and leaves debt, it will depend on the type of debt whether or not you will have to pay it. Most debt you will not have to pay. However, if a debt is a shared obligation and there is not enough money in your husband's estate to pay it in full, you may have to take care of that debt by using the money from the bank accounts, insurance proceeds or other assets that were not part of the probate process. You are also responsible for any debt secured with property.

 HOT TIP

Because the rules governing a widow's obligations for her dead husband's debts are different in community property states, check with your attorney if you live in one of these states.

Once again, the problems just described illustrate why it is important to keep joint credit to an absolute minimum and to avoid it completely if possible. Having at least some individual credit will maximize the number of options you have for dealing with money matters after your husband's death.

CHAPTER
NINE

Creating Divorce-Proof Credit

Mary E. was going through a difficult divorce when she came to my office with questions about how the divorce might affect her credit. She had never been concerned about her credit before. She and her husband had been happily married for many years, and she had never anticipated that things would change. Mary had allowed her husband to maintain all the accounts in his name, and whenever they needed new credit, her husband applied for it. One consequence of the divorce was the failure of her ex-husband's business. Therefore, Mary was anxious to learn what would happen to her credit rating if her husband filed for bankruptcy. As part of their divorce agreement, Mary's husband had agreed to assume responsibility for paying off the debt they had acquired during their marriage. Mary's salary barely covered her basic needs so she was concerned that with his serious financial troubles, her husband would no longer be able to live up to his promise. Mary wanted to know if she would be responsible for paying off the debts from her marriage if her husband couldn't.

As I prepared to give Mary the information and advice she would need to begin developing a credit identity for herself, I thought how much better her situation would have been if she had planned for the possibility of divorce at the outset of her marriage, not at the end. That information could have been used to help prevent many of her problems.

Because approximately 50 percent of all American marriages now end in divorce, the problems Mary faced are no different than those being faced by countless women and men who failed to plan adequately for the financial aspects of divorce.

The credit and money-related problems that can accompany a divorce used to affect women primarily. However, an increasing number of men are now confronting these issues because growing numbers of women are pursuing successful careers and starting their own businesses. In fact, some women are now the family's major wage earner, and it is their income and not their husbands' that qualifies these couples for joint credit. Additional evidence of their growing economic clout is the increasing number of women who now have the opportunity to begin their own businesses.

These changes mean that when couples split up, traditional divorce arrangements may not apply, and it may be the former husband, not the former wife, who will experience the financial problems that sometimes come with divorce. Therefore, no matter how happy your relationship, it is wise for *both* men and women to prepare financially for the possibility of divorce.

In this chapter I discuss some of the problems both sexes can face after divorce, how best to deal with them and how to avoid them. I also provide some new information related to divorce and bankruptcy as a result of the 1994 changes in the Bankruptcy Code.

Planning for a Divorce

If you are contemplating divorce, it is important to take certain steps before filing to minimize any potential financial damage the change in marital status may cause. These steps include the following:

- Make sure you have good credit separate from your spouse's. If you don't, delay your divorce if possible until you can get some credit and a bank account in your own name. For advice about building individual credit, read Chapter 5.

- Pay all mutually shared bills and credit card debts from joint funds. That way you don't risk their becoming your debt to be paid out of your income once you divorce.

- If you already have either joint or individual credit, obtain a copy of your credit report from each of the big three and address any problems you may find.

- If some of the accounts in your credit file are joint accounts with negative histories, and if the adverse information is the fault of your soon-to-be former spouse or the result of circumstances beyond your control, prepare a written explanation of the reason(s) for the negative information, and ask the credit bureau to make this explanation a permanent part of your credit history. Doing so may help disassociate you from the account's problems. It is also a good idea to attach the same explanation to any credit applications you complete.

- If you have a lawyer or a financial advisor you trust, talk with that person about what you should do to prepare for the change in your marital status.

If your spouse files for bankruptcy while you are in the process of divorce, it is likely that the divorce proceedings will be stopped until the bankruptcy is completed. During this time, talk with your lawyer about how to minimize the impact of your spouse's troubles on your financial situation.

Avoiding Trouble with Joint Accounts

Creditors consider spouses with joint accounts—national bankcards and loans, for example—to be equally liable for those accounts. Because of this, it is very important that you cancel all joint accounts as soon as possible. If you don't, you risk being liable for payments on account balances that your former spouse ran up and cannot pay. Furthermore, if your spouse is late in making payments on joint accounts or defaults on those accounts, that adverse information will be reflected in your credit record as well as in your spouse's as long as those accounts are open. You may then be faced with having to rebuild your own once-good credit.

Close joint accounts by writing to each creditor and indicating that as of the date of your letter you will not be responsible for any charges your spouse might incur.

When you are ready to close your joint accounts, remember that if you want individual credit with the same creditors, they have the right to require that you reapply for the credit if your joint accounts were based on your spouse's income. If the accounts were based on your income, however, or if either of you could have qualified for the credit at the time of application, you will probably not be required to reapply.

Avoid negotiating a divorce agreement that allows your spouse to maintain your joint accounts in exchange for paying off the outstanding balances on those accounts. Remember, as long as those joint accounts remain open—whether you use them or not—you will be legally liable for them regardless of what your divorce agreement says.

Other Credit Problems Created by Divorce

If you divorce without having separate credit in your own name, you are in a very vulnerable position. If the joint accounts are kept open, you risk becoming liable for your ex-spouse's debt. If all joint accounts are closed or if you are removed from an authorized-user account, you may be left without ready access to credit at a time when credit can be especially valuable. However, if you have your own credit identity separate from your former spouse, access to credit should be generally unaffected by a divorce—except in the case of joint account problems.

As noted in Chapter 8, creditors cannot deny a consumer who shared accounts with a former spouse continued use of those accounts, nor can creditors change the terms of credit simply because of a change in marital status. Creditors can, however, require that you reapply for that credit if you would not have qualified for the credit on your own at the time application was first made. In marriages where there is a significant disparity in earnings between spouses and the spouse with the smaller income shared accounts with the other, the person making less money risks losing the credit.

If you reapply for credit once held jointly or apply for completely new credit, potential creditors cannot discount or refuse to consider nonjob income such as child support and alimony. However, they do have the right to request that you prove the reliability of these sources of income, and they can deny you credit if they judge your income sources to be unreliable. If you will be relying on nonjob income to help you qualify for credit, it is a good idea to collect and save any documentation you may have that supports the reliability of that income. Such documentation might include canceled checks, legal documents such as your divorce agreement, a notarized letter from your ex-spouse and bank deposit slips.

In evaluating your creditworthiness, creditors also must consider the credit history of your former spouse *if* you can demonstrate that your former spouse's history reflects your history too. If that credit history is positive and you have no individual credit and never shared credit with your former spouse, you may want to use this provision to build your own credit record. This, however, is a long shot.

To demonstrate that your former spouse's history reflects yours, you may be able to provide copies of checks you wrote to pay on accounts, letters you may have written to creditors regarding accounts or similar evidence. If you are on good terms, you may also want to ask your former spouse to write a letter to the potential creditor on your behalf.

 HOT TIP

If you are a woman and take back your maiden name after a divorce, be certain to let your creditors know. Ask them to begin reporting account information to credit bureaus in your new name. Then wait a few months and check your credit record again to make sure your creditors are reporting correctly to credit bureaus.

If Your Spouse Files for Bankruptcy after Divorce

In today's economy, it's very possible that your former spouse may file for bankruptcy. Be aware that even though bankruptcy may wipe out debt that your former spouse owes you as part of your divorce agreement, it does not cancel alimony, maintenance or child support obligations nor does it wipe out tax debts. In other words, these obligations cannot be discharged through bankruptcy.

If your former spouse files a Chapter 13 reorganization of debt bankruptcy, he or she will have to pay all past due alimony, maintenance or support payments owed you while the reorganization plan is in effect. At the same time, your former spouse will be expected to make all current payments on time.

 HOT TIP

As a result of the 1994 changes in the Bankruptcy Code, alimony, maintenance and support obligations now have priority in a bankruptcy and thus must be paid before tax debts and most unsecured debts.

If your former spouse files a Chapter 7 liquidation of debt, you may not collect what you are owed until the bankruptcy is over and the *automatic stay* has been lifted. The automatic stay is a court action that prohibits all creditor collection actions against a debtor once the debtor has filed for bankruptcy. The protection of the automatic stay ends when the bankruptcy is over or when the court lifts the automatic stay. The automatic stay in no way affects the obligation of your former spouse to stay current on all support obligations to you during a Chapter 7 liquidation. That responsibility remains.

Another option if your former spouse files a Chapter 7 is to try and collect what you are owed from the assets that are not part of the bankruptcy estate while the bankruptcy is ongoing. Those assets are not affected by the automatic stay. Check with a bankruptcy attorney in your state to find out what property is part of your spouse's bankruptcy estate as every state is different.

There are two important exceptions to the nondischargeability of alimony, maintenance and support debts. (*Nondischargeability* is the inability to wipe out the obligation to pay in bankruptcy.) The first is that if you voluntarily assign these debts to a collection agency or some other entity with the hope that the agency will be able to get you what you are owed, the debts can be discharged through bankruptcy. In other words, your ex-spouse could use bankruptcy to wipe out the debt to you, but the obligation to make all *future* alimony, maintenance and support debts to you in full and on time remains.

The second exception comes into play if your former spouse asks the court to rule that a debt classified as child support, alimony or maintenance is really another type of debt related to his or her change in marital status—a property settlement obligation for example—and that it should therefore be discharged. If the court agrees, whether the ex-spouse is in Chapter 7 or Chapter 13, the debt will be wiped out.

Property Settlement and "Hold Harmless" Obligations

Until 1994, if you let your ex-spouse keep a certain asset in exchange for promising to pay you a set amount of money in installments or promising to pay off certain of your debts, or if you agreed to accept smaller alimony, maintenance or support payments in exchange for your being "held harmless" (i.e., not liable) for certain debts you incurred during your marriage, your ex-spouse could wipe out those obligations by filing for bankruptcy. This could have left you with substantial debts to pay and with little or no alimony, support or maintenance income—a situation that could possibly have plunged *you* into bankruptcy. The 1994 Bankruptcy Code changes amended the way that property settlement and "hold harmless" agreements that are part of a divorce can be treated in a bankruptcy.

Now bankruptcy does not necessarily release a former spouse from property settlement and "hold harmless" obligations if the court believes that the resources of your former spouse are sufficient to meet both alimony, support and maintenance-related obligations and basic living expenses. However, if your former spouse can prove that he or she cannot meet both categories of obligations, all or a portion of these obligations will be discharged. They will also be discharged if your ex-spouse can prove to the court that otherwise not enough money remains for continuing in business. Property and "hold harmless" obligations will not be discharged, however, if the court believes the potential harm done to you outweighs the benefits that your ex-spouse would realize by having them wiped out through bankruptcy.

There is an important catch to these exceptions: to benefit from them, you must file an adversary proceeding—the equivalent of a minilawsuit—against your ex-spouse within 60 days of the date of the first meeting of the creditors. To file within the necessary time frame means that you must know your former spouse has filed for bankruptcy and that you have the resources to hire an attorney or have the time and ability to initiate an adversary proceeding yourself.

Other Important Divorce-Related Changes Resulting from 1994 Bankruptcy Code Reforms

The 1994 reforms to the Bankruptcy Code included some other changes that affect divorced people. For example, the law now says that any actions necessary to establish the paternity of a child will not be affected by the filing of a bankruptcy. This means that if you have asked your state attorney general to help you get support for your child and the alleged father subsequently files for bankruptcy, the automatic stay will not affect your action to get support. It also means that if the alleged father is in fact identified as your child's actual father, he will be obligated to make child support payments regardless of his having filed for bankruptcy.

Another change in the Code now allows you to establish or modify an order for alimony, maintenance or support without getting the bankruptcy court's permission first. In the past, having to get permission first often created expense and delay for the former spouse seeking the change.

Before the 1994 changes in the Bankruptcy Code, if a debtor in a Chapter 7 liquidation paid some creditors but not others before filing for bankruptcy, the court might view those payments as "preferential" and require that they be returned for a fairer distribution among all of the debtor's eligible creditors. Payments to an ex-spouse used to be included in this prohibition. Now, they are not.

A final change you should know about relates to judicial liens. In the past under a division of property agreement, one spouse would promise to pay on a debt related to a division of property with a judicial lien against an asset of the other spouse (i.e., to pay the other spouse money, to fairly divide the marital property estate and to secure the promise to pay by giving a lien on property). It used to be that if the former spouse with the asset filed for bankruptcy, the law allowed the debtor to wipe out the lien if it were on exempt property. However, shortly before the 1994 changes to the law, the U.S. Supreme Court changed this and the amended law codified the Court's decision. Now, therefore, the law says that if a lien secures the obligation of one spouse under a division of property agreement, it cannot be erased through bankruptcy.

Special Concerns for Divorced People Living in Community Property States

Consumers living in community property states face special problems when there is a divorce. Community property states include: Arizona, California, Idaho, Louisiana, Nevada, New Mexico, Texas, Washington and Wisconsin (see page 116). In these states, both parties in a marriage are jointly liable for any debts that were incurred during that marriage—whether those debts were acquired individually or together. That means that if a former spouse signs a divorce agreement promising to pay off all debt incurred during the marriage but then fails to, creditors have the legal right to expect payment from the other party in the now-dissolved marriage. Otherwise, the creditors can look only to the property accumulated during the marriage to settle the claim.

In such a situation, you have two basic options—pay off the debt and try to save your own credit history, or file for bankruptcy. If you want to pay off the debt, and if those financial obligations are sizable, it is advisable to try negotiating a payment schedule with each of your creditors.

To arrange a workable payment plan, contact each creditor directly—by letter, telephone or in person. Tell your creditors what your situation is. Explain that you would like to meet your obligations but your income is such that you will need to work out a schedule of monthly payments that you can afford.

If you do not feel comfortable initiating these negotiations, call to schedule an appointment with a counselor at the Consumer Credit Counseling (CCC) office nearest you (800-388-2227). CCC counselors are professionals, have a lot of experience in creditor negotiations and are well respected by most creditors.

Do not opt for bankruptcy without giving it a lot of serious thought. A bankruptcy will remain on your credit record for up to ten years and will make it even more difficult for you to build a positive credit record. Before you choose bankruptcy, talk with a bankruptcy attorney to understand all the ramifications of that step, and make sure that all other options for dealing with your problem have been exhausted.

 HOT TIP

To learn more about consumer bankruptcy and how the process works, read *The Bankruptcy Kit*, 2nd edition, by John Ventura (Dearborn Financial Publishing, Inc.). The book can help you discover everything you need to know about the new changes in bankruptcy law and relief for your personal finances or small business. It also explains how bankruptcy affects taxes, mortgages, alimony, child support and more. The book is available through local bookstores nationwide, or call toll-free 800-829-7934.

CHAPTER
TEN

Protecting Your Financial Privacy

When Susan M. came to see me, she was angry about a phone call she had received. A man had called to discuss selling her a service for her home. In talking with her, it became clear that he knew a great deal about her personal and financial situation. She became suspicious and asked him how he knew so much about her. He responded evasively and hung up.

Susan wanted to know if I knew how this person could get information about her; she felt the man had invaded her privacy.

We talked for a while about the issue of privacy, and I told Susan how it was possible for companies to get detailed information about consumers through computerized databases. Susan was amazed that such personal information, some of which she had provided to creditors when she applied for credit, was available to direct marketers.

Susan also told me that she received a lot of offers from businesses in the mail and solicitations from charities as well. I explained that her name was probably on some mailing lists and that there were things she could do to cut down on the number of solicitations she was receiving.

We also talked about the general issue of privacy in today's technology-driven world and about some ways that Susan could help preserve her privacy. Finally, I suggested that Susan channel her anger by writing letters to her congressmen and senators to ask that the laws protecting consumers' privacy be strengthened.

I hope that after reading this chapter you will become as angry as Susan was. I hope that each of you will write to your elected officials to demand that something be done *now* to better protect consumer privacy and to demand that businesses of all kinds be more strictly limited in the ways that they can use the very personal consumer information they collect and maintain in their files. You should also demand that creditors who provide credit bureaus and other types of businesses with information about consumers be required by law to meet strict standards regarding the accuracy of that information. The FCRA needs to be amended to address the accuracy of the information creditors maintain on consumers and to provide sanctions against creditors who provide inaccurate information to credit bureaus.

In this chapter, I will talk about the ways that consumer privacy is being threatened by the development of increasingly sophisticated computer technology and by the buying and selling of information about consumers. Now, with the advent of the information superhighway and the prospect of an increasing amount of commerce on the Internet, this threat is increasing.

I will also discuss some of the sources of the threat to consumer privacy—credit bureaus and other information brokers, creditors, businesses that store consumer-related information in computer databases, direct marketers, government agencies, the medical industry and unscrupulous individuals. Finally, I will review the major federal privacy laws and will offer advice to those of you who want to have more control over who has access to your personal data and how that data are used.

Privacy in the Age of Information

Today, with a mere push of a button or by knowing a special code or account number, personal details about your life can be accessed. In fact, just about anything is available for collection and sale, including information as diverse as your in-store and credit card purchases and general buying habits, your medical history, your employment background, on-the-job injuries, telephone records, details about your home, your household income, and marital status. For example, Information America, Inc.'s People Finder Data Base includes information on 11 million individuals, 92 million households and 61 million telephone numbers! The database includes information drawn from telephone directories, post office change of address forms, voter registration records, and birth and wedding announcements. Another large information broker, California-based CBD Infotek, maintains thousands of different databases developed from a wide variety of public records, including motor vehicle records, filings at county, state and federal courts and tax rolls. Businesses have many uses for this kind of information: banks to check out potential borrowers or a personal injury attorney to learn about the assets of the driver who injured his client.

Sometimes the information in one database is combined with information from another to create marketable new information products or improve existing databases. In other cases, information from one database may be compared with that of another to help identify specific consumers or to make an existing database more comprehensive and accurate. Databases also are being linked electronically to create huge information networks.

Consumers' personal information has become a valuable commodity. Yet, most of the time individuals are unaware that information about their finances, personal habits, health, buying patterns and other such information is being bought, sold and exchanged. And, even worse, there is little they can do to stop it.

Unauthorized Access and Inappropriate Use of Credit Record Data

Technology has made unauthorized access to consumer credit files easier, especially now that online electronic access to the files of the big three has become commonplace. Not only are individuals misrepresenting themselves to gain access to credit bureau data, but in some instances those who have legitimate access to credit reporting data are using that information for illegal purposes in violation of federal law. For example, an August 1995 article in *Kiplinger's Personal Finance* magazine, entitled "Guarding Your Financial Privacy," pointed out that it is possible for unscrupulous employees at businesses with computer access to credit bureau data—car dealerships, brokerage houses, local banks—to get credit information on consumers and use it for fraudulent purposes. The article referred to a New Jersey car dealership where employees accessed the files of a credit bureau and ran up more than $800,000 of fraudulent credit card charges before they were caught.

The ease with which an unauthorized person can tap into a credit file was also highlighted in 1989 by the now famous incident of the *Business Week* reporter who used his personal computer to access former Vice President Dan Quayle's credit record through a superbureau. Since that time, others have reported using their personal computers to acquire credit record information on famous persons, and there have been instances of private detectives gaining unauthorized access to credit files to secure certain credit information.

Another problem, according to the FTC, is the way some companies and organizations that do not have a permissible purpose for obtaining a credit history under the FCRA nonetheless obtain credit reports through intermediaries. Although the FTC has cracked down on some of these companies, much remains to be done.

Another potential breach in security is created by the fact that not all credit bureaus adequately police what their subscribers do with credit record information once they have it. There is always the possibility that someone with a legitimate right to the information in your credit record under the FCRA may not actually use that information for the intended purpose. At this time there is no guaranteed way to protect against unauthorized access to your credit record or against the possibility that information in your file will be used inappropriately by a credit bureau subscriber. Your only real option for dealing with this problem is an after-the-fact approach. Therefore, carefully review the *Inquiries* section of your credit report, and call the credit bureau about any questionable inquiries.

Finally, there have been instances of credit bureaus that are in the business of purchasing credit information from the big three and reselling that data, sometimes to companies without a legal right to the information.

Consumer advocates suggest that credit bureaus help consumers monitor their records for illegal access by doing a better job of identifying the source of an inquiry. This would make it easier for you to know who has seen your credit records. Advocates would also like to see credit bureaus more aggressively investigate consumer complaints about inquiries. Unfortunately, these measures are of little help if an unauthorized individual or company circumvents a credit bureau's security system or acquires the computer access code and taps into the bureau's files. Ultimately, better security systems and tougher, more up-to-date laws are needed to thoroughly address the problem of credit record security.

Public Response to Privacy Problems

Privacy groups, consumer watchdogs and policymakers watching the privacy dilemma are alarmed. Critics believe it is wrong when you provide information about yourself for one purpose and then that information is bought and sold for other purposes. Critics are also concerned about the invasive nature of the databases that are being created and their potential for abuse. For example, Congressman Charles Schumer of New York said the following when testifying before the Subcommittee on Consumer Affairs and Coinage in June 1991:

> In the modern era, one punch of a computer button can instantly deliver to anyone with a terminal more confidential information about an American consumer than a private detective could unearth in a week. As a result of technology, the privacy of American citizens is imperiled more than at any other time in our history.

There is fear among other policymakers that the era of "Big Brother is watching you" has arrived, created by a combination of forces in both the public and the private sectors.

Consumers are worried too. A 1990 Harris poll commissioned by Equifax, *Equifax Report on Consumers in the Information Age,* revealed that 79 percent of all Americans are concerned about threats to their privacy and that 71 percent believe they have lost control over how their personal information is used by companies. Another poll commissioned by *Time* magazine and CNN further reinforces the fact that consumers are concerned. In that poll, conducted by the firm of Yankelovich, Clancy, Shulman, 78 percent of the respondents indicated they are very/somewhat concerned about the amount of computerized information that businesses and the government collect and store about them. Ninety-three percent indicated that they felt companies that sell information about consumers should be required by law to ask a consumer's permission before making information available to another individual, company or organization. Eighty-eight percent believe that these same companies should be required by law to make their information available to consumers so that possible inaccuracies can be corrected.

Although there are ten privacy-related federal laws and some state privacy laws, legislation for the most part does little to check the flow of consumer information.

Federal Privacy Laws

When the Constitution was written, the word *privacy* was not specifically mentioned because a citizen's privacy was considered adequately protected by safeguards against physical searches and seizures. Today, however, searches and seizures of some of the most personal details of your life are being accomplished by technology rather than by physical means. As a result, most of the federal privacy laws currently on the books, including the FCRA, are woefully inadequate. Not only do these laws tend to be outdated, many are full of exemptions and loopholes that make them easy to circumvent.

In addition to the FCRA, the most important federal privacy laws are the Privacy Act of 1974, the Right to Financial Privacy Act of 1978, the Video Privacy Protection Act and the Computer Matching and Privacy Protection Act.

The Privacy Act of 1974

The Privacy Act of 1974 applies to federal agencies, prohibiting them from obtaining information for one purpose and then sharing it for another. However, the exception that the information can be shared when it is for "routine use" makes the law essentially useless because nearly any use can be interpreted as "routine."

The Right to Financial Privacy Act

Although the Right to Financial Privacy Act is supposed to govern access of federal agencies to your bank records, exemptions allow the FBI and U.S. attorneys to review bank records. Nor does this law apply to private employers or to local and state governments. Furthermore, new exceptions are added to this law each year, whittling away the power of the law to truly protect your financial privacy.

The Video Privacy Protection Act

The Video Privacy Protection Act forbids retailers from providing—for free or for a price—a list of the videos you rent unless you approve the release of that information. Retailers are required, however, to release the information in the case of a court order.

The Computer Matching and Privacy Protection Act

The Computer Matching and Privacy Protection Act regulates the federal government's use of computer matching techniques that compare data in one computer file to data in another to determine your eligibility for federal benefits. The law also limits the federal government's use of matching techniques to help it collect money, such as back taxes, that you may owe the government. However, as a result of exemptions written into the law, the act does not apply to many potential matches, including those done for purposes of law enforcement and tax collection.

The Credit Industry and Privacy

Over the years, the larger credit bureaus—the big three and those who buy credit record information from the big three—have developed and marketed a variety of products and services that go beyond their original mission of helping creditors make credit granting decisions, helping employers to make hiring decisions, and aiding insurers in their decisions regarding coverage. These new products and services are the consequence of the loophole in the FCRA allowing consumer credit data to be given to "anyone with a legitimate business need." Such products and services are also the result of the dual fact that the FCRA has failed to keep pace with technological advances and that the FTC has too few resources and too little power to effectively police the industry. As a result, consumer watchdog groups and many policymakers are anxious to see the FCRA amended to place greater constraints on the development of products and services based on consumer credit information and to provide you with greater control over how the information in your credit files is used.

How Information Brokers Use Information

Some information brokers, but none of the big three, sell information that reflects your credit status to direct marketers and telemarketers—a violation of the FCRA. The big three do sell consumer identification information such as your age and address to direct marketers and telemarketers, which is not a violation of the FCRA.

Some information brokers also develop, maintain and market extensive demographic databases for targeted marketing. Although such databases are separate from those that credit bureaus, including the big three, maintain for credit granting purposes, they may be enhanced with information from the bureaus' credit files and outside data. These outside data might include phone book information, Census Bureau data, subscription lists, and real estate, insurance and consumer-purchase information. The databases that result can create very precise profiles of, among other things, your spending habits, lifestyle, hobbies, work, friends and family, and they can be extremely valuable to direct marketers and telemarketers who want to narrowly define their target markets for selling more.

Special Products and Services

Most of the privacy-related criticism directed at credit bureaus focuses on three very specific products/services: *prescreening, data enhancement* and *targeted marketing databases.*

Prescreening

Prescreening is a technique by which a credit bureau, using the information in its credit files, creates a list of consumers qualified to receive a preapproved offer of credit. Prescreening can be accomplished in one of two ways. First, a company may supply a credit bureau with a set of credit granting characteristics that describe its target market. For example, a national bankcard company may want to offer a preapproved card to all consumers who make more than $100,000 a year and have flawless credit records and several unused lines of credit of at least $5,000 per line.

The credit bureau doing the prescreening will compare the criteria specified by the bankcard company with the characteristics of the consumers in its database. From this comparison, it will develop a list of prescreened consumers to whom the company can make its credit card offer.

 HOT TIP

If you see the letters *prm* or the word *promotional* in the *Inquiries* section of your credit report, it means that your file was prescreened for an offer.

A company can also provide a credit bureau with a list of consumers and a set of criteria defining the types of consumers to whom it wants to make its offer. The company's list may have been obtained from a list broker or from the credit bureau itself. The credit bureau will then compare the information it has in its database with the criteria the creditor has specified so as to identify those who should receive the company's offer.

Critics of prescreening object to the practice because it is done without the knowledge or the approval of consumers. These critics are also concerned because—although prescreening has been going on since the 1970s—technological advances have greatly broadened the criteria that can be applied to credit bureau data. As a result, prescreening has become increasingly intrusive. Companies now can learn very specific details about your financial life without ever seeing your credit history.

Critics also allege that prescreening violates the intent of the FCRA because it doesn't relate to a consumer's solicitation of credit but rather to the company's solicitation of a consumer in order to *extend credit to the consumer.* On the other hand, supporters say that prescreening reduces the amount of unwanted solicitations a consumer receives by helping businesses better target their solicitations to those consumers most apt to be interested in them.

The FCRA has ruled that prescreening is legal so long as all those on a prescreened list receive the same solicitation. However, many consumer watchdogs and policymakers believe that if the practice is to continue, the FCRA should be amended to allow consumers the opportunity to opt out of prescreening. The big three in fact allow consumers to opt out of their prescreening programs and have begun sharing the names and addresses of consumers who do. This means that if you contact one of the big three about your desire to opt out, your request will automatically be communicated to the other two. Your name and address will be removed not only from the credit bureaus' prescreening programs but also from their direct marketing programs. Figure 10.1 provides the opt-out addresses for each of the big three.

 HOT TIP

Contacting the big three to have your name removed from prescreening and direct mail lists does not mean that you will no longer receive any such offers. That's because the big three are not the only companies that provide information for such lists.

Data Enhancement

The goal of data enhancement is to improve the quality of one database by adding selected information to it from other databases. Some critics argue that data enhancement allows a company to create marketing lists that are as effective as prescreened lists but with broader applications.

Credit bureaus that offer data enhancement services compare demographic and financial data about consumers in their own files to selected data in the files of another company or organization. When predefined information matches in the two files are identified, the appropriate credit bureau data are added to the other database.

An organization may use data enhancement because it wants to learn more about its customer base so that it can do a better job of marketing its products,

FIGURE 10.1   How To Opt Out

Here are the addresses to contact if you want your name removed from the prescreening and direct marketing programs of the big three. Don't forget you need only contact one of them. In your letter, include your full name, complete address and Social Security number.

Equifax Options
PO Box 740123
Atlanta, GA 30374-0123

Trans Union
Name Removal Option
PO Box 97328
Jackson, MS 39288

TRW Consumer Opt Out
TRW Credit Marketing
701 TRW Parkway
Allen, TX 75002

If you want to further reduce the number of solicitations you get via mail as well as phone, you should also contact the Direct Marketing Association, a national organization of direct marketers, including telemarketers.

Direct Marketing Association
Mail Preference Service
PO Box 9008
Farmington, NY 11735

Direct Marketing Association
Telephone Preference Service
PO Box 9014
Farmington, NY 11735

develop more detailed lists for direct marketing or sell the lists it develops through data enhancement.

Critics of data enhancement contend that the practice violates consumer privacy because the consumer information being transferred into another company's files was provided for credit granting purposes, not so it could be sold and used by another company for another purpose. Critics are also upset by the fact that once your personal data are in another company's files, you have no control over how that information will be used. Like prescreening, data enhancement is done without your knowledge or permission.

Targeted Marketing Databases

Targeted marketing databases are used by marketers to help them reach a narrowly defined audience with a specific product or service. The sales pitch often is delivered through telemarketing or promotional mailings. Some credit bureaus develop very detailed marketing databases, commonly selling them to mail order houses, credit card companies, real estate companies specializing in time-share vacations and the like.

Beyond the Big Three

Most privacy-related criticism directed at the credit reporting industry has focused on the big three because of the sheer volume of information they maintain in their databases, the many uses they have for such information and the fact that they are the credit bureaus consumers interact with most frequently. However, to focus only on the big three is to ignore a significant part of the problem in the credit reporting industry—information brokers that buy their consumer credit information from the big three and, in turn, sell it and other database information to businesses. Some of these other information brokers are reputed to sell their information to almost anyone willing to buy it, including debt collectors, private detectives and even a consumer's acquaintances and former spouses. There are a number of reasons why they are able to: They tend to operate less visibly than the big three and receive less public scrutiny; the FTC has a limited ability to "police" the credit reporting industry at all levels and to enforce the FCRA; and they know how to take advantage of weaknesses in the FCRA.

The *Business Week* editor referred to earlier in this chapter demonstrated just how easily consumer information can be obtained from these information brokers. The editor signed up with two such companies, telling them that he was an editor at McGraw Hill, Inc. and that he might be doing some hiring. He provided both with the names of some individuals he said were potential new hires and indicated that he would like to review their credit records. With no more than the most cursory check into the editor's identity, the brokers provided the editor with complete access to the files. One of them even provided the editor with instructions for using his home computer to tap into its database!

It appears that the further consumer credit information travels from the credit bureau that originally collected it, the more opportunities there are for this information to be used inappropriately and for unauthorized persons to acquire that data.

Government and Privacy

The federal government also collects and stores large volumes of information about consumers, thus posing another threat to individual privacy. In fact, it is the nation's largest data gatherer. Numerous federal agencies and departments maintain extensive databases on countless consumers—the FBI, the IRS, the Census Bureau and the DEA in particular.

 HOT TIP

Many state motor vehicle departments sell car registration and drivers license records to credit companies.

Despite the Federal Privacy Act, many federal agencies and departments link their databases as they look for consumer matches. Frequently, agencies also match the information in their computers with data purchased from private companies. The IRS, in fact, uses this technique to locate nonfilers.

Profiling

Presently, approximately 16 government agencies make use of a technique called *profiling* whereby a list of characteristics believed to be common to a particular group of people—tax evaders, drug smugglers, welfare cheaters, for example—is created. Then the government agency compares the individual characteristics of the population at large or of a particular group of persons to identify those who fit the profile.

Although no one can fault the IRS for wanting to crack down on nonfilers or the DEA for trying to reduce the amount of illegal drugs being smuggled into this country, their use of profiling is disturbing to privacy advocates. First, there are questions about the accuracy of profiling as well as concern because innocent people have been detained or prosecuted for no reason other than that they fit a profile. Second, because there are few restrictions on the use of the technique, there is nothing to stop government agencies from expanding its use.

The Private Sector and Privacy

As already reported, many companies other than the big three develop and maintain extensive databases. They include other credit reporting agencies, list brokers, credit card companies and firms in the financial services and direct marketing industries. These companies may augment or improve the data in their files by using a credit bureau's data enhancement service, purchasing direct marketing lists, purchasing Census Bureau information or buying information from information brokers that are not credit bureaus. Companies with extensive databases may also glean important consumer-specific information from warranty cards, subscriber or user surveys, mail order forms, credit applications and the like.

Some of these companies not only use the information in their databases for their own purposes but they also provide prescreening services similar to those offered by the larger credit reporting agencies; others may market their data to outside users. Some credit card companies, for example, sell information detailing the types of credit purchases their cardholders have made or market lists of people who have purchased a particular type of product with their card.

The Medical/Insurance Industry and Privacy

The medical industry is another big collector of consumer information. Hospitals, HMOs, doctors' offices, self-insured corporations and insurance companies all maintain extensive medical information databases on their clients, patients or employees.

Much of this information ends up with the *Medical Information Bureau* (MIB), a membership organization of about 680 life insurance companies. Established in 1902 by the medical directors of 15 insurance companies, the MIB's original purpose was to reduce fraudulent claims. Although it continues to serve this function, the MIB now has a broader potential impact on consumers. According to the FTC, the activities of the MIB are governed by the FCRA; but just as the general public hasn't been aware of the activities of credit bureaus other than the big three, so too has the MIB escaped public knowledge and scrutiny until recently.

The information in the MIB's files can influence your ability to get health, life or disability insurance, or reimbursement for a claim. It can also affect your employment opportunities if an insurer shares information from your MIB report with your employer or potential employer.

If you have medical insurance and require medical care, you or your doctor will file a claim with your insurance carrier to get reimbursed. The information on that claim will be shared with the MIB if your insurer is a member. In turn, the MIB will share the claim information with other member companies that provide you insurance or that are assessing you for insurance. Thus, the highly personal information you thought you were telling your doctor in strictest confidence may actually become part of a vast national medical information network.

The FTC is beginning to hold the MIB and other companies that provide information to insurers about consumers to the same standards as it holds credit reporting agencies. For example, the FTC has ruled that if an insurance company denies you health, life or disability insurance based on information in an MIB report, the insurer must tell you where the information came from, including the company's name and address. Usually that company will be the MIB. The insurer must provide you the same information if it raises your insurance premium based on information in a credit bureau report. If you request a copy of your report within 30 days of being denied the insurance, you are entitled to a free report.

If you have not been denied insurance but want to know what is being maintained about you by the MIB, you can obtain an MIB report for $8 by writing the Medical Information Bureau (Box 105, Essex Station, Boston, MA 02112; 617-426-3660).

How Employers Are Using Information about Consumers

The increased availability and specificity of consumer information, including credit-related information, is something that many employers are taking advantage of as part of their decision-making process.

Critics of using credit record information in making hiring decisions question the predictive value of credit information for screening employees. They are also concerned because some employers who review credit records as part of their hiring process are violating the FCRA. That law says that if a job applicant loses a job in whole or in part because of information in the applicant's credit records, the employer must disclose this and give the applicant the name and address of the credit bureau that reported the negative information. Despite the law, not all employers are doing this, leaving job seekers vulnerable to continued job rejections. Some states, including California and Minnesota, require an employer to notify a prospective employee before obtaining a report and require the agency providing the report to give the applicant a free copy of that report. In addition, it is the policy of members of Associated Credit Bureaus, Inc. not to sell credit reports for employment purposes unless the employer certifies in writing that the employee or potential employee is notified that the report will be reviewed. Bureau members also encourage employers to share with an employee or prospective employee, before an employment decision is made, a copy of the credit report so that the person involved can make sure there are no errors in it.

Private Databases

Private databases now exist that have been expressly designed to provide employers with information about potential employees that goes beyond the information in a traditional employment report provided by a credit bureau. Here are some examples:

- Employer's Information Services in Louisiana has developed a massive national database that contains the names of employees who have claimed on-the-job injuries with details of their claims and lawsuits. This information may be used by employers to screen job applicants. The information—accurate or not and without any consideration given to the circumstances of the injury and claim—may remove a candidate from consideration for a job. Without the candidate's knowledge, the data maintained by Employer's Information Services can wrongfully label workers as *troublemakers,* effectively blacklisting them from future employment.

- Pinkerton Investigative Services claims that it has access to a worldwide network of databases it uses to perform background checks on prospective employees. The defense industry has traditionally used this kind of check, but today other industries as well are making extensive use of background checks.

- Information Resource Service Company (IRSC) offers employers an opportunity to determine whether a prospective employee has ever been arrested, even if the arrest did not result in a conviction. To provide this service, IRC taps into more than 7,000 databases.

What is particularly alarming about the use of these databases in hiring decisions is that there is no way for you to know if the information is accurate. Any job applicant may thus lose an employment opportunity from misinformation. Furthermore, even if you can determine the source of any misinformation about yourself, unless that source is a credit bureau there is no law to assist you in correcting the error and no way of knowing the other databases that carry this misinformation.

Psychological Testing

Some employers are using psychological testing to help screen out *problem* job applicants. Often the questions asked are highly personal, covering such topics as religion, politics and sex. Such testing can put applicants in a precarious position—if they don't agree to the testing, they won't get the job, but if they answer, they may have to reveal highly personal information. And if these persons are hired and that personal information is retained in their employer's database, there is no way of knowing who might see the information and where it might end up.

Preserving Your Privacy in a High-Tech World

As this chapter has already indicated, it is becoming increasingly difficult for consumers to preserve their privacy in today's high-tech world. New laws must be written and existing laws strengthened to address the dramatic technological changes that have been taking place. However, no law can protect consumers completely because there will always be companies and individuals able to get around laws and get away with it. Consumers themselves therefore must do what they can to preserve their privacy. Here are some tips on how to do that:

- Monitor your credit record. Request a copy of it from each of the big three once a year and from any independent local or regional credit bureaus maintaining a file on you and check it carefully for problems, including inquiries you do not understand.

- Request a copy of your MIB file.

- Contact the big three to tell them that you want to opt out of prescreening and direct marketing programs. See Figure 10.1 for how to do this.

- Write to the Direct Marketing Association (DMA) to ask to be put on their list of people whose names cannot be released to direct marketing firms and telemarketing firms. Doing so will help reduce the number of companies and organizations that could gain access to information about you; it will also reduce the amount of junk mail and unsolicited phone calls that you receive. See Figure 10.1 for DMA addresses.

- Pay cash whenever possible rather than using credit. That way you won't be signing anything, and your transaction will be less likely to become a part of a company's databank. This will also help minimize the opportunity for developing credit problems.

- Read disclosure statements on any credit forms you sign.

- Check out your credit card's billing statements each month to spot any charges you do not understand or did not make.

- Don't give out personal information just because someone asks for it. For example, do not write your Social Security number on your check or on the part of a credit receipt that a business is going to keep. Your Social Security number is a basic identifying number that can be used to call up a variety of information about you. No law says you must provide your Social Security number for a credit transaction.

- Do not write your telephone number or address on a merchant's credit slip or receipt. No law requires this either, and some states actually prohibit merchants from asking consumers to provide such information on their receipts or sales slips.

- Keep your drivers license number to yourself as much as possible. Depending on your state, this number may be the same as your Social Security number.

- Think twice before responding to a telephone or written survey.

- Limit the amount of information that you write on a warranty card, product registration form, mail order form and the like.

- Call your bank, credit card companies and phone company to tell them you do not want them giving third parties your name or other personal information. Recognize that if you respond to a mail or phone offer, your name, address and telephone number will probably end up on at least one more list.

- Think twice before including your Social Security number, credit card account numbers or other personal information in an e-mail message.

- Find out how your Internet service provider protects the consumer credit-related information in its database.

- If you subscribe to an online service, avoid obvious passwords.

Appendix A

Public Law 91-508
Title VI

The Fair Credit Reporting Act
As amended, including September 23, 1994
Public Law No. 103-325

Enacted October 26, 1970
Effective April 24, 1971

TITLE VI—PROVISIONS RELATING TO CREDIT REPORTING SERVICES

AMENDMENT OF CONSUMER CREDIT PROTECTION ACT

SEC.601. The Consumer Credit Protection Act is amended by adding at the end thereof the following new title:

TITLE VI—CONSUMER CREDIT REPORTING

Sec.

§ 601. Short title

This title may be cited as the Fair Credit Reporting Act.

§ 602. Findings and purpose   15 U.S.C. 1681

(a)   The Congress makes the following findings:

(1) The banking system is dependent upon fair and accurate credit reporting. Inaccurate credit reports directly impair the efficiency of the banking system, and unfair credit reporting methods undermine the public confidence which is essential to the continued functioning of the banking system.

(2) An elaborate mechanism has been developed for investigating and evaluating the credit worthiness, credit standing, credit capacity, character, and general reputation of consumers.

(3) Consumer reporting agencies have assumed a vital role in assembling and evaluating consumer credit and other information on consumers.

(4) There is a need to insure that consumer reporting agencies exercise their grave responsibilities with fairness, impartiality, and a respect for the consumer's right to privacy.

(b) It is the purpose of this title to require that consumer reporting agencies adopt reasonable procedures for meeting the needs of commerce for consumer credit, personnel, insurance, and other information in a manner which is fair and equitable to the consumer, with regard to the confidentiality, accuracy, relevancy, and proper utilization of such information in accordance with the requirements of this title.

15 U.S.C. 1681a

§ 603. Definitions and rules of construction

(a) Definitions and rules of construction set forth in this section are applicable for the purposes of this title.

(b) The term "person" means any individual, partnership, corporation, trust, estate, cooperative, association, government or governmental subdivision or agency, or other entity.

(c) The term "consumer" means an individual.

(d) The term "consumer report" means any written, oral, or other communication of any information by a consumer reporting agency bearing on a consumer's credit worthiness, credit standing, credit capacity, character, general reputation, personal characteristics, or mode of living which is used or expected to be used or collected in whole or in part for the purpose of serving as a factor in establishing the consumer's eligibility for (1) credit or insurance to be used primarily for personal, family, or household purposes, or (2) employment purposes, or (3) other purposes authorized under section 604. The term does not include (A) any report containing information solely as to transactions or experiences between the consumer and the person making the report; (B) any authorization or approval of a specific extension of credit directly or indirectly by the issuer of a credit card or similar device; or (C) any report in which a person who has been requested by a third party to make a specific extension of credit directly or indirectly to a consumer conveys his decision with respect to such request, if the third party advises the consumer of the name and address of the person to whom the request was made and such person makes the disclosures to the consumer required under section 615.

(e) The term "investigative consumer report" means a consumer report or portion thereof in which information on a consumer's character, general reputation, personal characteristics, or mode of living is obtained through personal interviews with neighbors, friends, or associates of the consumer reported on or with others with whom he is acquainted or who may have knowledge concerning any such items of information. However, such information shall not include specific factual information on a consumer's credit record obtained directly from a creditor of the consumer or from a consumer reporting agency when such information was obtained directly from a creditor of the consumer or from the consumer.

(f) The term "consumer reporting agency" means any person which, for monetary fees, dues, or on a cooperative nonprofit basis, regularly engages in whole or in part in the practice of assembling or evaluating consumer credit information or other information on consumers for the purpose of furnishing consumer reports to third parties, and which uses any means or facility of interstate commerce for the purpose of preparing or furnishing consumer reports.

(g) The term "file", when used in connection with information on any consumer, means all of the information on that consumer recorded and retained by a consumer reporting agency regardless of how the information is stored.

(h) The term "employment purposes" when used in connection with a consumer report means a report used for the purpose of evaluating a consumer for employment, promotion, reassignment or retention as an employee.

(i) The term "medical information" means information or records obtained, with the consent of the individual to whom it relates, from licensed physicians or medical practitioners, hospitals, clinics, or other medical or medically related facilities

(j) (1) The term "overdue support" has the meaning given to such term in section 466(e) of the Social Security Act.

(2) The term "State or local child support enforcement agency" means a State or local agency which administers a State or local program for establishing and enforcing child support obligations.

15 U.S.C. 1681b

§ 604. Permissible purposes of reports

A consumer reporting agency may furnish a consumer report under the following circumstances and no other:

(1) In response to the order of a court having jurisdiction to issue such an order, or a subpoena issued in connection with proceedings before a Federal grand jury.

(2) In accordance with the written instructions of the consumer to whom it relates.

(3) To a person which it has reason to believe—

(A) intends to use the information in connection with a credit transaction involving the consumer on whom the information is to be furnished and involving the extension of credit to, or review or collection of an account of, the consumer; or

(B) intends to use the information for employment purposes; or

(C) intends to use the information in connection with the underwriting of insurance involving the consumer; or

(D) intends to use the information in connection with a determination of the consumer's eligibility for a license or other benefit granted by a governmental instrumentality required by law to consider an applicant's financial responsibility or status; or

(E) otherwise has a legitimate business need for the information in connection with a business transaction involving the consumer.

§ 605. Obsolete information

15 U.S.C. 1681c

(a) Except as authorized under subsection (b), no consumer reporting agency may make any consumer report containing any of the following items of information:

   (1) Cases under title 11 of the United States Code or under the Bankruptcy Act that, from the date of entry of the order for relief or the date of adjudication, as the case may be, antedate the report by more than 10 years.

   (2) Suits and judgments which, from date of entry, antedate the report by more than seven years or until the governing statute of limitations has expired, whichever is the longer period.

   (3) Paid tax liens which, from date of payment, antedate the report by more than seven years.

   (4) Accounts placed for collection or charged to profit and loss which antedate the report by more than seven years.[†]

   (5) Records of arrest, indictment, or conviction of crime which, from date of disposition, release or parole, antedate the report by more than seven years.

   (6) Any other adverse item of information which antedates the report by more than seven years.[†]

(b) The provisions of subsection (a) are not applicable in the case of any consumer credit report to be used in connection with—

   (1) a credit transaction involving, or which may reasonably be expected to involve, a principal amount of $50,000 or more;

   (2) the underwriting of life insurance involving, or which may reasonably be expected to involve, a face amount of $50,000 or more; or

   (3) the employment of any individual at an annual salary which equals, or which may reasonably be expected to equal $20,000, or more.

[†] The reporting periods have been lengthened for certain adverse information pertaining to U.S. Government insured or guaranteed student loans, or pertaining to national direct student loans. See sections 430A(f) and 463(c)(3) of the Higher Education Act of 1965, 20 U.S.C. 1080a(f) and 20 U.S.C. 1087cc(c)(3), respectively.

15 U.S.C. 1681d   **§ 606. Disclosure of investigative consumer reports**

(a) A person may not procure or cause to be prepared an investigative consumer report on any consumer unless—

     (1) it is clearly and accurately disclosed to the consumer that an investigative consumer report including information as to his character, general reputation, personal characteristics, and mode of living, whichever are applicable, may be made, and such disclosure (A) is made in a writing mailed, or otherwise delivered, to the consumer, not later than three days after the date on which the report was first requested, and (B) includes a statement informing the consumer of his right to request the additional disclosures provided for under subsection (b) of this section; or

     (2) the report is to be used for employment purposes for which the consumer has not specifically applied.

(b) Any person who procures or causes to be prepared an investigative consumer report on any consumer shall, upon written request made by the consumer within a reasonable period of time after receipt by him of the disclosure required by subsection (a)(1), shall ‡ make a complete and accurate disclosure of the nature and scope of the investigation requested. This disclosure shall be made in a writing mailed, or otherwise delivered, to the consumer not later than five days after the date on which the request for such disclosure was received from the consumer or such report was first requested, whichever is the later.

(c) No person may be held liable for any violation of subsection (a) or (b) of this section if he shows by a preponderance of the evidence that at the time of the violation he maintained reasonable procedures to assure compliance with subsection (a) or (b).

15 U.S.C. 1681e   **§ 607. Compliance Procedures**

(a) Every consumer reporting agency shall maintain reasonable procedures designed to avoid violations of section 605 and to limit the furnishing of consumer reports to the purposes listed under section 604. These procedures

---

‡ So in original. Probably should be omitted.

shall require that prospective users of the information identify themselves, certify the purposes for which the information is sought, and certify that the information will be used for no other purpose. Every consumer reporting agency shall make a reasonable effort to verify the identity of a new prospective user and the uses certified by such prospective user prior to furnishing such user a consumer report. No consumer reporting agency may furnish a consumer report to any person if it has reasonable grounds for believing that the consumer report will not be used for a purpose listed in section 604.

(b) Whenever a consumer reporting agency prepares a consumer report it shall follow reasonable procedures to assure maximum possible accuracy of the information concerning the individual about whom the report relates.

§ 608. Disclosures to governmental agencies

15 U.S.C. 1681f

Notwithstanding the provisions of section 604, a consumer reporting agency may furnish identifying information respecting any consumer, limited to his name, address, former addresses, places of employment, or former places of employment, to a governmental agency.

§ 609. Disclosures to consumers

15 U.S.C. 1681g

(a) Every consumer reporting agency shall, upon request and proper identification of any consumer, clearly and accurately disclose to the consumer:

(1) The nature and substance of all information (except medical information) in its files on the consumer at the time of the request.

(2) The sources of the information; except that the sources of information acquired solely for use in preparing an investigative consumer report and actually used for no other purpose need not be disclosed: *Provided,* That in the event an action is brought under this title, such sources shall be available to the plaintiff under appropriate discovery procedures in the court in which the action is brought.

(3) The recipients of any consumer report on the consumer which it has furnished—

(A) for employment purposes within the two-year period preceding the request, and

(B) for any other purpose within the six-month period

preceding the request.

    (4) The dates, original payees, and amounts of any checks upon which is based any adverse characterization of the consumer, included in the file at the time of the disclosure.

  (b) The requirements of subsection (a) respecting the disclosure of sources of information and the recipients of consumer reports do not apply to information received or consumer reports furnished prior to the effective date of this title except to the extent that the matter involved is contained in the files of the consumer reporting agency on that date.

15 U.S.C. 1861h

§ 610. Conditions of disclosure to consumers

  (a) A consumer reporting agency shall make the disclosures required under section 609 during normal business hours and on reasonable notice.

  (b) The disclosures required under section 609 shall be made to the consumer—

    (1) in person if he appears in person and furnishes proper identification; or

    (2) by telephone if he has made a written request, with proper identification, for telephone disclosure and the toll charge, if any, for the telephone call is prepaid by or charged directly to the consumer.

  (c) Any consumer reporting agency shall provide trained personnel to explain to the consumer any information furnished to him pursuant to section 609.

  (d) The consumer shall be permitted to be accompanied by one other person of his choosing, who shall furnish reasonable identification. A consumer reporting agency may require the consumer to furnish a written statement granting permission to the consumer reporting agency to discuss the consumer's file in such person's presence.

  (e) Except as provided in sections 616 and 617, no consumer may bring any action or proceeding in the nature of defamation, invasion of privacy, or negligence with respect to the reporting of information against any consumer reporting agency, any user of information, or any person who furnishes information to a consumer reporting agency, based on information disclosed pursuant to section 609, 610, or 615, except as to false information furnished with malice or willful intent to injure such consumer.

§ 611. Procedure in case of disputed accuracy

15 U.S.C. 1681i

(a) If the completeness or accuracy of any item of information contained in his file is disputed by a consumer, and such dispute is directly conveyed to the consumer reporting agency by the consumer, the consumer reporting agency shall within a reasonable period of time reinvestigate and record the current status of that information unless it has reasonable grounds to believe that the dispute by the consumer is frivolous or irrelevant. If after such reinvestigation such information is found to be inaccurate or can no longer be verified, the consumer reporting agency shall promptly delete such information. The presence of contradictory information in the consumer's file does not in and of itself constitute reasonable grounds for believing the dispute is frivolous or irrelevant.

(b) If the reinvestigation does not resolve the dispute, the consumer may file a brief statement setting forth the nature of the dispute. The consumer reporting agency may limit such statements to not more than one hundred words if it provides the consumer with assistance in writing a clear summary of the dispute.

(c) Whenever a statement of a dispute is filed, unless there is reasonable grounds to believe that it is frivolous or irrelevant, the consumer reporting agency shall, in any subsequent consumer report containing the information in question, clearly note that it is disputed by the consumer and provide either the consumer's statement or a clear and accurate codification or summary thereof.

(d) Following any deletion of information which is found to be inaccurate or whose accuracy can no longer be verified or any notation as to disputed information, the consumer reporting agency shall, at the request of the consumer, furnish notification that the item has been deleted or the statement, codification or summary pursuant to subsection (b) or (c) to any person specifically designated by the consumer who has within two years prior thereto received a consumer report for employment purposes, or within six months prior thereto received a consumer report for any other purpose, which contained the deleted or disputed information. The consumer reporting agency shall clearly and conspicuously disclose to the consumer his rights to make such a request. Such disclosure shall be made at or prior to the time the information is deleted or the consumer's statement regarding the disputed information is received.

15 U.S.C. 1681j

§ 612. Charges for certain disclosures

A consumer reporting agency shall make all disclosures pursuant to section 609 and furnish all consumer reports pursuant to section 611(d) without charge to the consumer if, within thirty days after receipt by such consumer of a notification pursuant to section 615 or notification from a debt collection agency affiliated with such consumer reporting agency stating that the consumer's credit rating may be or has been adversely affected, the consumer makes a request under section 609 or 611(d). Otherwise, the consumer reporting agency may impose a reasonable charge on the consumer for making disclosure to such consumer pursuant to section 609, the charge for which shall be indicated to the consumer prior to making disclosure; and for furnishing notifications, statements, summaries, or codifications to person designated by the consumer pursuant to section 611(d), the charge for which shall be indicated to the consumer prior to furnishing such information and shall not exceed the charge that the consumer reporting agency would impose on each designated recipient for a consumer report except that no charge may be made for notifying such persons of the deletion of information which is found to be inaccurate or which can no longer be verified.

15 U.S.C. 1681k

§ 613. Public record information for employment purposes

A consumer reporting agency which furnishes a consumer report for employment purposes and which for that purpose compiles and reports items of information on consumers which are matters of public record and are likely to have an adverse effect upon a consumer's ability to obtain employment shall—

(1) at the time such public record information is reported to the user of such consumer report, notify the consumer of the fact that public record information is being reported by the consumer reporting agency, together with the name and address of the person to whom such information is being reported; or

(2) maintain strict procedures designed to insure that whenever public record information which is likely to have an adverse effect on a consumer's ability to obtain employment is reported it is com-

plete and up to date. For purposes of this paragraph, items of public record relating to arrests, indictments, convictions, suits, tax liens, and outstanding judgments shall be considered up to date if the current public record status of the item at the time of the report is reported.

§ 614. Restrictions on investigate consumer reports   15 U.S.C. 1681l

Whenever a consumer reporting agency prepares an investigative consumer report, no adverse information in the consumer report (other than information which is a matter of public record) may be included in a subsequent consumer report unless such adverse information has been verified in the process of making such subsequent consumer report, or the adverse information was received within the three-month period preceding the date the subsequent report is furnished.

§ 615. Requirements on users of consumer reports   15 U.S.C. 1681m

(a) Whenever credit or insurance for personal, family, or household purposes, or employment involving a consumer is denied or the charge for such credit or insurance is increased either wholly or partly because of information contained in a consumer report from a consumer reporting agency, the user of the consumer report shall so advise the consumer against whom such adverse action has been taken and supply the name and address of the consumer reporting agency making the report.

b) Whenever credit for personal, family, or household purposes involving an consumer is denied or the charge for such credit is increased wholly or partly because of information obtained from a person other than a consumer reporting agency bearing upon the consumer's credit worthiness, credit standing, credit capacity, character, general reputation, personal characteristics, or mode of living, the user of such information shall, within a reasonable period of time, upon the consumer's written request for the reasons for such adverse action received within sixty days after learning of such adverse action, disclose the nature of the information to the consumer. The user of such information shall clearly and accurately disclose to the consumer his right to make such written request at the time such adverse action is communicated to the consumer.

(c) No person shall be held liable for any violation of this section if he shows by a preponderance of the evidence that at the time of the alleged violation he maintained reasonable procedures to assure compliance with the provisions of subsections (a) and (b).

15 U.S.C. 1681n **§ 616. Civil liability for willful noncompliance**

Any consumer reporting agency or user of information which willfully fails to comply with any requirement imposed under this title with respect to any consumer is liable to that consumer in an amount equal to the sum of—

(1) any actual damages sustained by the consumer as a result of the failure;

(2) such amount of punitive damages as the court may allow; and

(3) in the case of any successful action to enforce any liability under this section, the costs of the action together with reasonable attorney's fees as determined by the court.

15 U.S.C. 1681o **§ 617. Civil liability for negligent noncompliance**

Any consumer reporting agency or user of information which is negligent in failing to comply with any requirement imposed under this title with respect to any consumer is liable to that consumer in an amount equal to the sum of—

(1) any actual damages sustained by the consumer as a result of the failure;

(2) in the case of any successful action to enforce any liability under this section, the costs of the action together with reasonable attorney's fees as determined by the court.

15 U.S.C. 1681p **§ 618. Jurisdiction of courts; limitation of actions**

An action to enforce any liability created under this title may be brought in any appropriate United States district court without regard to the amount in controversy, or in any other court of competent jurisdiction, within two years from the date on which the liability arises, except that where a defendant has materially and willfully misrepresented any information required under this title to be disclosed to an individual and the information so misrepresented is material to the establishment of the defendant's liability to that individual under this title, the action may be brought at any time within two years after discovery by the individual of the misrepresentation.

§ 619. Obtaining information under false pretenses

15 U.S.C. 1681q

Any person who knowingly and willfully obtains information on a consumer from a consumer reporting agency under false pretenses shall be fined not more the $5,000 or imprisoned not more than one year, or both.

§ 620. Unauthorized disclosures by officers or employees

15 U.S.C. 1681r

Any officer or employee of a consumer reporting agency who knowingly and willfully provides information concerning an individual from the agency's files to a person not authorized to receive that information shall be fined not more than $5,000 or imprisoned not more than one year, or both.

§ 621. Administrative enforcement

15 U.S.C. 1681s

(a) Compliance with the requirements imposed under this title shall be enforced under the Federal Trade Commission Act by the Federal Trade Commission with respect to consumer reporting agencies and all other persons subject thereto, except to the extent that enforcement of the requirements imposed under this title is specifically committed to some other government agency under subsection (b) hereof. For the purpose of the exercise by the Federal Trade Commission of its functions and powers under the Federal Trade Commission Act, a violation of any requirement or prohibition imposed under this title shall constitute an unfair or deceptive act or practice in commerce in violation of section 5(a) of the Federal Trade Commission Act and shall be subject to enforcement by the Federal Trade Commission under section 5(b) thereof with respect to any consumer reporting agency or person subject to enforcement by the Federal Trade Commission pursuant to this subsection, irrespective of whether that person is engaged in commerce or meets any other jurisdictional tests in the Federal Trade Commission Act. The Federal Trade Commission shall have such procedural, investigative, and enforcement powers, including the power to issue procedural rules in enforcing compliance with the requirements imposed under this title and to require the filing of reports, the production of documents, and the appearance of witnesses as though the applicable terms and conditions of the Federal Trade Commission Act were part of this title. Any person violating any of the provisions of this title shall be subject to the penalties and entitled to the privileges and immunities provided in the Federal Trade Commission Act as though the applicable terms and provisions thereof were part of this title.

(b) Compliance with the requirements imposed under this title with respect to consumer reporting agencies and persons who use consumer reports from such agencies shall be enforced under—

(1) section 8 of the Federal Deposit Insurance Act, in the case of—

   (A) national banks, and Federal branches and Federal agencies of foreign banks, by the Office of the Comptroller of the Currency;

   (B) member banks of the Federal Reserve System (other than national banks), branches and agencies of foreign banks (other than Federal branches, Federal agencies, and insured State branches of foreign banks), commercial lending companies owned or controlled by foreign banks, and organizations operating under section 25 or 25(a) of the Federal Reserve Act, by the Board of Governors of the Federal Reserve System; and

   (C) banks insured by the Federal Deposit Insurance Corporation (other than members of the Federal Reserve System) and insured State branches of foreign banks, by the Board of Governors of the Federal Deposit Insurance Corporation;

(2) section 8 of the Federal Deposit Insurance Act, by the Director of the Office of Thrift Supervision, in the case of a savings association the deposits of which are insured by the Federal Deposit Insurance Corporation;

(3) the Federal Credit Union Act, by the Administrator of the National Credit Union Administration with respect to any Federal credit union;

(4) subtitle IV of Title 49, by the Interstate Commerce Commission with respect to any common carrier subject to such subtitle;

(5) the Federal Aviation Act of 1958, by the Secretary of Transportation with respect to any air carrier or foreign air carrier subject to that Act; and

(6) the Packers and Stockyards Act, 1921 (except as provided in section 406 of that Act), by the Secretary

of Agriculture with respect to any activities subject to that Act.

The terms used in paragraph 1 that are not defined in this title or otherwise defined in section 3(s) of the Federal Deposit Insurance Act shall have the meaning given to them in section 1(b) of the International Banking Act of 1978.

(c) For the purpose of the exercise by any agency referred to in subsection (b) of its powers under any Act referred to in that subsection, a violation of any requirement imposed under this title shall be deemed to be a violation of a requirement imposedunder that Act. In addition to its powers under any provision of law specifically referred to in subsection (b), each of the agencies referred to in that subsection may exercise, for the purpose of enforcing compliance with any requirement imposed under this title any other authority conferred on it by law.

§ 622. Information on overdue child support obligations

15 U.S.C. 1681s-1

Notwithstanding any other provision of this title, a consumer reporting agency shall include in any consumer report furnished by the agency in accordance with section 604, any information on the failure of the consumer to pay overdue support which—

(1) is provided (A) to the consumer reporting agency by a State or local child support enforcement agency, or (B) to the consumer reporting agency and verified by any local, State, or Federal government agency; and

(2) antedates the report by 7 years or less.

§ 623. Relation to State laws

15 U.S.C. 1681t

This title does not annul, alter, affect, or exempt any person subject to the provisions of this title from complying with the laws of any State with respect to the collection, distribution, or use of any information on consumers, except to the extent that those laws are inconsistent with any provision of this title, and then only to the extent of the inconsistency.

EFFECTIVE DATE

SEC. 602. Section 504 of the consumer Credit Protection Act is amended by adding at the end thereof the following new subsection:

> (d) Title VI takes effect upon the expiration of one hundred and eighty days following the date of enactment.

Approved October 26, 1970.

LEGISLATIVE HISTORY:

HOUSE REPORTS: No. 91-975 (Comm. on Banking and Currency) and
No. 91-1587 (Comm. of Conference).

SENATE REPORTS: No. 91-1139 accompanying S. 3678 (Comm. on Banking and Currency).

CONGRESSIONAL RECORD, Vol. 116 (1970):
May 25, considered and passed House.
Sept. 18, considered and passed Senate, amended.
Oct. 9, Senate agreed to conference report.
Oct. 13, House agreed to conference report.

ENACTMENT: Public Law No.   91-508 (October 26, 1970)

AMENDMENTS: Public Law Nos.   95-473 (October 17, 1978)
95-598 (November 6, 1978)
98-443 (October 4, 1984)
101-73 (August 9, 1989)
102-242 (December 19, 1991)
102-537 (October 27, 1992)
102-550 (October 28, 1992)
103-325 (September 23, 1994)

Appendix B

Federal Trade Commission Offices

FTC Headquarters

6th & Pennsylvania Ave., N.W.
Washington, DC 20580
202-326-2222
TDD 202-326-2502

FTC Regional Offices

1718 Peachtree St., N.W., Ste. 1000
Atlanta, GA 30367
404-347-4836

10 Causeway St., Ste. 1184
Boston, MA 02222-1073
617-565-7240

55 E. Monroe St., Ste. 1437
Chicago, IL 60603
312-353-4423

118 Saint Clair Avenue
Cleveland, OH 44114
216-522-4210

8303 Elmbrook Drive
Dallas, TX 75247
214-767-7050

1405 Curtis St., Ste. 2900
Denver, CO 80202-2393
303-844-2271

11000 Wilshire Blvd., Ste. 13209
Los Angeles, CA 90024
213-209-7890

26 Federal Plaza
New York, NY 10278
212-264-1207

901 Market St., Ste. 570
San Francisco, CA 94103
415-995-5220

2806 Federal Bldg.
915 Second Ave.
Seattle, WA 98174
206-422-4655

Appendix C

State and Local Consumer Protection Agencies

Usually the government agencies most responsive to our needs are those at the local and state levels. These agencies have a better understanding of the needs of the people in their area. Following is a list of the state and local government protection agencies that can provide the assistance you need to understand your rights and help you enforce them.

Alabama

State Offices

Consumer Affairs Division
Office of Attorney General
11 S. Union St.
Montgomery, AL 36130
205-242-7334
800-392-5658 (toll-free in AL)

Alaska

The Consumer Protection Section in the Office of the Attorney General has been closed. Consumers with complaints are being referred to the Better Business Bureau, small claims court and private attorneys.

Arizona

State Offices

Consumer Protection
Office of the Attorney General
1275 W. Washington St., Rm. 259
Phoenix, AZ 85007
602-542-3702
602-542-5763 (consumer information and complaints)
800-352-8431 (toll-free in AZ)

Assistant Attorney General
Consumer Protection
Office of the Attorney General
402 W. Congress St., Ste. 315
Tucson, AZ 85701
602-628-6504

County Offices

Apache County Attorney's Office
PO Box 637
St. Johns, AZ 85936
602-337-4364, ext. 240

Cochise County Attorney's Office
PO Drawer CA
Bisbee, AZ 85603
602-432-9377

Coconino County Attorney's Office
Coconino County Courthouse
100 E. Birch
Flagstaff, AZ 86001
602-779-6518

Gila County Attorney's Office
1400 E. Ash St.
Globe, AZ 85501
602-425-3231

Graham County Attorney's Office
Graham County Courthouse
800 W. Main
Safford, AZ 85546
602-428-3620

Greenlee County Attorney's Office
PO Box 1717
Clifton, AZ 85533
602-865-4108

LaPaz County Attorney's Office
1200 Arizona Ave.
PO Box 709
Parker, AZ 85344
602-669-6118

Mohave County Attorney's Office
315 N. 4th St.
PO Box 7000
Kingman, AZ 86402-7000
602-753-0719

Navajo County Attorney's Office
P.O. Box 668
Holbrook, AZ 86025
602-524-6161, ext. 303

Pima County Attorney's Office
1400 Great American Tower
32 N. Stone
Tucson, AZ 85701
602-740-5733

Pinal County Attorney's Office
PO Box 887
Florence, AZ 85232
602-868-6271

Santa Cruz County Attorney's Office
2100 N. Congress Dr., Ste. 201
Nogales, AZ 85621
602-281-4966

Yavapai County Attorney's Office
Yavapai County Courthouse
Prescott, AZ 86301
602-771-3344

Yuma County Attorney's Office
168 S. Second Ave.
Yuma, AZ 85364
602-329-2270

City Office

Supervising Attorney
Consumer Affairs Division
Tucson City Attorney's Office
110 E. Pennington St., 2nd Fl.
PO Box 27210
Tucson, AZ 85726-7210
602-791-4886

Arkansas

State Office

Director, Consumer Protection Division
Office of Attorney General
200 Tower Building
323 Center St.
Little Rock, AR 72201
501-682-2341 (voice/TDD)
800-482-8982 (toll-free voice/TDD in AR)

California

State Offices

Director, Calif. Dept. of Consumer Affairs
400 R St., Ste. 1040
Sacramento, CA 95814
916-445-1254 (consumer information)
916-522-1700 (TDD)
800-344-9940 (toll-free in CA)

Bureau of Automotive Repair
Calif. Dept. of Consumer Affairs
10240 Systems Pkwy.
Sacramento, CA 95827
916-255-4300
800-952-5210 (toll-free in CA, auto repair only)

Office of Attorney General
Public Inquiry Unit
PO Box 944255
Sacramento, CA 94244-2550
916-322-3360
800-952-5225 (toll-free in CA)
800-952-5548 (toll-free TDD in CA)

County Offices

Coordinator, Alameda County Consumer Affairs Commission
4400 MacArthur Blvd.
Oakland, CA 94619
510-530-8682

District Attorney
Contra Costa County
District Attorney's Office
725 Court St., 4th Fl.
PO Box 670
Martinez, CA 94553
510-646-4500

Senior Deputy District Attorney
Business Affairs Unit
Fresno County District Attorney's Office
2220 Tulare St., Ste. 1000
Fresno, CA 93721
209-488-3156

District Attorney
Civil Section
Kern County District Attorney's Office
1215 Truxtun Ave.
Bakersfield, CA 93301
805-861-2421

Director, Los Angeles County Dept. of Consumer Affairs
500 W. Temple St., Rm. B-96
Los Angeles, CA 90012
213-974-1452 (Public)

Director, Citizens Service Office
Marin County Mediation Services
Marin County Civic Center, Rm. 278
San Rafael, CA 94903
415-499-7454

District Attorney
Marin County District Attorney's Office
Hall of Justice, Rm. 183
San Rafael, CA 94903
415-499-6482

Deputy District Attorney
Consumer Protection Division
Marin County District Attorney's Office
Hall of Justice, Rm. 183
San Rafael, CA 94903
415-499-6450

District Attorney
Mendocino County District Attorney's Office
PO Box 1000
Ukiah, CA 95482
707-463-4211

Coordinator, Monterey County Office of Consumer Affairs
PO Box 1369
Salinas, CA 93902
408-755-5073

Deputy District Attorney
Consumer Affairs Division
Napa County District Attorney's Office
931 Parkway Mall
PO Box 720
Napa, CA 94559
707-253-4211

Deputy District Attorney in Charge
Consumer/Environmental Protection Unit
Orange County District Attorney's Office
405 West 5th Street, Suite 606
Santa Ana, CA 92701
714-568-1240
92702
714-541-7600

Deputy District Attorney
Economic Crime Division
Riverside County District Attorney's Office
4075 Main St.
Riverside, CA 92501
714-275-5400

Supervising Deputy District Attorney
Consumer and Environmental Protection Division
Sacramento County District Attorney's Office
PO Box 749
Sacramento, CA 95812-0749
916-440-6174

Director, Consumer Fraud Division
San Diego County District Attorney's Office
PO Box X-1011
San Diego, CA 92112-4192
619-531-3507 (fraud complaint line)

Attorney, Consumer and Environmental Protection Unit
San Francisco County District Attorney's Office
732 Brannan St.
San Francisco, CA 94103
415-552-6400 (public inquiries)
415-553-1814 (complaints)

Deputy District Attorney
Mediator
San Joaquin County District Attorney's Office
222 E. Weber, Rm. 412
PO Box 990
Stockton, CA 95202
209-468-2481

Director, Economic Crime Unit
Consumer Fraud Dept.
County Government Center
1050 Monterey St., Rm. 235
San Luis Obispo, CA 93408
805-781-5856

Deputy in Charge
Consumer Fraud and Environmental Protection Unit
San Mateo County District Attorney's Office
401 Marshall St.
Hall of Justice and Records
Redwood City, CA 94063
415-363-4656

Deputy District Attorney
Consumer Protection Unit
Santa Barbara County District Attorney's Office
1105 Santa Barbara St.
Santa Barbara, CA 93101
805-568-2300

Deputy District Attorney
Consumer Fraud Unit
Santa Clara County District Attorney's Office
70 W. Hedding St., West Wing
San Jose, CA 95110
408-299-7400

Coordinator, Santa Clara County Dept. of Consumer Affairs
70 West Hedding St., West Wing, Lower level
San Jose, CA 95110-1705
408-299-4211

Coordinators, Division of Consumer Affairs
Santa Cruz County District Attorney's Office
701 Ocean St., Rm. 200
Santa Cruz, CA 95060
408-425-2050

Deputy District Attorney
Consumer Affairs Unit
Solano County District Attorney's Office
600 Union Ave.
Fairfield, CA 94533
707-421-6860

Deputy District Attorney
Consumer Fraud Unit
Stanislaus County District Attorney's Office
PO Box 442
Modesto, CA 95353-0442
209-571-5550

Deputy District Attorney
Consumer and Environmental Protection Division
Ventura County District Attorney's Office
800 S. Victoria Ave.
Ventura, CA 93009
805-654-3110

Supervising Deputy District Attorney
Special Services Unit—Consumer/ Environmental
Yolo County District Attorney's Office
PO Box 245
Woodland, CA 95776
916-666-8424

City Offices

Supervising Deputy City Attorney
Consumer Protection Division
Los Angeles City Attorney's Office
200 N. Main St.
1600 City Hall East
Los Angeles, CA 90012
213-485-4515

Consumer Affairs Specialist
Consumer Protection, Fair Housing and Public Rights Unit
1685 Main St., Rm. 310
Santa Monica, CA 90401
310-458-8336

Colorado

State Offices

Consumer Protection Unit
Office of Attorney General
1525 Sherman St., 5th Floor
Denver, CO 80203
303-866-5189

Consumer and Food Specialist
Dept. of Agriculture
700 Kipling St., Ste. 4000
Lakewood, CO 80215-5894
303-239-4114

County Offices

District Attorney
Archuleta, LaPlata and San Juan Counties
District Attorney's Office
PO Drawer 3455
Durango, CO 81302
303-247-8850

District Attorney
Boulder County District Attorney's Office
PO Box 471
Boulder, CO 80306
303-441-3700

Executive Director
Denver District Attorney's Consumer Fraud
Office
303 W. Colfax Ave., Ste. 1300
Denver, CO 80204
303-640-3555 (inquiries)
303-640-3557 (complaints)

Chief Deputy District Attorney
Economic Crime Division
El Paso and Teller Counties District Attorney's
Office
326 S. Tejon
Colorado Springs, CO 80903-2083
719-520-6002

District Attorney
Pueblo County District Attorney's Office
Courthouse
215 W. Tenth St.
Pueblo, CO 81003
719-546-6030

District Attorney
Weld County District Attorney's Consumer
Office
PO Box 1167
Greeley, CO 80632
303-356-4010

Connecticut

State Offices

Commissioner
Dept. of Consumer Protection
State Office Building
165 Capitol Ave.
Hartford, CT 06106
203-566-2534
800-842-2649 (toll-free in CT)

Assistant Attorney General
Antitrust/Consumer Protection
Office of Attorney General
110 Sherman St.
Hartford, CT 06015
203-566-5374

City Office

Director, Middletown Office of Consumer Protection
City Hall
Middletown, CT 06457
203-344-3492

Delaware

State Offices

Director, Division of Consumer Affairs
Dept. of Community Affairs
820 N. French St., 4th Fl.
Wilmington, DE 19801
302-577-2500

Deputy Attorney General for Economic Crime and Consumer Protection
Office of Attorney General
820 N. French St.
Wilmington, DE 19801
302-577-3250

District of Columbia

Director, Dept. of Consumer and Regulatory Affairs
614 H St., N.W.
Washington, DC 20001
202-727-7120

Florida

State Offices

Director, Dept. of Agriculture and Consumer Services
Division of Consumer Services
407 South Calhoun Street
Mayo Bldg., 2nd Floor
Tallahassee, FL 32399-0800
904-488-2221
800-435-7352 (toll-free in FL)

Chief, Consumer Litigation Section
4000 Holywood Blvd.,
Ste 505-South
Hollywood, FL 33021
305-985-4780

Bureau Chief, Consumer Division
Office of Attorney General
4000 Hollywood Blvd.
Ste. 505-South
Hollywood, FL 33021
305-985-4780

County Offices

Director, Broward County Consumer Affairs Division
201 S. Andrews Ave., Ste. 201
Fort Lauderdale, FL 33301
305-765-5355

Consumer Advocate
Metropolitan Dade County
Consumer Protection Division
140 W. Flagler St., Ste. 902
Miami, FL 33130
305-375-4222

Chief, Dade County Economic Crime Unit
Office of State Attorney
1350 N.W. 12th Ave., 5th Floor
Graham Building
Miami, FL 33136
305-547-0671

Director, Hillsborough Commerce Department
Office of Consumer Affairs
P.O. Box 1110
Tampa, FL 33601
813-272-6750

Chief, Orange County Consumer Fraud Unit
250 N. Orange Ave.
PO Box 1673
Orlando, FL 32802
407-836-2490

Citizens Intake
Office of State Attorney
401 N. Dixie Highway, Ste. 1600
West Palm Beach, FL 33401
407-355-7108

Director, Palm Beach County Division of Consumer Affairs
3111 S. Dixie Hwy., Ste. 128
West Palm Beach, FL 33405
407-355-2670

Administrator, Pasco County Consumer Affairs Division
7530 Little Rd.
New Port Richey, FL 34654
813-847-8110

Director, Pinellas County Office of Consumer Affairs
PO Box 17268
Clearwater, FL 34622-0268
813-464-6200

City Offices

Chief of Consumer Affairs
City of Jacksonville
Division of Consumer Affairs
421 W. Church St., Ste. 404
Jacksonville, FL 32202
904-630-3667

Chairperson Lauderhill Consumer Protection Board
1176 N.W. 42nd Way
Lauderhill, FL 33313
305-321-2456

Chairman, Tamarac Board of Consumer Affairs
7525 N.W. 88th Ave.
Tamarac, FL 33321
305-722-5900, ext. 389
(Monday-Thursday—10 AM to Noon)

Georgia

State Office

Administrator
Governor's Office of Consumer Affairs
2 Martin Luther King, Jr. Dr., S.E.
Plaza Level—East Tower
Atlanta, GA 30334
404-651-8600
404-658-3790
800-869-1123 (toll-free in GA)

Hawaii

State Offices

Director, Office of Consumer Protection
Dept. of Commerce and Consumer Affairs
828 Fort St. Mall, Ste. 600B
PO Box 3767
Honolulu, HI 96812-3767
808-586-2636

Investigator, Office of Consumer Protection
Dept. of Commerce and Consumer Affairs
75 Aupuni St.
Hilo, HI 96720
808-933-4433

Investigator, Office of Consumer Protection
Dept. of Commerce and Consumer Affairs
3060 Eiwa St.
Lihue, HI 96766
808-241-3365

Investigator, Office of Consumer Protection
Dept. of Commerce and Consumer Affairs
54 High St.
Wailuku, HI 96793
808-243-5387

Idaho

State Office

Deputy Attorney General
Office of the Attorney General
Consumer Protection Unit
Statehouse, Rm. 119
Boise, ID 83720-1000
208-334-2424
800-432-3545 (toll-free in ID)

Illinois

State Offices

Director, Governor's Office of Citizens Assistance
222 S. College
Springfield, IL 62706
217-782-0244
800-642-3112

Chief, Consumer Protection Division
Office of Attorney General
100 W. Randolph, 12th Fl.
Chicago, IL 60601
312-814-3580
312-793-2852 (TDD)

Director, Dept. of Citizen Rights
100 W. Randolph, 13th Fl.
Chicago, IL 60601
312-814-3289
312-814-3374 (TDD)

Regional Offices

Assistant Attorney General
Carbondale Regional Office
Office of Attorney General
626A E. Walnut St.
Carbondale, IL 62901
618-457-3505
618-457-4421 (TDD)

Assistant Attorney General
Champaign Regional Office
34 E. Main St.
Champaign, IL 61820
217-333-7691 (voice/TDD)

Assistant Attorney General
East St. Louis Regional Office
Office of Attorney General
8712 State St.
East St. Louis, IL 62203
618-398-1006
618-398-1009 (TDD)

Assistant Attorney General
Granite City Regional Office
Office of Attorney General
1314 Niedringhaus
Granite City, IL 62040
618-877-0404

Assistant Attorney General
Kankakee Regional Office
Office of Attorney General
1012 N. 5th Ave.
Kankakee, IL 60901
815-935-8500

Assistant Attorney General
LaSalle Regional Office
Office of Attorney General
1222 Shooting Park Rd., Ste. 106
Peru, IL 61354
815-224-4861
815-224-4864 (TDD)

Mt. Vernon Regional Office
Office of Attorney General
3405 Broadway
Mt. Vernon, IL 62864
618-242-8200 (voice/TDD)

Assistant Attorney General
Peoria Regional Office
Office of Attorney General
323 Main St.
Peoria, IL 61602
309-671-3191
309-671-3089 (TDD)

Quincy Regional Office
Office of Attorney General
523 Main St.
Quincy, IL 62301
217-223-2221 (voice/TDD)

Director, Assistant Attorney General
Rockford Regional Office
Office of Attorney General
119 N. Church St.
Rockford, IL 61101
815-987-7580
815-987-7579 (TDD)

Assistant Attorney General
Rock Island Regional Office
Office of Attorney General
1710 3rd Ave.
Rock Island, IL 61201
309-793-0950
309-793-0953 (TDD)

Assistant Attorney General and Chief
Consumer Protection Division
Office of Attorney General
500 S. Second St.
Springfield, IL 62706
217-782-9020
800-252-8666 (toll-free in IL)

Assistant Attorney General
Waukegan Regional Office
Office of Attorney General
12 S. County St.
Waukegan, IL 60085
708-336-2207
708-336-2374 (TDD)

Assistant Attorney General
West Frankfort Regional Office
Office of Attorney General
607 W. Oak Street
West Frankfort, IL 62896
618-937-6421

Assistant Attorney General
Dupage Regional Office
Office of Attorney General
122A County Farm Rd.
Wheaton, IL 60187
708-653-5060 (voice/TDD)

County Offices

Supervisor, Consumer Fraud Division-303
Cook County Office of State's Attorney
303 Daley Center
Chicago, IL 60602
312-443-4600

State's Attorney
Madison County Office of State's Attorney
157 N. Main, Ste. 402
Edwardsville, IL 62025
618-692-6280

City Offices

Commissioner, Chicago Dept. of Consumer Services
121 N. LaSalle St., Rm. 808
Chicago, IL 60602
312-744-4006
312-744-9385 (TDD)

Administrator, Des Plaines Consumer Protection Commission
1420 Miner St., Room 502
Des Plaines, IL 60016
708-391-5363

Indiana

State Office

Chief Counsel and Director
Consumer Protection Division
Office of Attorney General
219 State House
Indianapolis, IN 46204
317-232-6330
800-382-5516 (toll-free in IN)

County Offices

Director, Consumer Protection Division
Lake County Police Dept.
2293 N. Main St.
Crown Point, IN 46307
219-755-3353

Marion County Prosecuting Attorney
560 City-County Building
200 E. Washington St.
Indianapolis, IN 46204-3363
317-236-3522

Vanderburgh County Prosecuting Attorney
108 Administration Building
Civic Center Complex
Evansville, IN 47708
812-426-5150

City Office

Director, Gary Office of Consumer Affairs
Annex E.
1100 Massachusetts St.
Gary, IN 46407
219-886-0145

Iowa

State Office

Assistant Attorney General
Consumer Protection Division
Office of Attorney General
1300 E. Walnut St., 2nd Fl.
Des Moines, IA 50319
515-281-5926

Kansas

State Office

Deputy Attorney General
Consumer Protection Division
Office of Attorney General
301 W. 10th
Kansas Judicial Center
Topeka, KS 66612-1597
913-296-3751
800-432-2310 (toll-free in KS)

County Offices

Head, Consumer Fraud Division
Johnson County District Attorney's Office
Johnson County Courthouse
PO Box 728
Olathe, KS 66051
913-764-8484, ext. 5318

Chief Attorney
Consumer Fraud and Economic Crime Division
Sedgwick County District Attorney's Office
Sedgwick County Courthouse
Wichita, KS 67203
316-266-7921

Assistant District Attorney
Shawnee County District Attorney's Office
Shawnee County Courthouse, Rm. 212
Topeka, KS 66603-3922
913-291-4330

City Office

Assistant City Attorney
Topeka Consumer Protection Division
City Attorney's Office
215 E. Seventh St.
Topeka, KS 66603
913-295-3883

Kentucky

State Offices

Director, Consumer Protection Division
Office of Attorney General
209 Saint Clair St.
Frankfort, KY 40601-1875
502-564-2200
800-432-9257 (toll-free in KY)

Administrator, Consumer Protection Division
Office of Attorney General
107 S. 4th St.
Louisville, KY 40202
502-588-3262
800-432-9257 (toll-free in KY)

Louisiana

State Office

Chief, Consumer Protection Section
Office of Attorney General
State Capitol Building
PO Box 94095
Baton Rouge, LA 70804-9095
504-342-9368

County Office

Chief, Consumer Protection Division
Jefferson Parish District Attorney's Office
5th Floor, Gretna Courthouse Annex
Gretna, LA 70053
504-364-3644

Maine

State Offices

Superintendent, Bureau of Consumer Credit Protection
State House Station No. 35
Augusta, ME 04333-0035
207-582-8718
800-332-8529 (toll-free in ME)

Chief, Consumer and Antitrust Division
Office of Attorney General
State House Station No. 6
Augusta, ME 04333
207-626-8849 (9 AM–1 PM)

Maryland

State Offices

Chief, Consumer Protection Division
Office of Attorney General
200 St. Paul Pl.
Baltimore, MD 21202-2021
410-528-8662 (9 AM–3 PM)
410-576-6372 (TDD in Baltimore area

Director, Licensing & Consumer Services
Motor Vehicle Administration
6601 Ritchie Hwy., N.E.
Glen Burnie, MD 21062
301-768-7420

Consumer Affairs Specialist
Eastern Shore Branch Office
Consumer Protection Division
Office of Attorney General
201 Baptist St., Ste. 30
Salisbury, MD 21801-4976
410-543-6620

Director, Western Maryland Branch Office
Consumer Protection Division
Office of Attorney General
138 E. Antietam St., Ste. 210
Hagerstown, MD 21740-5684
301-791-4780

County Offices

Administrator, Howard County Office of Consumer Affairs
9250 Rumsey Rd.
Columbia, MD 21045
410-313-7220
410-313-2323 (TDD)

Executive Director
Prince George's County Office of Citizen and Consumer Affairs
County Administration Bldg., Ste. L15
Upper Marlboro, MD 20772
301-952-4700
301-925-5167 (TDD)

Massachusetts

State Offices

Chief, Consumer Protection Division
Dept. of Attorney General
1 Ashburton Place
Boston, MA 02103
617-727-8400
(information and referral to local consumer
offices that work in conjunction with the
Dept. of Attorney General)

*Secretary, Executive Office of Consumer
Affairs and Business Regulation*
One Ashburton Place, Rm. 1411
Boston, MA 02108
617-727-7780
(information and referral only)

*Assistant Attorney, Western Massachusetts
Consumer Protection Division*
Dept. of Attorney General
436 Dwight St.
Springfield, MA 01103
413-784-1240

County Offices

Division Manager
Consumer Fraud Prevention
Franklin County District Attorney's Office
238 Main St.
Greenfield, MA 01301
413-774-5102

Director, Consumer Fraud Prevention
Hampshire County District Attorney's Office
1 Court Square
Northhampton, MA 01060
413-586-9225

Director
Consumer Council of Worcester County
484 Main St., 2nd Floor
Worcester, MA 01608
508-754-1176 (9:30 AM–4 PM)

City Offices

*Commissioner, Mayor's Office of Consumer
Affairs and Licensing*
Boston City Hall, Rm. 613
Boston, MA 02201
617-635-4165

Director, Consumer Information Center
Springfield Action Commission
PO Box 1449 Main Office
Springfield, MA 01101
413-737-4376
(Hampton and Hampshire Counties)

Michigan

State Offices

Assistant in Charge
Consumer Protection Division
Office of Attorney General
PO Box 30213
Lansing, MI 48909
517-373-1140

Director
Bureau of Automotive Regulation
Michigan Dept. of State
Lansing, MI 48918-1200
517-373-4777
800-292-4204 (toll-free in MI)

County Offices

Chief Investigator
Bay County Consumer Protection Unit
Bay County Building
Bay City, MI 48708-5994
517-895-4139

Director, Consumer Protection Dept.
Macomb County
Office of the Prosecuting Attorney
Macomb Court Building, 6th Fl.
Mt. Clemens, MI 48043
313-469-5350

*Director, Washtenaw County Consumer
Services*
4133 Washtenaw St.
PO Box 8645
Ann Arbor, MI 48107-8645
313-971-6054

City Office

Director, City of Detroit
Dept. of Consumer Affairs
1600 Cadillac Tower
Detroit, MI 48226
313-224-3508

Minnesota

State Offices

Director, Consumer Services Division
Office of Attorney General
1400 NCL Tower, 445 Minnesota St.
St. Paul, MN 55101
612-296-3353

County Office

Citizen Protection Unit
Hennepin County Attorney's Office
C-2000 County Government Center
Minneapolis, MN 55487
612-348-4528

City Office

Director
Minneapolis Dept. of Licenses & Consumer
Services
One C City Hall
Minneapolis, MN 55415
612-673-2080

Mississippi

State Offices

Special Assistant Attorney General
Director, Office of Consumer Protection
PO Box 22947
Jackson, MS 39225-2947
601-354-6018

Director, Bureau of Regulatory Services
Dept. of Agriculture and Commerce
500 Greymont Ave.
PO Box 1609-1609
Jackson, MS 39215
601-354-7063

Missouri

State Offices

Office of the Attorney General
Division of Consumer Protection
PO Box 899
Jefferson City, MO 65102
314-751-3321
800-392-8222 (toll-free in MO)

Chief Counsel, Consumer Protection
Office of Attorney General
PO Box 899
Jefferson City, MO 65102
314-751-3321
800-392-8222 (toll-free in MO)

Montana

State Office

Consumer Affairs Unit
Dept. of Commerce
1424 Ninth Ave.
Box 200501
Helena, MT 59620-0501
406-444-4312

Nebraska

State Office

Assistant Attorney General
Consumer Protection Division
Dept. of Justice
2115 State Capitol
PO Box 98920
Lincoln, NE 68509
402-471-2682

Nevada

State Offices

Commissioner of Consumer Affairs
Dept. of Commerce
State Mail Rm. Complex
Las Vegas, NV 89158
702-486-7355
800-992-0900 (toll-free in NV)

Consumer Services Officer
Consumer Affairs Division
Dept. of Commerce
4600 Kietzke Lane, B-113
Reno, NV 89502
702-688-1800
800-992-0900 (toll-free in NV)

County Office

Investigator, Consumer Fraud Division
Washoe County District Attorney's Office
PO Box 11130
Reno, NV 89520
702-328-3456

New Hampshire

State Office

Chief, Consumer Protection and Antitrust Bureau
Office of Attorney General
State House Annex
Concord, NH 03301
603-271-3641

New Jersey

State Offices

Director, Division of Consumer Affairs
124 Halsey St.
PO Box 45027
Newark, NJ 07101
201-504-6534

Deputy Attorney General
New Jersey Division of Law
124 Halsey St., 5th Floor
PO Box 45029
Newark, NJ 07101
201-648-7579

County Offices

Director, Atlantic County Consumer Affairs
1333 Atlantic Ave., 8th Fl.
Atlantic City, NJ 08401
609-345-6700

Director, Bergen County Division of Consumer Affairs
21 Main St., Rm. 101-E
Hackensack, NJ 07601-7000
201-646-2650

Director, Burlington County Office of Consumer Affairs
49 Rancocas Rd.
Mount Holly, NJ 08060
609-265-5054

Director, Camden County Office of Consumer Affairs
1800 E. Davis St., Ste. 315
Camden, NJ 08104
609-757-8397

Director, Cape May County Consumer Affairs
4 Moore Road
Cape May Court House, NJ 08210
609-889-0440

Director, Cumberland County Dept. of Consumer Affairs and Weights and Measures
788 E. Commerce St.
Bridgeton, NJ 08302
609-453-2203

Director, Essex County Consumer Services
15 South Munn Ave., 2nd Fl.
E. Orange, NJ 07018
201-678-8071
201-678-8928

Director, Gloucester County Dept. of Consumer Protection/Weights & Measures
152 N. Broad. St.
Woodbury, NJ 08096
609-853-3349
609-848-6616 (TDD)

Director, Hudson County Division of Consumer Affairs
595 Newark Ave.
Jersey City, NJ 07306
201-795-6295

Director, Hunterdon County Consumer Affairs
PO Box 283
Lebanon, NJ 08833
908-236-2249

Division Chief
Mercer County Consumer Affairs
640 S. Broad. St., Rm. 229
PO Box 8068
Trenton, NJ 08650-0068
609-989-6671

Director, Middlesex County Consumer Affairs
10 Corporate Place South
Piscataway, NJ 08854
908-463-6000

Director, Monmouth County Consumer Affairs
50 E. Main St.
PO Box 1255
Freehold, NJ 07728-1255
908-431-7900

Director, Ocean County Consumer Affairs
PO Box 2191
County Administration Building, Rm. 107-1
Toms River, NJ 08754-2191
908-929-2105

Director, Passaic County Consumer Affairs
County Administration Building
309 Pennsylvania Ave.
Paterson, NJ 07503
201-881-4547, 4499

Somerset County Consumer Affairs
County Administration Building
PO Box 3000
Somerville, NJ 08876
908-231-7000, ext. 7400

Director, Union County Consumer Affairs
300 North. Ave. East.
PO Box 186
Westfield, NJ 07091
201-654-9840

Director, Warren County Consumer Affairs
Dumont Administration Bldg., Route 519
Belvedere, NJ 07823
908-475-6500

City Offices

Director, Brick Consumer Affairs
Municipal Building
401 Chambers Bridge Rd.
Brick, NJ 08723
908-262-1033

Director, Cinnaminson Consumer Affairs
Municipal Building
1621 Riverton Rd.
Cinnaminson, NJ 08077
609-829-6000

Director, Clark Consumer Affairs
430 Westfield Ave.
Clark, NJ 07066
908-388-3600

Director, Elizabeth Consumer Affairs
City Hall
50-60 W. Scott Plaza
Elizabeth, NJ 07201
908-820-4183

Director, Fort Lee Consumer Protection Board
Borough Hall
309 Main St.
Fort Lee, NJ 07024
201-592-3654

Director, Franklin Consumer Affairs
David Herzenberg Dr.
P.O. Box 254
Franklin, NJ 07416
201-827-4450

Consumer Advocate
City Hall
94 Washington St.
Hoboken, NJ 07030
201-420-2038

Director, Livingston Consumer Affairs
357 S. Livingston Ave.
Livingston, NJ 07039
201-535-7976

Director, Maywood Consumer Affairs
459 Maywood Ave.
Maywood, NJ 07607
201-845-2900
201-845-7822

Director, Middlesex Borough Consumer Affairs
1200 Mountain Ave.
Middlesex, NJ 08846
908-356-8090

Director, Mountainside Consumer Affairs
1455 Coles Ave.
Mountainside, NJ 07092
908-232-6600

Deputy Mayor, Director Consumer Affairs
Municipal Building
N. Bergen, NJ 07047
201-330-7291; 201-330-7292

Director, Nutley Consumer Affairs
Public Safety Building
228 Chestnut St.
Nutley, NJ 07110
201-284-4936

Director, Parsippany Consumer Affairs
Municipal Building, Rm. 101
1001 Parsippany Blvd.
Parsippany, NJ 07054
201-263-7011

Director, Perth Amboy Public Information
City Hall
1 Olive St.
Perth Amboy, NJ 08861
908-826-1690, ext. 16, 17

Director, Plainfield Action Services
510 Watchtung Ave.
Plainfield, NJ 07060
908-753-3519

Director, Secaucus Dept. of Consumer Affairs
Municipal Government Center
Secaucus, NJ 07094
201-330-2019

Director, Union Township Consumer Affairs
Municipal Building
1976 Morris Ave.
Union, NJ 07083
908-688-6763

Director, Wayne Township Consumer Affairs
475 Valley Rd.
Wayne, NJ 07470
201-694-1800, ext. 3290

Director, Weehawken Consumer Affairs
400 Park Ave.
Weehawken, NJ 07087
201-319-6005

Director, W. New York Consumer Affairs
428 60th St.
West New York, NJ 07093
201-861-2522

Woodbridge Consumer Affairs
Municipal Building
One Main Street
Woodbridge, NJ 07095
908-634-4500, ext. 2697

New Mexico

State Office

Consumer Protection Division
Office of Attorney General
PO Drawer 1508
Santa Fe, NM 87504
505-827-6060
800-678-1508 (toll-free in NM)

New York

State Offices

Chairperson and Executive Director
New York State Consumer Protection Board
99 Washington Ave.
Albany, NY 12210-2891
518-474-8583

Assistant Attorney General
Bureau of Consumer Frauds and Protection
Office of Attorney General
State Capitol
Albany, NY 12224
518-474-5481

Chairperson and Executive Director
New York State Consumer Protection Board
250 Broadway, 17th Fl.
New York, NY 10007-2593
212-417-4908 (complaints)
212-417-4482 (main office)

Assistant Attorney General
Bureau of Consumer Frauds and Protection
Office of Attorney General
120 Broadway
New York, NY 10271
212-416-8345

Regional Offices

Assistant Attorney General in Charge
Binghamton Regional Office
Office of Attorney General
59-61 Court St., 7th Fl.
Binghamton, NY 13901
607-762-1013

Assistant Attorney General in Charge
Buffalo Regional Office
Office of Attorney General
65 Court St.
Buffalo, NY 14202
716-847-7184

Assistant Attorney General in Charge
Plattsburgh Regional Office
Office of Attorney General
70 Clinton St.
Plattsburgh, NY 12901
518-563-8012

Assistant Attorney General in Charge
Poughkeepsie Regional Office
Office of Attorney General
235 Main St.
Poughkeepsie, NY 12601
914-485-3920

Assistant Attorney General in Charge
Rochester Regional Office
Office of Attorney General
144 Exchange Blvd.
Rochester, NY 14614
716-546-7430

Assistant Attorney General in Charge
Suffolk Regional Office
Office of Attorney General
300 Motor Pkwy.
Hauppauge, NY 11788
516-231-2400

Assistant Attorney General in Charge
Syracuse Regional Office
Office of Attorney General
615 Erie Blvd. West
Syracuse, NY 13204-2465
315-448-4848

Assistant Attorney General in Charge
Utica Regional Office
Office of Attorney General
207 Genesee St.
Utica, NY 13501
315-793-2225

County Offices

Director of Consumer Affairs
Broome County Bureau of Consumer Affairs
Governmental Plaza, PO Box 1766
Binghamton, NY 13902
607-778-2168

*Director, Dutchess County Dept. of
Consumer Affairs*
38-A Dutchess Turnpike
Poughkeepsie, NY 12603
914-471-6322

Assistant District Attorney
Consumer Fraud Bureau
Erie County District Attorney's Office
25 Delaware Ave.
Buffalo, NY 14202
716-858-2424

*Commissioner, Nassau County Office of
Consumer Affairs*
160 Old Country Rd.
Mineola, NY 11501
516-535-2600

Executive Director
New Justice Conflict Resolution Services Inc.
210 E. Fayette St., Ste. 700
Syracuse, NY 13202
315-471-4676

*Commissioner, Orange County Dept. of
Consumer Affairs and Weights and
Measures*
99 Main St.
Goshen, NY 10924
914-294-5151, ext. 1762

District Attorney
Orange County District Attorney's Office
255 Main St.
County Government Center
Goshen, NY 10924
914-294-5471

Putnam County Office Facility
Dept. of Consumer Affairs
Myrtle Ave.
Mahopac Falls, NY 10542-0368
914-621-2317

Director/Coordinator
Rockland County Office of Consumer
Protection
County Office Building
18 New Hempstead Rd.
New City, NY 10956
914-638-5282

*Director, Steuben County Dept. of Weights,
Measures and Consumer Affairs*
3 E. Pulteney Square
Bath, NY 14810
607-776-9631
607-776-9631, ext. 2101 (voice/TDD)

Commissioner, Suffolk County Dept. of Consumer Affairs
Suffolk County Center
Hauppauge, NY 11788
516-360-4600

Director, Ulster County Consumer Fraud Bureau
285 Wall St.
Kingston, NY 12401
914-339-5680, ext. 240

Chief, Frauds Bureau
Westchester County
District Attorney's Office
111 Grove St.
White Plains, NY 10601
914-285-3303

Director, Westchester County Dept. of Consumer Affairs
Rm. 104, Michaelian Office Building
White Plains, NY 10601
914-285-2155

City Offices

Director, Babylon Consumer Protection Board
Town Hall Office Annex
281 Phelps Lane
N. Babylon, NY 11703
516-422-7636

Town of Colonie Consumer Protection
Memorial Town Hall
Newtonville, NY 12128
518-783-2790

Commissioner, Mt. Vernon Office of Consumer Affairs
City Hall
Mt. Vernon, NY 10550
914-665-2433

Commissioner, New York City Dept. of Consumer Affairs
42 Broadway
New York, NY 10004
212-487-4444

Bronx Neighborhood Office
New York City Dept. of Consumer Affairs
1932 Arthur Ave., Rm. 104-A
Bronx, NY 10457
212-579-6766

Brooklyn Neighborhood Office
New York City Dept. of Consumer Affairs
1360 Fulton St., Rm. 320
Brooklyn, NY 11216
718-636-7092

Director, Queens Neighborhood Office
New York City Dept. of Consumer Affairs
120-55 Queens Blvd., Rm. 301A
Kew Gardens, NY 11424
718-261-2922

Director, Staten Island Neighborhood Office
New York City Dept. of Consumer Affairs
Staten Island Borough Hall, Rm. 422
Staten Island, NY 10301
718-390-5154

Director, City of Oswego Office of Consumer Affairs
City Hall
West Oneida St.
Oswego, NY 13126
315-342-8150

Chairwoman, Ramapo Consumer Protection Board
Ramapo Town Hall
237 Rte. 59
Suffern, NY 10901-5399
914-357-5100

Schenectady Bureau of Consumer Protection
City Hall, Rm. 22
Jay St.
Schenectady, NY 12305
518-382-5061

Director, White Plains Dept. of Weights and Measures
77 S. Lexington Ave.
White Plains, NY 10601-2512
914-422-6359

Director, Yonkers Office of Consumer Protection, Weights and Measures
201 Palisade Ave.
Yonkers, NY 10703
914-377-6807

North Carolina

State Office

Special Deputy Attorney General
Consumer Protection Section
Office of Attorney General
Raney Building
PO Box 629
Raleigh, NC 27602
919-733-7741

North Dakota

State Offices

Office of Attorney General
600 E. Blvd. Ave.
Bismarck, ND 58505
701-224-2210
800-472-2600 (toll-free in ND)

Director, Consumer Fraud Section
Office of Attorney General
600 E. Blvd. Ave.
Bismarck, ND 58505
701-224-3404
800-472-2600 (toll-free in ND)

County Office

Executive Director
Quad County Community Action Agency
27 1/2 S. Third St.
Grand Forks, ND 58201
701-746-5431

Ohio

State Offices

Consumer Frauds and Crimes Section
Office of Attorney General
30 E. Broad. St.
State Office Tower, 25th Fl.
Columbus, OH 43266-0410
614-466-4986 (complaints)
614-466-1393 (TDD)
800-282-0515 (toll-free in OH)

Office of Consumers' Counsel
77 S. High St., 15th Fl.
Columbus, OH 43266-0550
614-466-9605 (voice/TDD)
800-282-9448 (toll-free in OH)

County Offices

Director, Economic Crime Division
Franklin County Office of Prosecuting
Attorney
369 S. High St.
Columbus, OH 43215
614-462-3555

County Prosecutor
Consumer Protection Division
Lake County Office of Prosecuting Attorney
Lake County Court House
Painesville, OH 44077
216-357-2683
800-899-5253 (toll-free in OH)

Assistant Prosecuting Attorney
Montgomery County Fraud Section
301 W. 3rd St.
Dayton Montgomery County
Courts Building
Dayton, OH 45402
513-225-5757

Prosecuting Attorney
Portage County Office of Prosecuting
Attorney
466 S. Chestnut St.
Ravenna, OH 44266-0671
216-296-4593

Prosecuting Attorney
Summit County Office of Prosecuting
Attorney
53 University Ave.
Akron, OH 44308-1680
216-379-2800

City Offices

*Chief, Cincinnati Office of Consumer
Services*
Division of Human Services
City Hall, Rm. 126
Cincinnati, OH 45202
513-352-3971

*Director, Youngstown Office of Consumer
Affairs and Weights and Measures*
26 S. Phelps St.
City Hall
Youngstown, OH 44503-1318
216-742-8884

Oklahoma

State Offices

Assistant Attorney General
Office of Attorney General
420 W. Main, Ste. 550
Oklahoma City, OK 73102
405-521-4274

Administrator, Dept. of Consumer Credit
4545 Lincoln Blvd., Ste. 104
Oklahoma City, OK 73105-3408
405-521-3653

Oregon

State Office

Attorney in Charge
Financial Fraud Section
100 Dept. of Justice
Justice Building
Salem, OR 97310
503-378-4320

Pennsylvania

State Offices

Director, Bureau of Consumer Protection
Office of Attorney General
Strawberry Square, 14th Fl.
Harrisburg, PA 17120
717-787-9707
800-441-2555 (toll-free in PA)

Consumer Advocate
Office of Consumer Advocate-Utilities
Office of Attorney General
1425 Strawberry Square
Harrisburg, PA 17120
717-783-5048 (utilities only)

Deputy Attorney General
Bureau of Consumer Protection
Office of Attorney General
27 N. Seventh St.
Allentown, PA 18101
215-821-6690

Director, Bureau of Consumer Services
Pennsylvania Public Utility Commission
PO Box 3265
203 N. Office Building
Harrisburg, PA 17105-3265
717-787-4970 (out-of-state calls only)
800-782-1110 (toll-free in PA)

Deputy Attorney General
Bureau of Consumer Protection
Office of Attorney General
919 State St., Rm. 203
Erie, PA 16501
814-871-4371

Attorney in Charge
Bureau of Consumer Protection
Office of Attorney General
132 Kline Village
Harrisburg, PA 17104
717-787-7109
800-441-2555 (toll-free in PA)

Deputy Attorney General
Bureau of Consumer Protection
Office of the Attorney General
IGA Building, Rte. 219 N.
PO Box 716
Ebensburg, PA 15931
814-949-7900

Deputy Attorney General
Bureau of Consumer Protection
Office of Attorney General
21 S. 12th St., 2nd Fl.
Philadelphia, PA 19107
215-560-2414
800-441-2555 (toll-free in PA)

Deputy Attorney General
Bureau of Consumer Protection
Office of Attorney General
Manor Complex, 5th Fl.
564 Forbes Ave.
Pittsburgh, PA 15219
412-565-5394

Deputy Attorney General
Bureau of Consumer Protection
Office of Attorney General
State Office Building, Rm. 358
100 Lackawanna Ave.
Scranton, PA 18503
717-963-4913

County Offices

Director, Beaver County Alliance for Consumer Protection
699 Fifth St.
Beaver, PA 15009-1997
412-728-7267

Director/Chief Sealer, Bucks County Consumer Protection, Weights and Measures
50 N. Main
Doylestown, PA 18901
215-348-7442

Director, Chester County Bureau of Consumer Protection, Weights and Measures
Courthouse, 5th Fl., North Wing
High and Market Sts.
Westchester, PA 19380
215-344-6150

Consumer Mediator, Cumberland County Consumer Affairs
One Courthouse Square
Carlisle, PA 17013-3387
717-240-6180

Director, Delaware County Office of Consumer Affairs, Weights and Measures
Government Center Building
Second and Olive Sts.
Media, PA 19063
215-891-4865

Director, Montgomery County Consumer Affairs Dept.
County Courthouse
Norristown, PA 19404
215-278-3565

City Office

Chief, Economic Crime Unit
Philadelphia District Attorney's Office
1421 Arch St.
Philadelphia, PA 19102
215-686-8750

Puerto Rico

Secretary, Dept. of Consumer Affairs (DACO)
Minillas Station, PO Box 41059
Santurce, PR 00940
809-721-0940

Secretary, Dept. of Justice
PO Box 192
San Juan, PR 00902
809-721-2900

Rhode Island

State Offices

Director, Consumer Protection Division
Dept. of Attorney General
72 Pine St.
Providence, RI 02903
401-277-2104
401-274-4400, EXT. 354 (voice/TDD)
800-852-7776 (toll-free in RI)

Executive Director
Rhode Island Consumers' Council
365 Broadway
Providence, RI 02909
401-277-2764

South Carolina

State Offices

Assistant Attorney General
Consumer Fraud and Antitrust Section
Office of Attorney General
PO Box 11549
Columbia, SC 29211
803-734-3970

Administrator, Dept. of Consumer Affairs
PO Box 5757
Columbia, SC 29250-5757
803-734-9452
803-734-9455 (TDD)
800-922-1594 (toll-free in SC)

State Ombudsman
Office of Executive Policy and Program
1205 Pendleton St., Rm. 308
Columbia, SC 29201
803-734-0457
803-734-1147 (TDD)

South Dakota

State Office

Assistant Attorney General
Division of Consumer Affairs
Office of Attorney General
500 E. Capitol
State Capitol Building
Pierre, SD 57501-5070
605-773-4400

Tennessee

State Offices

Deputy Attorney General
Antitrust and Consumer Protection Division
Office of Attorney General
450 James Robertson Pkwy.
Nashville, TN 37243-0485
615-741-2672

Director, Division of Consumer Affairs
Dept. of Commerce and Insurance
500 James Robertson Pkwy., 5th Fl.
Nashville, TN 37243-0600
615-741-4737
800-342-8385 (toll-free in TN)
800-422-CLUB (toll-free health club hotline in TN)

Texas

State Offices

Assistant Attorney General and Chief, Consumer Protection Division
Office of Attorney General
Supreme Court Building
PO Box 12548
Austin, TX 78711
512-463-2070

Assistant Attorney General
Consumer Protection Division
Office of Attorney General
714 Jackson St., Ste. 700
Dallas, TX 75202-4506
214-742-8944

Assistant Attorney General
Consumer Protection Division
Office of Attorney General
6090 Surety Dr., Rm. 260
El Paso, TX 79905
915-772-9476

Assistant Attorney General
Consumer Protection Division
Office of Attorney General
1019 Congress St., Ste. 1550
Houston, TX 77002-1702
713-223-5886

Assistant Attorney General
Consumer Protection Division
Office of Attorney General
1208 14th St., Ste. 900
Lubbock, TX 79401-3997
806-747-5238

Assistant Attorney General
Consumer Protection Division
Office of Attorney General
3600 N. 23rd St., Ste. 305
McAllen, TX 78501-1685
512-682-4547

Assistant Attorney General
Consumer Protection Division
Office of Attorney General
115 E. Travis St., Ste. 925
San Antonio, TX 78205-1607
512-225-4191

Office of Consumer Protection
State Board of Insurance
816 Congress Ave., Ste. 1400
Austin, TX 78701-2430
512-322-4143

County Office

Assistant District Attorney and Chief of Dallas County District Attorney's Office
Specialized Crime Division
133 N. Industrial Blvd., LB 19
Dallas, TX 75207-4313
214-653-3820

Assistant District Attorney and Chief Harris County Consumer Fraud Division
Office of District Attorney
201 Fannin, Ste. 200
Houston, TX 77002-1901
713-221-5836

City Office

Director, Dallas Consumer Protection Division
Health and Human Services Dept.
320 E. Jefferson Blvd., Ste. 312
Dallas, TX 75203
214-948-4400

Utah

State Offices

Director, Division of Consumer Protection
Dept. of Commerce
160 E. 3rd S.
PO Box 45802
Salt Lake City, UT 84145-0802
801-530-6601

Assistant Attorney General for Consumer Affairs
Office of Attorney General
115 State Capitol
Salt Lake City, UT 84114
801-538-1331

Vermont

State Offices

Assistant Attorney General and Chief, Public Protection Division
Office of Attorney General
109 State St.
Montpelier, VT 05609-1001
802-828-3171

Supervisor, Consumer Assurance Section
Dept. of Agriculture, Food and Market
120 State St.
Montpelier, VT 05620-2901
802-828-2436

Virgin Islands

Commissioner, Dept. of Licensing and Consumer Affairs
Consumer Affairs
Property and Procurement Building
Subbase #1, Rm. 205
St. Thomas, VI 00802
809-774-3130

Virginia

State Offices

Chief, Antitrust and Consumer Litigation Section
Office of Attorney General
Supreme Court Building
101 N. Eighth St.
Richmond, VA 23219
804-786-2116
800-451-1525 (toll-free in VA)

Director, Division of Consumer Affairs
Dept. of Agriculture and
Consumer Services
Rm. 101, Washington Building
1100 Bank St.
PO Box 1163
Richmond, VA 23219
804-786-2042

Investigator, Northern Virginia Branch
Office of Consumer Affairs
Dept. of Agriculture and
Consumer Services
100 N. Washington St., Ste. 412
Falls Church, VA 22046
703-532-1613

County Offices

Section Chief, Office of Citizen and Consumer Affairs
#1 Court House Plaza, Ste. 314
2100 Clarendon Blvd.
Arlington, VA 22201
703-358-3260

Director, Fairfax County Dept. of Consumer Affairs
3959 Pender Dr., Ste. 200
Fairfax, VA 22030-6093
703-246-5949
703-591-3260 (TDD)

Administrator, Prince William County Office of Consumer Affairs
4370 Ridgewood Center Dr.
Prince William, VA 22192-9201
703-792-7370

City Offices

Director, Alexandria Office of Citizens' Assistance
City Hall
PO Box 178
Alexandria, VA 22313
703-838-4350
703-838-5056 (TDD)

Coordinator, Division of Consumer Affairs
City Hall
Norfolk, VA 23501
804-441-2821
804-441-2000 (TDD)

Assistant to the City Manager
Roanoke Consumer Protection Division
364 Municipal Building
215 Church Ave., S.W.
Roanoke, VA 24011
703-981-2583

Director, Consumer Affairs Division
Office of the Commonwealth's Attorney
3500 Virginia Beach Blvd., Ste. 304
Virginia Beach, VA 23452
804-431-4610

Washington

State Offices

Investigator, Consumer and Business Fair Practices Division
Office of the Attorney General
111 Olympia Ave., NE
Olympia, WA 98501
206-753-6210

Director of Consumer Services
Consumer and Business Fair Practices Division
Office of the Attorney General
900 Fourth Ave., Ste. 2000
Seattle, WA 98164
206-464-6431
800-551-4636 (toll-free in WA)

Chief, Consumer and Business Fair Practices Division
Office of the Attorney General
W. 1116 Riverside Ave.
Spokane, WA 99201
509-456-3123

Contact Person, Consumer and Business Fair Practices Division
Office of the Attorney General
1019 Pacific Ave., 3rd Fl.
Tacoma, WA 98402-4411
206-593-2904

City Offices

Director, Dept. of Weights and Measures
3200 Cedar St.
Everett, WA 98201
206-259-8810

Chief Deputy Prosecuting Attorney
Fraud Division
1002 Bank of California
900 4th Ave.
Seattle, WA 98164
206-296-9010

Director, Seattle Dept. of Licenses and Consumer Affairs
102 Municipal Building
600 4th Ave.
Seattle, WA 98104-1893
206-684-8484

West Virginia

State Offices

Director, Consumer Protection Division
Office of Attorney General
812 Quarrier St., 6th Fl.
Charleston, WV 25301
304-348-8986
800-368-8808 (toll-free in WV)

Director, Division of Weights and Measures
Dept. of Labor
1800 Washington St., East
Building #3, Rm. 319
Charleston, WV 25305
304-348-7890

City Office

Director, Dept. of Consumer Protection
PO Box 2749
Charleston, WV 25330
304-348-8172

Wisconsin

State Offices

Administrator, Division of Trade and Consumer Protection
Dept. of Agriculture, Trade and Consumer Protection
801 W. Badger Rd.
PO Box 8911
Madison, WI 53708
608-266-9836
800-422-7128 (toll-free in WI)

Regional Supervisor, Division of Trade and Consumer Protection
Dept. of Agriculture, Trade and Consumer Protection
927 Loring St.
Altoona, WI 54720
715-839-3848
800-422-7218 (toll-free in WI)

Regional Supervisor, Division of Trade and Consumer Protection
Dept. of Agriculture, Trade and Consumer Protection
200 N. Jefferson St., Ste. 146A
Green Bay, WI 54301
414-448-5111
800-422-7128 (toll-free in WI)

Regional Supervisor, Consumer Protection Regional Office
Dept. of Agriculture, Trade and Consumer Protection
3333 N. Mayfair RD., Ste. 114
Milwaukee, WI 53222-3288
414-257-8956

Assistant Attorney General
Office of Consumer Protection and Citizen Advocacy
Dept. of Justice
PO Box 7856
Madison, WI 53707-7856
608-266-1852
800-362-8189 (toll-free)

Assistant Attorney General
Office of Consumer Protection
Dept. of Justice
Milwaukee State Office Building
819 N. 6th St., Rm. 520
Milwaukee, WI 53203-1678
414-227-4948
800-362-8189 (toll-free)

County Offices

District Attorney
Marathon County District Attorney's Office
Marathon County Courthouse
Wausau, WI 54401
715-847-5555

Assistant District Attorney
Milwaukee County District Attorney's Office
Consumer Fraud Unit
821 W. State St., Rm. 412
Milwaukee, WI 53233-1485
414-278-4792

Consumer Fraud Investigator
Racine County Sheriff's Dept.
717 Wisconsin Ave.
Racine, WI 53403
414-636-3125

Wyoming

State Office

Assistant Attorney General
Office of Attorney General
123 State Capitol Building
Cheyenne, WY 82002
307-777-7874

Information in this section was taken from the *Consumers' Resource Handbook*, 1992 edition, U.S. Office of Consumer Affairs.

Appendix D

Sample Small Claims Forms

This appendix features small claims court forms for the municipality and county of San Francisco, California. The forms typify small claims court paperwork and are included to help you decide whether to use small claims court. If you wish to bring your case to small claims court, it is a good idea to contact your local small claims court clerk to obtain information on the procedures in your area.

MUNICIPAL COURT OF THE
CITY AND COUNTY OF SAN FRANCISCO
(415) 554-4565

SMALL CLAIMS OFFICE
575 POLK STREET
SAN FRANCISCO, CA 94102
(415) 292-2129

Enclosed you will find forms to file a Small Claims action by mail.

1. **INFORMATION FOR THE SMALL CLAIMS PLAINTIFF (Form SC-150)**
   Please read the entire form. It will explain Small Claims procedures.

2. **SMALL CLAIMS INFORMATION - FEES AND SCHEDULE**

3. **BEFORE FILING A CLAIM IN SMALL CLAIMS COURT**

4. **PLAINTIFF'S CLAIM AND ORDER TO DEFENDANT (Form SC-100)**
   This form must be completely filled out, you may either type or *neatly* print. It must be signed and dated by the party(s) bringing the action. A separate check or money order must be remitted with each claim you file, made payable to "Clerk, Municipal Court". The fee is $15.00 per claim if you have filed less than 12 claims in the 12 months preceding. The fee is $30.00 per claim if you have filed more than 12 claims. Please attach a note indicating first and second choices of the hearing time you prefer: 8:30 am, 10:30 am, 1:30 pm, 3:30 pm, 5:30 pm or 7 pm.

5. **SERVICE BY RETURN RECEIPT MAIL BY THE CLERK (Form SCF-26)**
   If you want this office to mail your claim to the defendant by Certified Mail, one form must be completed and returned for each defendant. Enclose a check for $6.00, payable to "Clerk, Municipal Court", *for each defendant* you wish to serve. Do not fill in the section headed, "Clerk's Certificate of Mailing Claim by Certified Mail". NOTE: If the person to whom the Certified Mail is addressed does not sign, or if the signature is clearly by someone other than the addressee, such service is invalid. If the signature is illegible, the court *may* (at the time of the hearing) review the signature and hold that it is not acceptable take the case off calendar and ask that you re-serve the claim prior to a new court hearing date. Please call the office not later than 20 days after filing your claim to learn if the defendant was properly served.

6. **DECLARATION PURSUANT TO CCP 116.540 (Form SCF-222)**
   If the plaintiff is a corporation or other business entity, you must complete and return this form to this office.

7. **FICTITIOUS BUSINESS NAME DECLARATION (Form SC-103)**
   If you, as plaintiff, are suing under a fictitious business name, this form must be completed and returned to this office.

8. **INFORMATION SERVICE OF PLAINTIFF'S CLAIM AND ORDER**

9. **INSTRUCTIONS TO THE SHERIFF**

LEGAL ADVISOR DAYS & HOURS: Monday to Friday **EXCEPT** for Wednesday
                          9:15 am to II:30 am **AND** 1:30 pm to 3:30 pm
   TELEPHONE — DAYS & HOURS: (415) 292-2124 or (415) 554-4528 — Monday to Friday, 8:00 am to 12:00 pm
   RECORDED INFORMATION TELEPHONE: (415) 292-2121

Claims are processed upon receipt. Please provide a self-addressed stamped (.32¢), legal size envelope for plaintiff's packet or a 5 x 7 manila envelope ($1.00 postage) for the packet and a handbook. The copies of the claim will be returned to you with the assigned court hearing date. If you do not choose Certified Mailing (#5 above) to be done by the Small Claims office, there will be 2 copies of the claim for you to serve upon the deft. The proof-of-service form must be filed with the court after service of process is completed.

INFORMATION FOR THE SMALL CLAIMS PLAINTIFF

This information sheet is written for the person who sues in the small claims court. It explains some of the rules of and some general information about the small claims court. It may also be helpful for the person who is sued.

WHAT IS SMALL CLAIMS COURT?

Small claims court is a special court where disputes are resolved quickly and inexpensively. The rules are simple and informal. The person who sues is the **plaintiff**. The person who is sued is the **defendant**. In small claims court, you may ask a lawyer for advice before you go to court, but you cannot have a lawyer in court. Your claim cannot be for more than $5,000 (*see below*). If you have a claim for more than this amount, you may sue in the civil division of the municipal court or you may sue in the small claims court and give up your right to the amount over $5,000. You cannot, however, file more than two cases in small claims court for more than $2,500 each during a calendar year.

WHO CAN FILE A CLAIM?

1. You must be at least *18 years old* to file a claim. If you are not yet 18, you may ask the court to appoint a **guardian ad litem.** This is a person who will act for you in the case. The guardian ad litem is usually a parent, relative, or adult friend.
2. A person who sues in small claims court must first make a **demand** if possible. This means that you have asked the defendant to pay, and the defendant has refused. If your claim is for possession of property, you must ask the defendant to give you the property.
3. Unless you fall within two technical exceptions, you must be the **original owner** of the claim. This means that if the

claim is assigned, the buyer cannot sue in the small claims court. **You must also appear at the small claims hearing yourself unless you filed the claim for a corporation or other entity that is not a natural person.**
4. If a corporation files a claim, an employee, officer, or director must act on its behalf. If the claim is filed on behalf of an association or other entity that is not a natural person, a regularly employed person of the entity must act on its behalf. A person who appears on behalf of a corporation or other entity must not be employed or associated solely for the purpose of representing the corporation or other entity in the small claims court. **You must file a declaration with the court to appear in any of these instances.**

WHERE CAN YOU FILE YOUR CLAIM?

You must sue in the right court and **judicial district**. This rule is called **venue**.

If you file your claim in the wrong court, the court will dismiss the claim unless all defendants personally appear at the hearing and agree that the claim may be heard.

The right district may be any of these:
1. Where the defendant lives or where the business involved is located;
2. Where the damage or accident happened;
3. Where the contract was signed or carried out;

4. If the defendant is a corporation, where the contract was broken;
5. For a retail installment account or sales contract or a motor vehicle finance sale:
   a. Where the buyer lives;
   b. Where the buyer lived when the contract was entered into;
   c. Where the buyer signed the contract;
   d. Where the goods or vehicle are permanently kept.

SOME RULES ABOUT THE DEFENDANT

1. You must sue using the defendant's *exact legal name.* If the defendant is a business or a corporation and you do not know the exact legal name, check with: the state or local licensing agency; the county clerk's office; or the Office of the Secretary of State, corporate status unit. Ask the clerk for help if you do not know how to find this information. If you do not use the defendant's exact legal name,

the court may be able to correct the name on your claim at the hearing or after the judgment.
2. If you want to sue a government agency, you must first file a claim with the agency before you can file a lawsuit in court. Generally, you must do this no later than *six months* after the act or event you are suing about.

HOW DOES THE DEFENDANT FIND OUT ABOUT THE CLAIM?

You must make sure the defendant finds out about your lawsuit. This has to be done according to the rules or your case may be dismissed or delayed. The correct way of telling the defendant about the lawsuit is called *service of process*. This means giving the defendant a copy of the claim. **YOU CANNOT DO THIS YOURSELF.** Here are four ways to serve the defendant:

1. **Service by a law officer**
   You may ask the marshal or sheriff to serve the defendant. A fee will be charged.
2. **Process server**
   You may ask anyone who is *not a party* in your case and who is at least *18 years old* to serve the defendant. The person is called a *process server* and must personally give a copy of your claim to the defendant. The person must

also sign a proof of service form showing when the defendant was served. Registered process servers will do this for you for a fee. You may also ask a friend or relative to do it.
3. **Certified mail**
   You may ask the clerk of the court to serve the defendant by certified mail. The clerk will charge a fee. You should check back with the court prior to the hearing to see if the receipt for certified mail was returned to the court. **Service by certified mail must be done by the clerk's office. You cannot serve the defendant this way yourself.**
4. **Substituted service**
   This method lets you serve another person instead of the defendant. You must follow the procedures carefully. You may also wish to use the marshal or sheriff or a registered process server.

* The $5,000 limit does not apply, and a $2,500 limit applies, if a "defendant guarantor . . . is required to respond based upon the default, actions, or omissions of another."

(Continued on reverse)

Form Adopted by the
Judicial Council of California
SC 150 (Rev. January 1, 1995)

INFORMATION FOR THE PLAINTIFF
(Small Claims)

Calif. Rules of Court, rule 982.7

4. **Substituted service** *(continued)*
   A copy of your claim must be left
   — at the defendant's business with the person in charge; or,
   — at the defendant's home with a competent person who is at least 18 years old. The person who receives the claim must be told about its contents. Another copy must be mailed, first class, postage prepaid, to the defendant at the address where the paper was left. The service is not complete until *10 days* after the copy is mailed.

No matter which method of service you choose, the defendant must be served by a certain date or the trial will be postponed. If the defendant lives in the county, service must be completed at least *10 days* before the trial date. This period is *15 days* if defendant lives outside the county.

The person who serves the defendant must sign a court paper showing when the defendant was served. This paper is called a **Proof of Service**. It must be signed and returned to the court clerk as soon as the defendant has been served.

WHAT IF THE DEFENDANT ALSO HAS A CLAIM?

Sometimes the person who was sued (the **defendant**) will also have a claim against the person who filed the lawsuit (the **plaintiff**). This claim is called the **Defendant's Claim**. The defendant may file this claim in the same lawsuit. This helps to resolve all of the disagreements between the parties at the same time.

If the defendant decides to file the claim in the small claims court, the claim may not be for more than $5,000 (**see reverse*). If the value of the claim is more than this amount,

the defendant may either give up the amount over $5,000 and sue in the small claims court or file a motion to transfer the case to the appropriate court for the full value of the claim.

The defendant's claim must be served on the plaintiff at least *5 days* before the trial. If the defendant received the plaintiff's claim *10 days* or less before the trial, then the claim must be served at least *1 day* before the trial.

Both claims will be heard by the court at the same time.

WHAT HAPPENS AT THE TRIAL?

Be sure you are on time for the trial. The small claims trial is informal. You must bring with you all witnesses, books, receipts, and other papers or things to prove your case. You may ask the witnesses to come to court voluntarily. You may also ask the clerk of the court to issue a **subpena**. A subpena is a court order that *requires* the witness to go to trial. The witness has a right to charge a fee for going to the trial. If you do not have the records or papers to prove your case, you may also get a court order prior to the trial date requiring the papers

to be brought to the trial. This order is called a **Subpena Duces Tecum**.

If you settle the case before the trial, you must file a **dismissal** form with the clerk.

The court's decision is usually mailed to you after the trial. It may also be hand delivered to you in court when the trial is over and after the judge has made a decision. The decision appears on a form called the **Notice of Entry of Judgment**.

WHAT HAPPENS AFTER JUDGMENT?

The court may have ordered one party to pay money to the other party. The party who wins the *case and collects the money* is called the **judgment creditor**. The party who loses the case and owes the money is called the **judgment debtor**.

Enforcement of the judgment is **postponed** until after the time for appeal ends or until after the appeal is decided. This

means that the judgment creditor cannot collect any money or take any action until after this period is over. Generally, both parties may be represented by lawyers after judgment.

More information about your rights after judgment is available on the back of the **Notice of Entry of Judgment** form. The clerk may also have this information on a separate sheet.

HOW TO GET HELP WITH YOUR CASE

1. **Lawyers**
   Both parties may ask a lawyer about the case, but a lawyer may not represent either party in court at the small claims trial. Generally, after judgment and on appeal, both parties may be represented by a lawyer.

2. **Interpreters**
   If you do not speak English, you may take a family member or friend to court with you. The court should also keep a list of interpreters who will interpret for you. You may choose an interpreter from the court's list. Some interpreters may be free, and some may charge a fee. If an interpreter is not available, the court must postpone the hearing one time only so that you have time to get one.

3. **Waiver of Fees**
   The court charges fees for some of its procedures. Fees are also charged for serving the defendant with the claim. The court may excuse you from paying these fees if you

cannot afford them. Ask the clerk for the **Information Sheet on Waiver of Court Fees and Costs** to find out if you meet the requirements so that you do not have to pay the fees.

4. **Night and Saturday Court**
   If you cannot go to court during working hours, ask the clerk if the court has trials at **night** or on **Saturdays**.

5. **Parties Who Are in Jail**
   If you are in jail, the court may excuse you from going to the trial. Instead, you may ask another person who is not an attorney to go to the trial for you. You may mail written declarations to the court to support your case.

6. **Advisors**
   The law requires each county to provide assistance in small claims cases free of charge. Here is some important information about the small claims advisor program in this county: Telephone: 292-2124
   Recorded Information: 292-2121

THE MUNICIPAL COURT OF THE
CITY AND COUNTY OF SAN FRANCISCO

Small Claims
575 Polk Street
San Francisco, CA 94102

SMALL CLAIMS INFORMATION

OFFICE DAYS & HOURS: Monday to Friday, 8:00 am to 4:30 pm

GENERAL INFORMATION TELEPHONE: (415) 292-2129

RECORDED INFORMATION TELEPHONE: (415) 554-4565

HEARINGS ARE HELD ON THE FOLLOWING DAYS & TIMES:
    Monday — 8:30 am, 1:30 pm, 3:30 pm, 5:30 pm, and 7:00 pm
    Tuesday — 8:30 am, 10:30 am, 1:30 pm, and 3:30 pm
    Wednesday — 8:30 am, 1:30 pm, 3:30 pm
    Thursday — 8:30 am, 10:30 am, 1:30 pm, and 3:30 pm
    Friday — 8:30 am, 10:30 am, 1:30 pm, and 3:30 pm

LEGAL ADVISOR DAYS & HOURS: Monday to Friday **EXCEPT** for Wednesday
                    9:15 am to 11:30 am **AND** 1:30 pm to 3:30 pm
    TELEPHONE — DAYS & HOURS: (415) 292-2124 or (415) 554-4528 — Monday to Friday,
        8:00 am to 12:00 pm
    RECORDED INFORMATION TELEPHONE: (415) 292-2121

ORDER OF EXAMINATIONS DAYS & TIMES: Monday and Wednesday — 11:00 am

FEES EFFECTIVE ON SEPTEMBER 7, 1993

Filings:	Plaintiff's Claim	$ 15.00
	Defendant's Claim	15.00
	Over 12 Plaintiff's or Defendant's Claim filed by the same party in the preceding 12 calendar months	30.00
Issuance:	Writ of Execution	$ 7.00
	Abstract of Judgment	7.00
	Order of Examination of Judgment Debtor	14.00
MISCELLANEOUS:	Postponement (Continuance or Reset) of Hearings	$ 10.00
	Service of Claim by Certified Mail	6.00
	Certification of Documents	1.75
	Photocopy per Page	.50
	Notice of Appeal	68.00
	Certificate of Facts re: Unsatisfied Judgment to Court	5.00
	" " DMV	20.00
	Officer's Witness per Diem (to be paid to Agency)	150.00
	Payment of Judgment to the Court	25.00
	All Motions	14.00
	Exemplification (Sister State Judgment)	20.00

2/95

SAN FRANCISCO SMALL CLAIMS LEGAL ADVISOR'S OFFICE

BEFORE FILING A CLAIM IN SMALL CLAIMS COURT

IS A SMALL CLAIMS CASE YOUR BEST CHOICE?

Before filing a small claims case, you should decide whether small claims court is the best place to resolve your dispute. Instead of going to court, you can try to settle the problem through conciliation, mediation, or arbitration. This usually means that a "neutral third party" -- someone, or several people, who have nothing to do with the dispute -- either helps both sides find a way to settle their differences or makes a decision for them. The process is informal, voluntary, and private. The charges are free to moderate.

WHAT KINDS OF DISPUTES CAN BE SETTLED BY ALTERNATIVE DISPUTE RESOLUTION?

Here are examples of some -- but not all -- kinds of disputes that can be settled without going to court.

*   Landlord/Tenant: security deposits, nonpayment of rent, repairs, evictions, apartment entry, lockout.

*   Neighborhood: noise, pets, nuisances, use of common property lines, parking.

*   Consumer/merchant: refunds, warranties, repairs, deposits, services.

*   Employer/employee: contracts, wages, dismissal.

*   Domestic: problems with roommates, friends, family members.

Note: While most dispute resolution programs work on problems quickly, you should be aware of the time limits, called statutes of limitation, that may apply to your case. If the time limit is about to expire, then don't delay in filing your small claims case, or you may be too late to use the court.

DISPUTE RESOLUTION PROGRAMS IN SAN FRANCISCO

COMMUNITY BOARDS
(415) 863-6100

DISTRICT ATTORNEY
   CONSUMER FRAUD UNIT
(415) 553-1814

CALIFORNIA LAWYERS
   FOR THE ARTS
(415) 775-7200

CALIFORNIA COMMUNITY
   DISPUTE SERVICES
(415) 434-2200

BUREAU OF AUTO REPAIR
(415) 468-6700

CONTRACTOR'S STATE
   LICENSE BOARD
(415) 469-6200

SMALL CLAIMS DIVISION
575 Polk Street
San Francisco, CA 94102
(415) 292-2129

Name and Address of Court:

SMALL CLAIMS CASE NO.

— NOTICE TO DEFENDANT — **YOU ARE BEING SUED BY PLAINTIFF** To protect your rights, you must appear in this court on the trial date shown in the table below. You may lose the case if you do not appear. The court may award the plaintiff the amount of the claim and the costs. Your wages, money, and property may be taken without further warning from the court.	**— AVISO AL DEMANDADO —** ***A USTED LO ESTAN DEMANDANDO*** *Para proteger sus derechos, usted debe presentarse ante esta corte en la fecha del juicio indicada en el cuadro que aparece a continuación. Si no se presenta, puede perder el caso. La corte puede decidir en favor del demandante por la cantidad del reclamo y los costos. A usted le pueden quitar su salario, su dinero, y otras cosas de su propiedad, sin aviso adicional por parte de esta corte.*

PLAINTIFF/DEMANDANTE *(Name, address, and telephone number of each)*:

Telephone No.:

Telephone No.:

Fict. Bus. Name Stmt. No.   Expires:

DEFENDANT/DEMANDADO *(Name, address, and telephone number of each)*:

Telephone No.:

Telephone No.:

☐ See attached sheet for additional plaintiffs and defendants.

PLAINTIFF'S CLAIM

1. Defendant owes me the sum of $ _____ , not including court costs, because *(describe claim and date)*:

2. a. ☐ I have asked defendant to pay this money, but it has not been paid.
    b. ☐ I have NOT asked defendant to pay this money because *(explain)*:

3. This court is the proper court for the trial because ☐ *(In the box at the left, insert one of the letters from the list marked "Venue Table" on the back of this sheet. If you select D, E, or F, specify additional facts in this space.)*

4. I ☐ have ☐ have not   filed more than one other small claims action anywhere in California during this calendar year in which the amount demanded is more than $2,500.

5. I ☐ have ☐ have not   filed more than 12 small claims, including this claim, during the previous 12 months.

6. I understand that
    a. I may talk to an attorney about this claim, but I cannot be represented by an attorney at the trial in the small claims court.
    b. I must appear at the time and place of trial and bring all witnesses, books, receipts, and other papers or things to prove my case.
    c. **I have no right of appeal on my claim,** but I may appeal a claim filed by the defendant in this case.
    d. If I cannot afford to pay the fees for filing or service by a sheriff, marshal, or constable, I may ask that the fees be waived.

7. I have received and read the information sheet explaining some important rights of plaintiffs in the small claims court.

I declare under penalty of perjury under the laws of the State of California that the foregoing is true and correct.

Date:

▶

. . . . (TYPE OR PRINT NAME) . . . .   (SIGNATURE OF PLAINTIFF)

ORDER TO DEFENDANT

You must appear in this court on the trial date and at the time LAST SHOWN IN THE BOX BELOW if you do not agree with the plaintiff's claim. Bring all witnesses, books, receipts, and other papers or things with you to support your case.

		DATE	DAY	TIME	PLACE	COURT USE
TRIAL DATE	1.					
	2.					
FECHA DEL JUICIO	3.					
	4.					

Filed on *(date)*:

Clerk, by _____ , Deputy

— The county provides small claims advisor services free of charge. Read the information on the reverse. —

Form Adopted by the
Judicial Council of California
SC-100 [Rev. January 1, 1995]

PLAINTIFF'S CLAIM AND ORDER TO DEFENDANT
(Small Claims)

Calif. Rules of Court, rule 982.7

(The space above is for the court's use)

—CONSEJEROS PARA RECLAMOS DE MENOR CUANTÍA—
El condado ofrece este servicio gratis. Pida al actuario (Court Clerk) que le dé el teléfono en su condado.

—INTÉRPRETES—
Si usted no habla inglés, puede presentarse ante la corte con un miembro de su familia o un amigo o amiga para que le sirva de intérprete. La corte debe también mantener una lista de intérpretes que le ofrecerán servicios de interpretación. Es posible que algunos intérpretes no cobren y que otros sí cobren por sus servicios.

INFORMATION FOR DEFENDANT

1. **What is the small claims court?** The small claims court is a special court in which disagreements are resolved quickly and cheaply. A small claim must be for $5,000 (*see below)* or less. No person may file more than two small claims actions in which the amount demanded is more than $2,500 anywhere in the state in a calendar year. The person who sues is called a **plaintiff**. The person who is sued is called a **defendant**. Neither party can be represented by a lawyer at the trial, but both parties may talk to a lawyer about the case before the trial.

2. **What can you do if you are sued in the small claims court?**
   a. **SETTLE** — You may settle your case before the trial. If you do, be sure that the plaintiff files a dismissal form with the court. If you would like help in settling your case, ask the small claims advisor (see No. 5, below) to refer you to an alternative dispute resolution provider.
   b. **DEFAULT** — If you do not go to the trial, it is called a **default**. The plaintiff may win the amount of the claim and costs. The plaintiff may then be able to use legal procedures to take your money or property to pay the claim.
   c. **APPEAR AND CONTEST** — You may go to the trial and disagree with the plaintiff's claim. If you do, bring all witnesses, books, receipts, and other papers or things to prove your case. You may ask the witnesses in your case to go to the trial or, before the trial, you may ask the clerk of the court to issue a **subpena**. A subpena is a court order that requires the witness to go to the trial.
   d. **APPEAR AND REQUEST PAYMENTS** — You may agree with the plaintiff's claim, but you may be unable to pay the money all at once. You may then choose to go to the trial and ask the court to order payments you can afford.
   e. **POSTPONE** — If you live in the county where the claim was filed, the plaintiff must serve a copy of the claim on you *10 days before the trial*. If you live outside the county, you must be served *15 days before the trial*. If you did not receive the claim within these time limits, you may ask the court for a postponement.
   If you cannot attend the hearing on the date scheduled, write to the court before the hearing date and tell why, and ask the court to postpone the hearing. The court charges a fee to request a postponement.
   f. **CHALLENGE VENUE** — If you believe the plaintiff's claim was filed in the wrong court (see Venue Table, below), write to the court before the hearing date, explain why you think so, and ask the court to dismiss the claim.

3. **What can you do if you also have a claim against the person who sued you?** A claim against the person who sued you is called a **Defendant's Claim**. Ask the clerk for this form to file your claim. The claim must not be for more than $5,000.* If you received your copy of the plaintiff's claim *less than 10 days* before the trial date, you must serve the plaintiff with your claim *at least 1 day* before the trial date. If you received your claim *more than 10 days* before the trial date, you must serve the plaintiff with your claim *at least 5 days* before the trial date. The court will hear both claims at the same time.

4. **What happens after trial?** The court will deliver or mail to you a copy of a form called the **Notice of Entry of Judgment**. This form tells you how the case was decided. If you disagree with the court's decision, you may appeal the judgment on the plaintiff's claim. You may not appeal your own claim. If you appeared at the trial, you must begin your appeal by filing a **Notice of Appeal** and pay the required fees within *30 days* after the date the Notice of Entry of Judgment was mailed or handed to you at the time of the small claims hearing. If you did not appear at the trial, you must first ask the court to vacate or cancel the judgment. To make this request, you must file a **Motion to Vacate the Judgment** and pay the required fees within *30 days* after the date the Notice of Entry of Judgment was mailed to you. If your request is denied, you then have *10 days* from the date the notice of denial was mailed to file an appeal.

5. **How can you get help with your case?**
   a. **MINORS** — If you are under 18 years old, you should tell the clerk. You are too young to act for yourself in the case. You must ask the court to appoint someone to act for you. That person is called a **guardian ad litem**.
   b. **INTERPRETERS** — If you do not speak English, you may take a family member or friend to court with you. The court should also keep a list of interpreters who will interpret for you. You may choose an interpreter from the court's list. Some interpreters may be free and some may charge a fee. If an interpreter is not available, the court must postpone the hearing one time only so that you have time to get one.
   c. **SMALL CLAIMS ADVISORS** — The law requires each county to provide assistance in small claims cases free of charge. Here is some important information about the small claims advisor program in this county:

   Legal Advisor days & hours
   M, T, Thurs., Fri.: 9:15 am to 11:30 am and
   1:30 pm to 3:30 pm
   Telephone - M-Fri.: 292-2124   Recorded - 292-2121

VENUE TABLE

(The plaintiff must file the claim in the proper court and geographical area. This rule is called **venue**. The box on this page describes possible reasons for filing the claim in this court.)

If you are the plaintiff, insert the proper letter from the list below in item 3 on the other side of this sheet and specify additional facts for D, E, or F.

This court is the proper court for the trial of this case because
A. a defendant lives in this judicial district or a defendant corporation or unincorporated association has its principal place of business in this judicial district.
B. a person was injured or personal property was damaged in this judicial district.
C. a defendant signed or entered into a contract in this judicial district, a defendant lived in this judicial district when the contract was entered into, a contract or obligation was to be performed in this judicial district, or, if the defendant was a corporation, the contract was breached in this judicial district.
D. the claim is on a retail installment account or contract subject to Civil Code section 1812.10. *(Specify facts on the other side of this sheet.)*
E. the claim is on a vehicle finance sale subject to Civil Code section 2984.4. *(Specify facts on the other side of this sheet.)*
F. other. *(Specify facts on the other side of this sheet.)*

---

* The $5,000 limit does not apply, and a $2,500 limit applies, if a ''defendant guarantor . . . is required to respond based upon the default, actions or omissions of another.''

SC-100 (Rev. January 1, 1995)

PLAINTIFF'S CLAIM AND ORDER TO DEFENDANT
(Small Claims)

Page two

MUNICIPAL COURT, SMALL CLAIMS DIVISION CITY AND COUNTY OF SAN FRANCISCO

575 Polk Street
San Francisco, CA 94102
(415) 554-4565   CASE NUMBER S.C. _____

(To protect your rights, notify the court if you change your address.)

SERVICE BY RETURN RECEIPT MAIL BY THE CLERK

1. The clerk will attempt to serve your claim by certified mail, return receipt requested, restricted delivery (to be signed by addressee only) for a fee of $6.00 for each party to be served. **THIS SERVICE IS NOT GUARANTEED AND VERY UNRELIABLE. THERE ARE NO REFUNDS IF THE PARTY IS NOT SERVED.** To determine when a party is served by return receipt mail, read number 2. below.

   Check with the clerk for more reliable methods of having your claim served. However, if you wish the clerk to attempt service by return receipt mail, read numbers 2 & 3. on this side of the form and the instructions on the reverse of this form before completing numbers 4 & 5. on this side.

2. THE COURT WILL NOT CALENDAR FOR TRIAL ANY CLAIM WHICH HAS BEEN SENT RETURN RECEIPT MAIL WHEN:

   a. The return receipt is signed by someone other than the addressee. (See the reverse of this form, the last two lines in number 4. for the one exception) (19% of mail)

   b. The Postal Service has returned the certified mail as unclaimed or refused by addressee or undeliverable as addressed unable to forward (31% of mail)

   c. The Postal Service has neither returned a signed receipt nor the certified letter.

   d. The certified letter is not addressed to the proper party to be served. Read the reverse, numbers 1. through 4., to determine who is the proper party to be served.

   e. The return receipt mail is sent by someone other than the clerk of the Small Claims Division.

   f. The return receipt is signed outside California, unless the owner of record of real property in California resides in another state and had no lawfully designated agent for service of process.

3. NOTE: THE COURT WILL NOT NOTIFY YOU IF THE CLAIM HAS BEEN SERVED!!
   You must call the Small Claims Office 554-4565 292-2129, not less than 20 days after the mailing of your claim to learn if the defendant has been served.

4. TO THE CLERK OF THE SMALL CLAIMS DIVISION:
   I have read numbers 1., 2., & 3. above and the instructions on the reverse of this form. I wish the clerk to attempt delivery of my claim as I have written below.

   _____   _____
   Dated   Signature of litigant

5.   READ INSTRUCTIONS ON REVERSE BEFORE COMPLETING

   Name: _____   Name: _____
   Street: _____   Title: _____
   City & Zip: _____   Company: _____
                                     Street: _____
                                     City & Zip: _____

Clerk's Certificate of Mailing Claim by Certified Mail

Fee(s) paid: $_____ on receipt No. _____ Court Date _____
I certify that I am not a party of this action, and that I mailed a copy of the subject claim by certified mail, restricted return receipt requested, postage prepaid, in a sealed envelope, addressed to the party's as shown above in item #5 of Form SCF 26 at San Francisco on (date) _____.

GORDON PARK-LI
Clerk/Administrator, San Francisco Municipal Court

by _____, Deputy Clerk

SCF 26   3/95

INSTRUCTIONS: HOW TO PROPERLY ADDRESS THE RETURN RECEIPT MAIL

To effect service upon the defendant, the return receipt mail must name and identify the proper person to be served. The proper person to be served varies with the legal entity of the defendant. The four categories of legal entities appearing below, (i.e. individuals, sole proprietorships, partnerships and corporations), comprise the vast majority of parties to small claims actions. Before completing item #5 on the reverse of this form, examine the appropriate section below to determine to whom the mail should be addressed.

1. Defendant is an INDIVIDUAL: The return receipt mail must be addressed to that individual and the receipt signed by that individual an no other.

    For Example:

(at home address)		(at work address)	
Name:	John Doe	Name:	John Doe
Street:	500 Washington Street	Title:	in care of
City & Zip:	San Francisco, CA 94131	Company:	Plastics Manufacturing Inc.
		Street:	750 10th Street
		City & Zip:	Oakland, CA 94610

2. Defendant is a SOLE PROPRIETORSHIP: John Doe IND & DBA John's Towing Service.
    The mail must be addressed to the proprietor (owner) and the receipt must be signed by the proprietor and no other person.

    For Example:

Name:	John Doe
Title:	owner & individual
Company:	John's Towing Service
Street:	600 Brannan Street
City & Zip:	San Francisco, CA 94103

3. Defendant is a PARTNERSHIP: AZY Cleaners, a partnership consisting of John Doe & Mary Doe and each individually. To serve the partnership and each partner as individuals, a separate letter must be addressed to each partner.

    For Example:

Name:	John Doe	Name:	Mary Doe
Title:	partner & individual	Title:	partner & individual
Company:	AZY Cleaners	Company:	AZY Cleaners
Street:	500 Geary Blvd.	Street:	500 Geary Blvd.
City & Zip:	San Francisco, CA 94118	City & Zip:	San Francisco, CA 94118

    In the above example, if only one of the partners signs the return receipt, the partnership and the partner who signed the receipt would be deemed served. The other partner as an individual would not have been deemed served.
    To serve only the partnership and not the partners as individuals; the return receipt mail must be addressed to: one of the partners, the general manager (not the same as manager), or the designated agent for service of process. The mail must name the person and their title and the return receipt must be signed by that person and no other.

    Note: Most partnerships have neither a general manager nor an agent for service of process other than the partners themselves.

4. Defendant is a CORPORATION: Jones Oil Co., Inc. The return receipt mail must be addressed to and the receipt signed by one of the following: president, vice-president, general manager (not the same as manager); secretary or assistant secretary; treasurer or assistant treasurer; or a person authorized by the corporation to receive service of process.

    Note: The return receipt mail must contain the name and title of the person, and the receipt must be signed by the person it is addressed to and no other.

    For Example:

Name:	Mary Jones	Name:	John Doe	Name:	C.T. Corporation
Title:	President	Title:	authorized agent for receipt of process for	Title:	authorized agent for receipt of process for
Company:	Jones Oil Co., Inc.	Company:	Jones Oil Co., Inc.	Company:	Jones Oil Co., Inc.
Street:	100 Windfall Way	Street:	600 Montgomery Street	Street:	700 So. Flower Street, Suite 1010
City & Zip:	Richmond, CA 94712	City & Zip:	San Francisco, CA 94118	City & Zip:	Los Angeles, CA 90017

    Note: In the second and third examples the mail is sent to the agent's address not the address of the defendant (the agent's address does not appear on the claim however). In the third example, if a corporation has authorized a second corporation for receiving service of process, the person at the agent corporation may sign the receipt.

SMALL CLAIMS DIVISION
575 POLK STREET
SAN FRANCISCO, CA 94102
(415) 554-4565 or 292-2129
Declaration pursuant to CCP 116.540 (a) (b) (c) (d, 1 2) (e)

Case Number SC_____

I, _____, am a   FULL TIME   PART TIME   employee of
     (declarant's name, print)   (circle one)

(print name of corporation or entity) _____;

my job title is _____, and I am not employed

exclusively for the representation of the corporation, or entity, in small

claims court.

I declare under penalty of perjury that the foregoing is true and correct,
executed in San Francisco, California, on

Dated _____   Signed _____

CODE OF CIVIL PROCEDURE 116.540

(a) Except as permitted by this section, no individual other than the plaintiff and the defendant may take part in the filing, conduct, or defense of a small claims action.

(b) A corporation may appear in small claims court only through a regular employee, or a duly appointed or elected officer or director, who is employed, appointed, or director, who is employed, appointed, or elected for the purpose other than solely representing the corporation in small claims court.

(c) A party other than corporation or a natural person may appear in a small claims action only through a regular employee, or a duly appointed or elected officer or director, or in the case of a partnership, a partner, engaged for purposes other than solely representing the party in small claims court.

(d) The personal presence of the plaintiff or defendant at the hearing is not required if both of the following conditions are met:

(1) The claim can be proved or disputed by evidence of an account that constitutes a business record as defined in Section 1271 of the Evidence Code, and there is no other issue of fact in the case.

(2) The individual appearing for the plaintiff is a regular employee, or a duly appointed or elected officer or director of the party, who is employed, appointed, or elected for purposes other than solely representing the party in small claims actions and is qualified to testify to the identity and mode of preparation of the business record.

(e) At the hearing of a small claims action, the court shall require any individual who is appearing on behalf of a corporation or other entity which is not a natural person or who is appearing under subdivision (d) to submit a declaration stating (1) that the individual is authorized to appear for the party, (2) the basis for that authorization, and (3) that the individual is not employed solely to represent the party in small claims court.

SCF 222,   91

Name and Address of Court:

_____

SMALL CLAIMS CASE NO.:

_____

— INSTRUCTIONS —

A. If you regularly do business in California for profit under a fictitious business name, you must execute, file, and publish a fictitious business name statement. This is sometimes called a "dba" which stands for "doing business as." This requirement applies if you are doing business as an individual, a partnership, a corporation, or an association. The requirement does not apply to nonprofit corporations and associations or certain real estate investment trusts. You must file the fictitious business name statement with the clerk of the county where you have your principal place of business, or in Sacramento County if you have no place of business within the state.

B. If you do business under a fictitious business name and you also wish to file an action in the small claims court, you must declare under penalty of perjury that you have complied with the fictitious business name laws by filling out the form below.

C. If you have not complied with the fictitious business name laws, the court may dismiss your claim. You may be able to refile your claim when you have fulfilled these requirements.

FICTITIOUS BUSINESS NAME DECLARATION

1. I wish to file a claim in the small claims court for a business doing business under the fictitious name of *(specify name and address of business)*:

2. The business is doing business as
   - [ ] an individual
   - [ ] a partnership
   - [ ] a corporation
   - [ ] an association
   - [ ] other *(specify)*:

3. The business has complied with the fictitious business name laws by executing, filing, and publishing a fictitious business name statement in the county of *(specify)*:

4. The number of the statement is *(specify)*:   and the statement expires on *(date)*:

I declare under penalty of perjury under the laws of the State of California that the foregoing is true and correct.

Date:

....   ▶   _____
(TYPE OR PRINT NAME)   (SIGNATURE OF DECLARANT)

Form Approved by the
Judicial Council of California
SC-103 [Rev. January 1, 1992]

FICTITIOUS BUSINESS NAME DECLARATION
(Small Claims)

Rule 982.7(b)
Code of Civil Procedure, § 116.430

SMALL CLAIMS OFFICE
575 POLK STREET
SAN FRANCISCO, CA 94102
(415) 292-2129

INFORMATION - SERVICE OF PLAINTIFF'S CLAIM AND ORDER

1. **CERTIFIED MAIL**
   COST: $6.00 per Defendant

   Service by certified mail must be done by the Clerk's Office; you may not mail it yourself. Certified mail can be issued by the addressee. The defendant does not have to sign for the certified letter. If the addressee is not at home, the postman leaves a notice that requests the party to pick up the letter at the Post Office; if the party ignores this notice, the letter will be returned to the Clerk's Office unserved. If any party other than the named defendant or addressee signs the green certified card, or if the signature is illegible, it may not be accepted by the Court as a valid service. The final determination of whether any service is valid or not rests with the Judge who hears the matter. You should allow at least 20 days before the Court date to accomplish service by certified mail. It is impractical to attempt certified service on a P.O. Box address.

2. **SHERIFF DEPARTMENT**
   COST: $25.00

   You can arrange to have the Sheriff of the County in which your defendant resides serve the paper. The fee is the same for every county in California. You may ask for personal or substitute service of process. It is recommended that you circle substitute service on the Sheriff's form. Information regarding service can be obtained from the Sheriff's Department, Civil Division. Service by the Sheriff is done Monday thru Friday from 8:00 am to 5:00 pm. Night service is on the 1st Tuesday of the month. The San Francisco Sheriff does service **only for the City and County of San Francisco**. The San Francisco Sheriff sends the original Proof of Service to the Court before the court date and mails you a copy so that you know the defendant has been served. Allow at least 20 days before the court date for the Sheriff to serve the paper.

3. **DISINTERESTED PARTY OVER 18**
   COST: No fee required

   Anyone over 18 may serve a paper and sign the Proof of Service form under penalty of perjury. The server must fill in the Proof of Service form as to the *exact name* of the party served, the address where service occurred, the date and time of service, and so on. Substitute Service may be done by the disinterested party by making an extra copy of the paper and serving it on someone over the age of 18 at defendant's home or place of business. Get the name of the person, their relation to the defendant (wife, mother, secretary, etc.) tell them they are being served on behalf of the defendant, then mail a copy of the paper to the defendant. Fill out a Proof of Service form and file it at he Clerks Office; proof of service should be filed before the court hearing date. A defendant who lives in this county must be served a least 10 calendar days before the court date.* If the defendant lives outside this county, he must be served at least 15 days before the court date, when doing personal service. A defendant who lives in the county must be served at least 20 calendar days before court date; outside this county 25 days before court date; when doing substitute service.

4. **PROCESS SERVER**
   COST: Must contact Process Server regarding costs

   Professional process servers are listed in the telephone book. The Clerk's Office **CANNOT** recommend one server over the others. The process server should return the original Proof of Service to the Clerk's Office before the court date; he should also notify you that your party has been served.

*REMEMBER that court costs and all serving costs should **NOT** be added to the amount of your claim. Costs for filing and service will be awarded at the discretion of the Judge at the time of the hearing. Be sure you bring all of your costs to his attention.

TODAY'S DATE _____   **SHERIFF#** _____

IN THE _____ COURT

OF _____ COUNTY OF _____

COURT CASE # _____

INSTRUCTIONS TO THE SHERIFF OF THE CITY AND COUNTY OF SAN FRANCISCO:
(The Sheriff must have written and signed instructions by the Plaintiff or the Plaintiff's Attorney for court documents in accordance with California Civil Procedure 262

_____ vs. _____
             PLAINTIFF   *DEFENDANT*

TYPE OF SERVICE REQUESTED:
☐ Claim of Plaintiff and Order (Small Claims)
☐ Summons & Complaint
☐ Other: _____

PERSON OR BUSINESS TO BE SERVED: (Type or Print CLEARLY/NEATLY)

NAME: _____

ADDRESS: _____

CITY: San Francisco, California (ZIP CODE): _____

AND   (Circle if more than one person is to be served. Include additional copy of the document to be served and additional service fee)

NAME: _____

ADDRESS: _____

CITY: San Francisco, California (ZIP CODE) _____

SUBSTITUTE SERVICE	(Sheriff will serve anyone 18 years or older at the address specified above - Circle yes or no)
YES NO	

PRINT NAME: _____
                        FIRST   LAST

SIGNED: _____
                PLAINTIFF OR PLAINTIFF'S ATTORNEY

NOTE: Once your documents are processed, or after an attempt has been made, whether or not the service is successful, the Sheriff is entitled to his fee.

ADDRESS: _____

CITY: _____ ZIP: _____

TELEPHONE: (____) _____

F# 0008

Index